PROJECT LEADERSHIP

— AND —

TEAM BUILDING

IN GLOBAL PROJECT MANAGEMENT

PROJECT LEADERSHIP AND TEAM BUILDING
IN GLOBAL PROJECT MANAGEMENT
BEST PRACTICES

PRANAV BHOLA

PARTRIDGE

To order additional copies of this book, contact
Partridge India
000 800 10062 62
orders.india@partridgepublishing.com

www.partridgepublishing.com/india

ACKNOWLEDGEMENTS

I thank God for His blessings and giving me strength to go through this intense, however, compelling and enlightening time.

I would like to thanks my parents and family who supported and inspired me for this work with patience and love.

I also heartily thank my fellow colleagues, staff, and friends for providing me the guidance, support and necessary information in completing this book.

Thanks to all learners, teachers, scholars, receivers and givers, all multilingual inhabitants in the global world, and to each person who has crossed my path during these thought-provoking times; whose diversities, social heritages, ethnicities, cultures and world views has opened my eyes and mind.

Pranav Bhola

DECLARATION

The author thereby declares that he has authored the entire book himself unless otherwise referenced. The author is also cognizant of cheating and plagiarism rules.

This book discusses the project management process, traits of the project leader and team building.

As per the author's experience, Engineering Businesses today run through projects. Business performance today is driven by the competitive advantage, which is possible only through successful project management. Projects are successful when we have an effective project leader. An effective global project leader builds efficient and collaborative teams across local and geographically distributed locations. This results in high level of organizational performance, and realization of sustainable competitive advantage through innovation, people development, and capability development. Project management is, therefore, the need of today's corporate for amplified business development, bottom-line payoffs, and agility and for attaining overwhelming and outstanding business performance in local and in global markets.

Project Leaders implement projects for the introduction of new products and other competitive product and services; organizations deploy projects for process improvements, which further step-ups profitability and growth of the business.

This book discusses the aspects of project management processes, project leadership and team building in context to Project Management. It encompasses how Project Leaders should nurture agile thinking, build performance, engagement, and trust among stakeholders. It also gives insights how Project Leader should develop a vision for creating business value through an emphasis on results instead of completion of activities; maintain transparency, accountability, fast decision making, and interventions when change drives are not moving in the right direction.

Pranav Bhola

TABLE OF CONTENTS

GLOSSARY

PM	Project Management
PMI	Project Management Institute
CSF	Critical Success Factors
ISO	International Standards Organization
PLM	Project Lifecycle Management
TOC	Theory of Constraints
IT	Information Technology
Prince 2	Projects in Controlled Environments –Methodology
PMBoK	Project Management Body of Knowledge
KPI	Key Performance Indicators
KRA	Key Results Area
OEM	Original Equipment Manufacturer
SBU	Strategic Business Unit
USD	United State Dollar
RFQ	Request for Quotation
GM	General Manager
APQP	Advance Product Quality Planning
QC	Quality Control
QCD	Quality Control Department
LPM	Lean Project Management
NPDD	New Product Design and Development Projects
SGPD	Stage- Gate Product Development System
TPDS	Toyota Product Development System

NPD	New Product Development
IS	Information Systems
CCPM	Critical Chain Project Management
SS	Six Sigma
LSS	Lean Six Sigma

CHAPTER 1

1. Introduction

1.1 Definition of Project Management

Project management is the usage of a set of processes, tool and techniques with a structured methodology to manage the business of the company through projects (Kerzner, 2010), (PMI, 2008). In exact terms, project management is the management of risks to eliminate/reduce possibility of delivering non-conforming products and services to clients, meeting on time delivery (OTD) targets, within budgeted cost.

Project management is regarded as a complex task that encompasses collecting knowledge for the project, creating schedules and setting project milestones and deadlines, taking critical decisions, recognizing and classifying project priorities, and building overall information system in the project (Söderlund, 2004). It classically encompasses numerous and diverse stakeholders such as the customer, the company and the manager of the project (Lia, Nga, & Skitmo, January 2013), (Olander, 2007), (Yang & Peng, 2008) wherein the Project Leader is the link between the customer and the company. The Project Leader must strive and concentrate especially on meeting expectations of their significant and legitimate stakeholders (Haverila & Fehr, 2016) in-order to increase the likelihood of the project's success (Post, Preston, & Sachs, 2005). Corporate today are driven by forces such as capital projects, customer expectations, competitiveness, executive understanding, new project development, or increasing efficiency and effectiveness (Kerzner, 2009, p.p. 47).

Projects are required as they provide a massive opportunity for accomplishing competitive advantage and value for an organization. (Hamel & Prahalad, 1994). Projects are executed in organizations for achieving desired goals that contribute to strategic objectives (Shenhar A., Dvir, Levy, & Maltz, 2001) (Grundy, 2000). However, the success of these projects is only possible if delivery of these projects is successful. Projects need to be managed strategically rather than just tactically or operationally to yield advantage of the vast opportunities that they epitomize (Larson. & Gobeli, May 1989), (Shenhar, Poli, & Lechler, 2001).

Research by PMI (PMI, 2010) reveals that the companies indulging in project management have a low standard of apprehension of the scope and processes of Project Management due to which they have restricted the view of what it contains and delivers. Research in this field has consistently revealed that companies concentrate more on project implementation and spend very less time on project initiation and planning phases of the project, which is the biggest problem in cost, and time overruns. It also revealed that companies' gives more concentration to hire managers with business acumen but with less expertise in Project Management to manage engineering project.

Therefore, for a successful project implementation, it is important that Top Management appoints professional project leaders in the organization, or imparts project management training to the current managers.

1.2 Need for Project Manager

Successful projects require a dynamic and powerful leader with strategic thinking and strong expertise in managing teams to execute projects within specified deadlines. Implementation of the project cannot be successful without a proper team.

Author, while working in engineering organizations with Strong Matrix Organizational structure, observed that organizations convert their new development activities into a project. While implementing those projects, companies select project leaders and team members from various functions in the organization and are then assign them to the project. However, it is observed that either a dedicated PM or a functional manager is given additional responsibility to manage the project. Table 1.1 lists out some behavior differences found between the PM (Project Manager) and the FM (Functional Manager).

Dimensions	Project Manager	Functional Manager
Reporting Structure	Complex reporting structure	Simple reporting structure.
Authority	Very less authority	High authority because of the title of their destination.
Performance reviews	No role in giving performance reviews to the employees.	Full right to provide full performance reviews of his direct subordinates.
Position	Position may be temporary.	Position of the functional manager would be permanent.
Salary	Many a times, PM has low grades than his/her team members.	Usually paid higher than his/her subordinates.

Table 1.1: Behaviour Difference between Project Manager and Functional Manager. Adopted from Kerzner, (2010, pp 378)

Functional or line managers are customarily appointed as project managers to handle engineering projects. These functional managers are usually expert in their respective fields but lack professional knowledge in project management methodologies and PM best practices for managing global and local projects, and therefore, follow a conventional approach towards project implementation. However, in today's dynamic business environment, organizations are employing projects as a mechanism for managing innovation and change. In addition to it, companies implement for not only executing things faster within fixed constraints of time and cost but for generating profit and business growth. These results in a quick upsurge in the importance of project leader and a need for a unique project management methodology suited to the firm for accomplishing the business goals and objectives. Moreover, to enable this, the organization needs to build project strategies aligned to organizational goals, create dynamic, collaborative, and high performing project teams, and cultivate a culture for development of a competent and proactive project leadership. Through these initiatives, the organization will achieve their business goals in a structured and cost-effective way.

Therefore, Project Leaders are required.

1.3 Current state

In current business scenario's, there is a shortfall of experienced and skilled Project Leaders with proficiency in managing cost, schedule, and quality problems while restraining scope creeps (PMI, 2012).

Therefore, it is important that Project Leader focusses on best practices in project management, project leadership traits, team-building practices. Project Leader should focus on building strong project teams, creating project strategy in line with global business and stakeholder requirements after understanding the impact of organizational and geographical culture for successful project delivery, and deploy an improved framework for comprehensive project management methodology.

CHAPTER 2

2. Project Life Cycle

2.1 Definition of Project Lifecycle

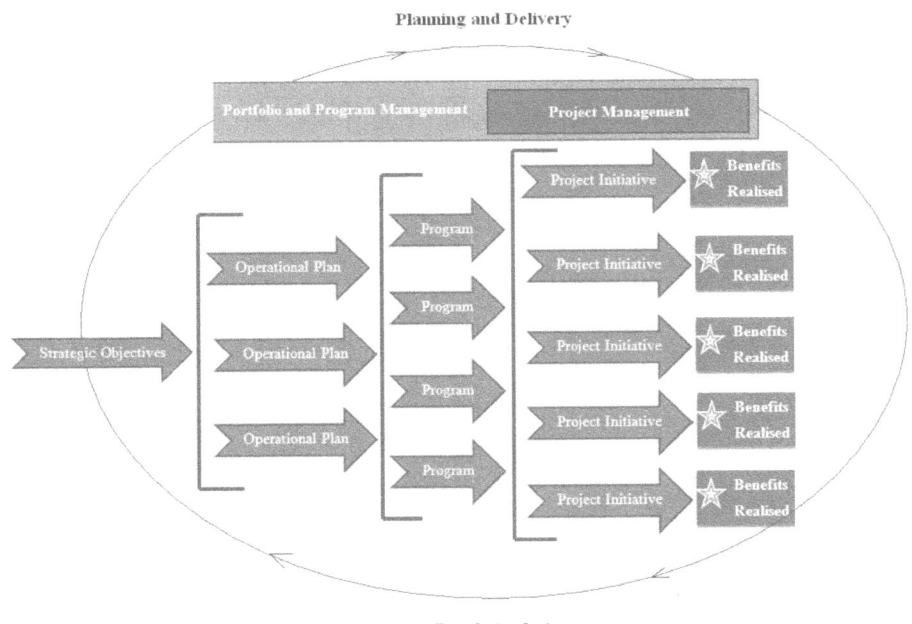

**Figure 2.1: Project Lifecycle. Source: Adopted
from (Means & Adams, 2005)**

Figure 2.1 illustrates the various stages in a project's development is referred to as project life cycle. Project Lifecycle Process Flow in a business environment is described. In the initial stage, the strategic objectives of the business are established, tested and adopted. After that, business strategy is formulated into operational plans to support those strategic objectives followed by program initiatives with fixed goals and measurable targets to execute those plans. Project Leaders builds the projects with these programs to achieve the selected goals and objectives. Benefits attained from the completion of these projects connect back to the programs, operational plans, and strategies. Project Leader measures performance, reflects on project experience and learnings and repeats the cycle.

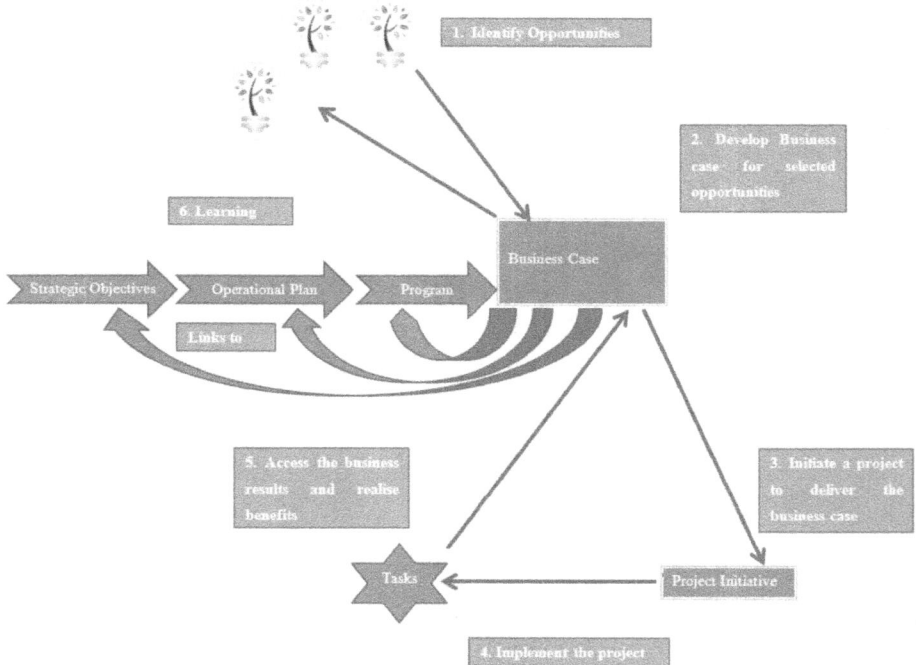

Figure 2.2: Product Lifecycle in a Single Project.
Source: Adapted from Means & Adams (2005).

Figure 2.2 illustrates the project lifecycle for a single project. Project Leader identifies opportunities and then develops business case listing all the financial costs, economic and non-financial benefits enabling business growth. After that, Project Leader initiates the project to deliver the business case, which is prepared after aligning the project with the strategic business objectives. Tasks are implemented by creating Operational Plans and Programs in a planned manner to realize business benefits. Project Leader then records the learning and documents it for future reference. Continuous business reviews are done, and new business cases are developed in alignment with business strategy. For accomplishing strategic objectives, Project Leader initiates new projects.

Product Lifecycle Process Flow in a Single Project is described. Firstly, Project Leader initiates the project with an idea aligned to the business strategy and with an opportunity for change. Project progresses through the following phases to explore the potential of the opportunity. Project leader performs Business analysis to build a solution that is finally implemented. The company owns the solutions once the transition process is over. Lastly, Project Leader monitors the performance and records the learning.

3. Project Management Methodologies

3.1 Introduction

Project management is being practiced for 1000s of years since the Egyptian and Romans Era (Kwak, 2003). There has been a significant change in the models of management projects, and these changes will carry on especially in managing multinational projects. Today, survival of the companies is not only dependent on complex and exceptional project management systems, but also on the methodologies that are being followed for project implementation and execution (Morris P., ed), (Garel, 2013), (Baptista, Santos, & Páscoa, March 2016).

Projects, being an ongoing activity, can surely bring business success, however, if not managed in a professional way, can lead to disasters. Therefore, it is vital that for successful project implementation, Project Leader charts an applicable project management methodology for project success (Baptista, Santos, & Páscoa, March 2016).

It is evident that PMI (Project Management Institute) was created with an intention to standardize project management models. PMI created PMBOK - Project Management Body, which uses a standard methodology that reinforces many other methods that are emerged in organizations depending on their needs.

The PMBOK methodology is divided into nine main features (Project Manager Institute-PMI, 2013):

1.   Management Integration
2.   Stress Management
3.   Time management and deadlines

4. Cost Management
5. Quality Management
6. Human Resource Management
7. Management of Communications
8. Risk Management
9. Procurement and Supplies Management

In this era, it is apparent that despite all adopted methodologies for project management in organizations, individual barriers often hinder implementation of some models. Projects between 1960 and 1990s had traditional business models whereas projects beyond 1990's follow a new generation of methodologies called modern project management methodologies (Project Manager Institute-PMI, 2013), (Baptista, Santos, & Páscoa, March 2016).

This chapter reviews the current project management processes, methods and approaches applied in Global Projects locally and at the Global Arena.

3.2 PM Paradigm

Success or failure in a project depends on upon different factors. Kolltveit, Karlsen, & Gronhaug, 1997 identified six various paradigms:

1. Leadership paradigm compassing effectiveness and leadership styles.
2. Task paradigm dominating PMBOK.
3. System model (e.g., lacking the requisite technology infrastructure).
4. Stakeholder model (e.g. accord about project goals).
5. Transaction cost standard (e.g., allegiance to the project team about project objectives).
6. Business-by-project paradigm (e.g., emphasis on project results).

For measuring business results, key stakeholders must comprehend and approve outcomes with their concurrence on clear success metrics. Moreover, project participant must have ownership in success and failure of the project.

Initially, the project is approved based on the business case, however, upon approval, the Project Leader manages the project by budget and schedule instead of a business case. It is important that Project Leader should not only adhere to the business case for approving or rejecting a project, but also guide the team during project implementation, and focus on managing value, effective change management and expected deliverables. Effective communication, scope management, effective budgeting, executive sponsorships are critical success factors emanating from the traditional (PMBOK) paradigm (Hidding & Nicholas, 2014).

An extensive and ever increasing array of methodologies enriches project management research (Miller R., 2015). Execution of Highly innovative projects in the uncertain, dynamic and complex environment require different project management approaches rather than traditional project management approaches as these projects have unclear goals, shifting milestones and evolving and unfolding activities (Midler, Killen, & Kock, 2016). Aerospace projects are involved in manufacturing and servicing of aircraft, missiles, airframes, helicopters, space equipment and aero engines. For large aerospace projects to be successful, highly formalized systems are required due to a large number of levels of product assembly and degree of repetition in Aerospace projects. Moreover, aerospace projects require management accounting, along with planning, reporting, and control system (Graham, 1999, p.p. 219). Discussion on various types of projects implemented in Industry is done in the next section.

3.3 Traditional Project Management Approach

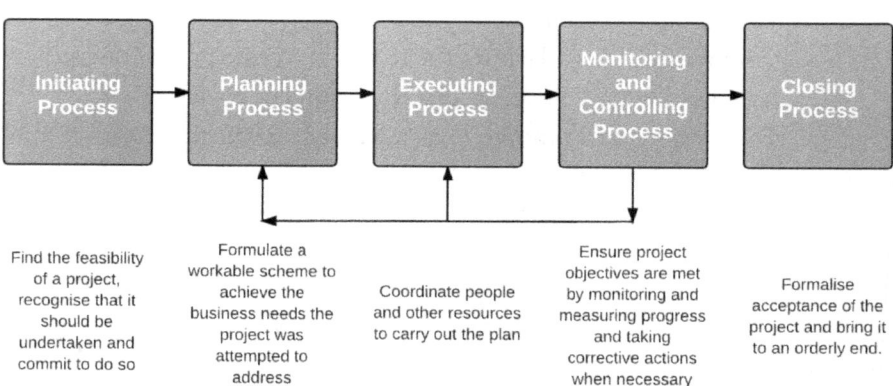

Figure 3.1: Traditional Project Management Approach

Figure 3.1 illustrates the traditional Project Management Approach. It consists of 5 phases starting from Project Initiation phase to Project Closing phase.

Project Leader performs Project Monitoring and Controlling in Planning and Executing process phases. These processes are explained further.

3.3.1 Project Initiation

In this phase, project leader conceptualizes the project by definition of project objectives, goals, and technical specifications of the project (Pinto, 2007, p.p.32).

After the recognition of problem or opportunity, Project Leader carries out the initial investigation or pre-feasibility study for understanding the problem and evaluating the alternative ways of solving those challenges. Project Leader analyses the preliminary risks in the project and its impact on company resources and impact on cost, time and performance evaluated (Kerzner, 2009, p.p.68). Proposed projects are then prescreened to check whether the proposed projects align with the business objective (Nicholas & Steyn, 2012, p.p.,92). Project Leader then prepares the Project Charter, identifies resources such as people, money, and builds the plant followed by signing off the stakeholders (Pinto, 2007, p.p.32).

3.3.2 Project Planning

In this phase called Project Planning, Project definition and system, Project Leader defines the system requirement in coordination with the project team for determining the system requirements and preparation of project plan (Nicholas & Steyn, 2012, p.p.92).

Project Leader develops a comprehensive list comprising of specifications, schedules, and plans through detailed analysis of the new concept. Actual and accurate time, cost and performance parameters along with process flow are determined by breaking down the work packages into small tasks and further documented (Kerzner, 2009, p.p.68). Project Kickoff Meeting is planned in this phase. Project teams prepare Project Scope and Project Plans in this phase. (Nicholas & Steyn, 2012, p.p.92).

3.3.3 Project Execution

In this phase, the project team executes the activities scheduled in the project plan (Nicholas & Steyn, 2012, p.p.90). In this phase, the project moves from an idea to a final product or service and is integrated into the organization. Product or service design, production and implementation work occurs during this phase. Major work of the project completes in this phase due to which the maximum cost incurs during this period (Pinto, 2007, p.p.32).

3.3.4 Project Monitoring and Control

Performance and daily progress of the project are monitored in this phase through project Scorecards or Balanced Scorecards (Norton & Kaplan, 1992). Research conducted by Kostelac, Vukomanović, & Ikonić (2012) demonstrated that Project Leaders should use Balance Scorecards (BCS) along with Enterprise Portfolio Project Management (EPPM) for developing a collaborative strategic control system for evaluating CSQS (Cost, Schedule, Quality, and Scope). Connecting BCS and EPPM might require lots of time. However, it can result in the evolution of complementary models. It finds its application in the real business environment for the development of strategic goals and an integrated system for strategic planning, monitoring and controlling the execution of the strategic objectives across all levels in the enterprise (Kostelac, Vukomanović, & Ikonić, 2012). Smart Key performance indicators (KPIs) should be decided and included in the strategic project plan to assess the performance of project leadership and project teams (Nixon, Harrington, & Parker, 2012).

3.3.5 Project Closing

In this final phase, Project Leader deploys the actual solution and later delivers to the customer. Project Leader reallocates the project resources and closes the project. Later, Project Leader prepares Final documentation after evaluation of the total system (Kerzner, 2009, p.p.68). Project Leader evaluates and documents *"What went wrong"* and *"What went right."* Costs are minimal in this phase.

3.3.6 Summary

The challenges in the project and program implementation lie in the implementation stage and the stage after the successful implementation. Problems include lack of awareness, organizational issues, and challenge to align and influence the management of project execution and lack of commitment from business leaders during the transition to the organization from projectization to programs. Six stage approaches are proposed for a successful transition. The stages include awareness, planning, understanding, planning, piloting, implementation, consolidation and customization (Shehu & Akintoye, 2010, p.p. 218).

3.4 New Approaches in Project Management.

There is the necessity of new methods for understanding operations as well as management in organizations where implementation of small, mid-sized and few large projects take place.

3.4.1 Prince2 (Project In Controlled Environment)

Prince2 is structured approach containing all the required process and basic concepts for active PM. It is process-based project management, designed to deliver specific products according to the Business Case. Prince2 employs a method based on processes for managing projects accomplished through identification of various management activities during the whole project management process and then further modularizing them (Lianying, Jing, & Xinxing, 2012). Prince2 can be applied to a project of any kind or any size and can be embedded across and organization, and tailored to suit the size, importance, and environment of the project (Bentley, 2010, p.p. 241).

Prince2 comprises of seven unique management processes, 7 Themes and seven Principles (Bentley, 2010). These processes are split into 40 subprocesses. Prince2 breaks the project into realizable and controlled stages, monitors milestones and further outlines the organization structure of the project team. It gives concentration to the product of the project through product based planning. Prince2 also gives emphasis to Quality control techniques and change controls (Ghosh, et.al., 2012). However, Prince2 does not cover Procurement and does not provide any information for handling Human Resources in the project environment. Further, there is no emphasis on project leadership capabilities (Ghosh, et.al., 2012).

3.4.2 Critical Chain Project Management (CCPM)

Developed by Dr.Eliyahu M. Goldratt (1997), Critical Chain Project Management is a new approach for managing projects funded on TOC (Theory of Constraints). This method explains that there is a constraint in every repetitive manufacturing system and that the overall system can be improved by boosting the performance of the constrained resource (Raz, Barnes, & Dvir, 2003). TOC applied in a project environment is called CCPM, and is an alternative to the methods employed in Project Planning and Control (Newbold, 1998), (Simpson & Lynch, 1999). Further to this,

CCPM leads to the elimination of multi-tasking, reduction of schedule or time, reduction in resource requirements, increase in profit, meeting of allocated budget and overall performance objectives (Robinson & Richards, 2010). Table 3.1 explains the methodology for managing single and multiple projects through critical chain method.

Critical Chain Project Management	
Locate the constraint (bottleneck) in the system that is restraining the overall system performance.	
In case of Single Project	**In case of Multiple projects**
1. Identify the critical chain of the project.	1. Identify the bottleneck resource(s) employed/used throughout numerous projects.
2. Monitor the critical chain, and ensure effectiveness and performance of the tasks.	2. Improve the performance of the system by using existing resources.
3. Give attention to decrease ambiguity in due date performance. Ensure non-critical tasks do not hinder or delay vital missions in the project.	3. Prioritize the projects; avoid multitasking to enable the bottleneck resource to complete all tasks in one operation before proceeding to the next project. The addition of slack or usage of overcapacity in non-bottleneck resources improves the performance of the bottleneck resources.
4. In case, no improvement is visible in system performance, increase the capacity of the bottleneck resource with a focus on bottleneck resource. Invest in additional resources or infrastructure.	4. Keep the bottleneck resources idle so that Project Leader can use these resources throughout diverse projects.
	5. In case, no improvement is visible, add extra capacity of the bottleneck resource.

Table 3.1: Steps for managing project(s) through Critical chain method. Source: Adapted from Lechler, Ronen, & Stohr (2005)

Through Critical Path (CP) methodology, the project leader prepares the initial project schedule to minimize project duration under resource constraints, and to meet the triple constraints of cost, time and performance on a single project (Umble & Umble, 2002). The scope is often reduced to meet on-time delivery targets. However, Critical Chain (CC) method, applicable to single as well as multiple projects scenarios, focuses, in the beginning, to reduce the scope of the projects as part of focused management approach (Pass & Ronen, 2004). Upon fine-tuning of the project scope, focus shifts to meeting on-time delivery targets, and bringing high throughput in scheduling and execution phases further resulting in excellent cost performance and meeting the triple constraints as well as (Lechler, Ronen, & Stohr, 2005). CC is best suited to handle projects with complexity and uncertainty as CC deals in the development of baseline schedule, and management of project during the execution phase. It is important that project leaders to focus on one critical chain at the time even if there are multiple chains, and concentrate on identification and management of one bottleneck resource in multi-project environments.

For handling risk and uncertainty in the project, apart from building contingency plans and risk analyses, traditional project management approach uses the safety margins built into individual activity estimates and the floats between non-critical project tasks as buffers against any variation in non-critical path projects. However, CC follows a different approach. Safety margins, added in individual activity estimates for giving activity duration a greater probability of meeting plans, are removed and added in global buffers (Goldratt E., 1997).

Project leader needs to take care of behavioral aspects of the project such as prevent compulsion on resources to multitask especially in a multi-project environment wherein Project Leaders force for execution of their project first (Patrick, 1998) (Patrick F., 1998b). Project leaders should learn to handle behavioral significance of CC because of its preference to throughput which causes managers to plan globally instead of locally (Rand, 2000).

Project Leaders need to handle the behavioral issue such as accountability of different activities. CP concentrates on meeting due dates of local activities and schedule adherence. On the other hand, CC focuses on the global perspective of adhering due dates of the entire project and schedule management through buffers monitoring. All this necessitates a behavioral transformation and a change from local to a global perspective and from one's accountability to shared goal accountability (Lechler, Ronen, & Stohr, 2005).

3.4.3 Agile Project Management

Agile Project Management is an extension of Agile Product Development and follows a real world and repeatable approach for creating a profound as well as flexible project process that aligns with the rapidly changing business priorities (Chin, 2004). Agile Project development stresses on minimization of risk through concentration on small iterations of clearly defined deliverables. Agile Project Leader concentrates on maintaining direct communication with partners in the development process rather than through project documentation. This enables the project team to adapt rapidly to the ever-changing as well as constantly changing circumstances for enabling execution of development projects. Project Leader often uses Scrum with Agile Project Management to manage and control IT software and product development in rapidly changing environment. It also helps in managing diverse and conflicting requirements of the team members, and enhancing the performance of the team, and protecting the team from work interruptions (Cervone, 2011).

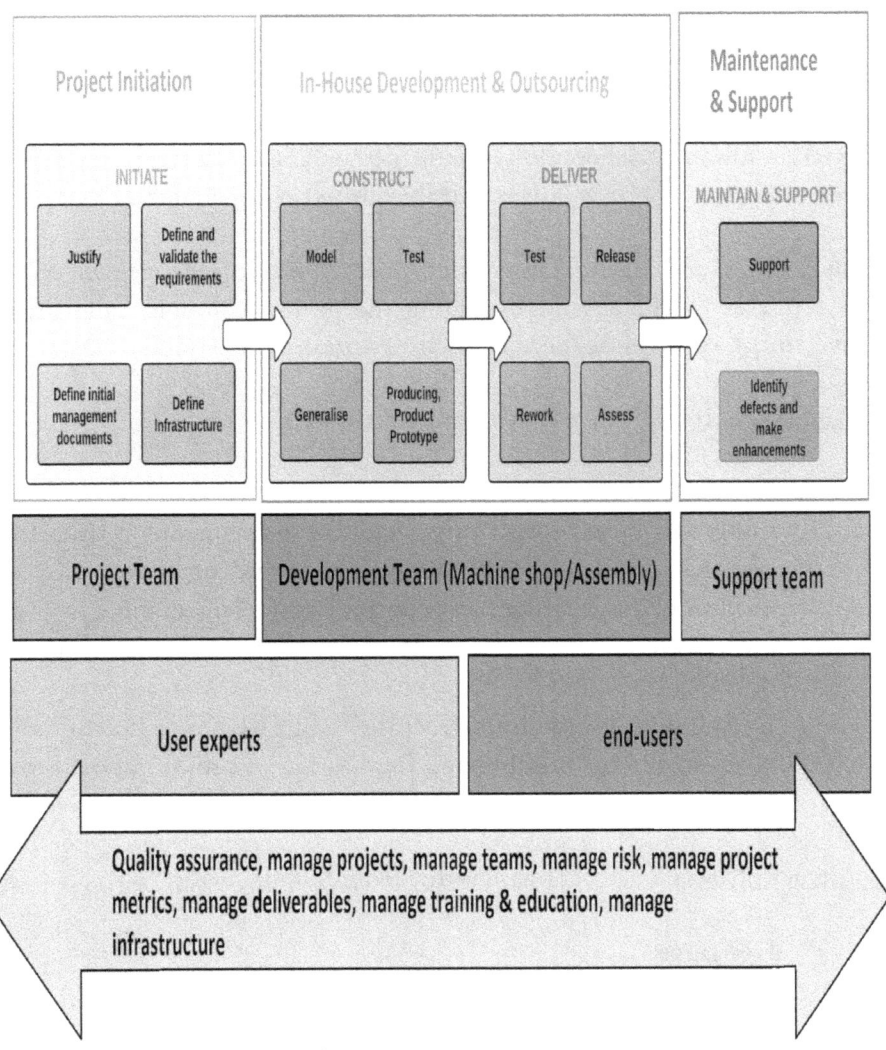

Figure 3.1: Agile Project Management Framework. Adapted
from Ambler (1998) and Modified by the Author

However, lately, Project Leaders have moved beyond that approach for disciplined agile as they devised agile methodologies for application in small projects. Potential benefits have made agile methods attractive for larger projects and big corporations in spite the fact that implementation of agile methodology is complex for large enterprises due to integration with human resources, marketing and sales, and product management. Nevertheless, due to project complexity, team members disintegrate with development teams. Still, there is growing inclination towards the adoption of agile methodologies. In recent times, large corporations, with globally dispersed teams, focus on distributed agile.

Agile Project Management Framework divides the project management process into 4 phases. The steps for managing the project through Agile Project Management as per Molhanec (2010) are mentioned here under:

<u>Initiate Phase:</u> Initial phase is further divided into four stages

1.   Assessment studies, technical, operational and financial (including budgeting) feasibility study including assessment of risks from previous projects, identification of new and potential risks, and analysis of another alternative for project implementation.
2.   Definition and authentication of requirements. Definition of primary documents.
3.   Definition of project infrastructure leading to the creation of Project Charter, Project funding and finalization of project scope. Project Leader defines Project Teams, processes and tools at this stage.

<u>Construct Phase</u>: Construct phase is divided into four stages

1.   Designing.
2.   Modelling.
3.   Analysis along with low-level testing.
4.   Production (manufacturing) of components of prototyping.

<u>Deliver Phase</u>: Deliver phase is divided into four stages

1.   The release of assemblies.
2.   Assembly level testing.

3.   Reworking (repairing).
4.   Assessing.

<u>Maintain & Support Phase</u>: Support phase is divided into three stages

1.   Supporting and identification of defects.
2.   Improvements.
3.   Change management and issued linked to operation cessation or product disposals.

Along with this, Project Leader performs activities such as quality assurance, risk management, monitoring of project metrics, training, knowledge management, management of deliverables and infrastructure management in this phase.

However, fruitful implementation of Agile also requires SWOT analysis for feasibility studies; FMEA for defect forecasting; and CMMI (Capability Maturity Model Approach) along with Information and Communication Technology (ICT) and Knowledge Management (KM) tools (Molhanec, 2010). Agile Project management methodology is applied in IT Projects globally. But, implementation of Agile Project Management for large complex projects may be very challenging as Agile is more suited for small and new product development projects. Nevertheless, Agile Projects give Project Leaders a capability to sell low-cost, high valued products in shortest delivery times in varying capacities by the adaptation of end user needs and hence providing increased value for customers (Franková, Drahošová, Balco, 2016).

<u>Success factors for Agile Projects</u>

- Set realistic goals and expectations.
- Determine the scope of the project based on the number and quality of data sources available.
- Select an iterative approach.
- Assemble the right team.
- Remove communication barriers between managers and ones entrusted with the implementation.
- Impart training in the organization.
- Acquire information on current data and identifying data sources for the future.

- Establish safety limits of the project.
- Restrict poor quality and inappropriate data.
- Ensure the preparation of the information.
- Include the complexity of the data (i.e. metadata).
- Do not to overlook granularity of data.
- Get support from management.
- Define the total operating costs.
- Avoid data lakes and ensure cooperation between departments.
- Define return on investment.
- Take right set of data into context.

3.4.4 Lean Project Management

Lean Manufacturing is a systematic approach to eliminating waste and improve project and systems processes by identifying and reducing waste throughout the value stream by continuous improvement (Alacca & Ceylan, 2011) resulting in improved value-added products to customers (Singgih & Tjiong, 2011). Shigeo Shingo identified seven wastes (Indrawati & Ridwansyah, 2015)

1. Overproduction.
2. Defect.
3. Unnecessary inventory.
4. Inappropriate processing.
5. Excessive transportation.
6. Waiting /idle.
7. Unnecessary motion.

Lean project management (LPM) is not integrated into the conventional project management techniques mentioned in the PMBoK (AGI-Goldratt Institute, 2009), but is an integration of lean theories into project management context. LPM finds its application in Infrastructure and Large Engineering and Industrial Projects such as Power Plant Projects, Refinery projects.

Developed by Ballard (2000), LPDS is an established framework for implementing projects on time, within budgets, eliminating rework, minimizing waste, maximizing value, sustaining high quality and with least safety incidents. Lean Project Delivery System (LPDS) have following benefits as corroborated from Forbes & Ahmed (2011).

- LDPS promotes collaboration, close coordination between all project participants, facilitating the formation of cross-functional teams resulting in the better decision and outcomes and maximizes positive iterations.
- Increases trust, openness, learning, and innovation through increased employee participation and commitment towards the project.
- Enables team members to collaborate and identify solutions best for the project but also increase trust and reduces conflict between team members.
- LDPS consists of multiple phases like traditional project management; however, applies product design principles for the augmenting delivery of the entire project from pre-design to completion phase.
- Promotes continuous learning through timely observation and assessment of project milestones through feedback enhances continuous improvement of project costs, project schedules, and project value.

Forbes & Ahmed, (2009) devised the five big ideas of Lean Project Delivery System (LPDS)

1. Collaborate, really collaborate.
2. Optimize the whole.
3. Tightly couple learning w/ action.
4. Projects as Networks of commitment.
5. Increase relatedness.

According to that, positive iterations are maximized, and negative iterations are reduced through collaborative design and planning. Relationships within participants are developed which increases trust and enables them to share their mistakes and improve learning opportunities. Project Leader maintains consistency in the maintenance of commitments at the time of uncertain future and sets the direction for the team to build jointly with project participants. Project Leader concentrates on optimization of the whole process rather than just reduction of cost and increase in speed, and collects immediate feedbacks in-order to incorporate learning acquired by project team members, and bring continuous improvements of cost and schedule (LCI, 2008), (Forbes & Ahmed, 2009).

LPDS has five steps. Work Structure and Production control span these phases. Table 3.2 describes the five steps of LPDS process.

Product Definition	↓	1. Project alternatives are developed at conceptual level, risks and economic payoff are identified and a financial plan in developed.
Lean design phase	↓	1. Output from the production definition's phase is worked upon to create designs.
		2. Cross functional teams members collaborate and interact with each other to perform project reviews and take decisions that are best for the product as well as the process.
Lean Supply	↓	1. Product and process designs are defined as per owner requirement along with the time of delivery.
		2. Workflow reliability is increased through identification and removal of project constraints.
		3. Transparency of projects is improved across value streams through web-based project management.
		4. Production workflow is connected with material supply which helps in reduction of incorrect calculation of material or material shortages which can halt the project.
Lean Assembly	↓	1. Schedules for each phase of the project are created.
		2. Work structuring, an integration of process design with product design for implementing a project, extends across entire production system and culminates in the form of schedules representing specific project goals.
		3. Lean assemblies comprises of fabrication, logistics, installation and commissioning. Prefabrication technique is followed to reduce non-value added activity in case of construction LPS.
"Use"	↓	1. "Use" represents the completed product which is further tested for reliability and maintenance.
		2. "Learning Loop" refers to the learning obtained from the project through weekly root cause analysis of LPS. This is conducted to review PPC and reliability values.

**Table 3.2: LPDS Process. Adapted from
Forbes & Ahmed (2011, p.p. 74-78).**

According to LPDS process, Project Leader manages and controls the whole project through Production control and Work Structuring (Ballard, 1999). Production control consists of production unit monitoring and workflow control. Project Leader splits the entire project work into chunks, which are different from one production unit to another, which improves flow, increase throughput, and organizes the work (Forbes & Ahmed, 2011).

Value Stream Mapping, Kaizen events, 5S, Visual Management, Kanban, PokaYoke, A3 reports, and preventive and predictive maintenance are the different approaches applied in the LPS. The performance of LPS is measured through measures such as Cycle time, Lead-time, Value Creating time, Takt Time, and production efficiency (Forbes & Ahmed, 2011). Project Leaders uses Pull scheduling in the project and frequently updates it to reveal the important milestone dates. PDCA cycle is applied in each phase of LPS for continuous improvement.

3.4.5 Six Sigma

Six Sigma, which started in the 1980s at Motorola and later practiced by GE, follows a structured, disciplined and statistical methodology for bringing product and business process improvements (Hahn, et.al, 1999) across an organization. In Six Sigma, Project Leader gives more significance to customers and stakeholder with a focus on improving product quality and company productivity (Gaspersz, 2007). Process Activity Mapping is used for grouping detailed activity into value added (VA), necessary non-value added (NVA) and non-value added (NVA). Project Leader uses Process Activity Mapping to identify non-value activities that occur on each production process (Indrawati & Ridwansyah, 2015).

3.4.5.1 Definition

Six Sigma uses statistical tools to measure process variability and states that in a normal distribution, 99.99966% of the population falls between -6σ and $+6\sigma$ of the mean, where σ is the standard deviation (Nicholas & Steyn, 2008). A process is said to be Six Sigma if the process has not more than 3.4 defects per million opportunities (DPMO) (Aboelmaged, 2010).

Winters-Miner, et al. (2015) describes the Key technologies and concepts in Six Sigma projects.

Statistical Process Control (SPC) is a technique employed for attaining quality control in the manufacturing process. Walter A. Shewhart and W. Edwards Deming brought in these techniques for advancement in aircraft production; however, the principles were ignored in the United States until many years after World War II (Darr, 1994). Post-war Japan, this technique was also led by Deming and his ideas were readily accepted.

Total Quality Management is a more novel model for improvement in medical care introduced by W. Edwards Deming. In this model, Project Leaders evaluates the systems of care for process issues that contribute to errors in care. Extensive application of this model by Japanese manufacturers amplified the demands of the Japanese goods worldwide.

Deming's Principles facilitates a reduction in variation diminishes dependence on inspection to attain quality, promotes leadership, encourages on the job training. It further eliminates inter-departmental barriers, endorses continual improvement, promotes education and self-improvement, disregards slogans, incitements and targets, disregards management by objective, removes the exercise of awarding a contract by cheapest costs, and engages team members for efficacious transformation.

3.4.5.2 Six Sigma Methodologies

Six Sigma employs two methodologies, DMAIC, and DFSS methodologies. DMAIC (*"Define, Measure, Analyze, Improve, Control"*) method is applied in Six Sigma for improvement of existing processes through the definition of the optimum measures for process improvement through data analysis, and then implementation and tracking of those measures for removal of defects (Nicholas & Steyn, 2008). Six Sigma initiatives improve existing processes to stay within tolerance, actions and controls critical to quality processes to meet customer requirements and customer needs.

In projects, Six Sigma approach is translated into clear objectives that align with the strategic goals of the organization. DMAIC process is employed in Six Sigma projects with phases of DMAIC defined as project stages. Through the implementation of Six Sigma improvement projects, Project Leaders improves organizational profitability, effectiveness and overall. This is accomplished by controlling the process variability through identification and removal of defects (Desai, Antony, & Patel, 2012), (Desai,2008).

Benefits of Six Sigma Project:

- It increases competitive advantage of an organization by increasing Overall Equipment Effectiveness (OEE)
- Reduces Cost of Poor Quality.
- Six Sigma Project enhances organizational learning and culture through the addition of new skills and competencies such as problem-solving through scientific methods.
- Improves decision making.
- Adds leverage to the company strategy increases cost flow (MAST, 2006).
- Increases customer satisfaction through identification of CTQs (Cost to Quality) characteristics (Evans & Lindsay, 2005).

By setting clearly defined improvement goals (Lindermana, et. al, 2004), Six Sigma project aligns the team, enables measures for team success and allows feedback for performance (Gabelica, Bossche, Segers, & Gijselaers, 2011)

3.4.5.3 Project Leadership for Six Sigma project

Project leader plays a vital role in successful implementation of Six Sigma projects. For successful Six Sigma Projects, Six Sigma provides a hierarchical structure where Project Leaders (Champions) initiates, supports and reviews key improvement projects. Champions involve in project selection, preparation of project charters, selection of Black Belts and related resources, conducting project and tollgate reviews with Black Belts. The role of Project Leader is played by Black Belts, who further provide coaching to the Green Belts in project execution through problem solving (Schroedera, et.al., 2008), (Gitlow & Levine, 2005), (Snee & Hoerl, 2003). Six Sigma employs tools such as FMEA, Cause and Effects Diagram, and Statistical Process Controls (Breyfogle III, 2003), (Ishikawa, 1985), (Kume & Loftus, 1985) for bringing process improvements.

For successful implementation of Six Sigma project, top management should understand SS methodologies and should actively participate and involve in project selection and execution. Successful Six Sigma Leaders as per Kumar, et.al. (2008), Snee & Hoerl (2003), Desai, Antony, & Patel (2012), Henderson &Evans (2000), Mahanti & Antony (2009) do following:

1. Selects Six Sigma project by potential financial returns.
2. Apprises the project financially.
3. Prioritizes projects that have direct impact on financial goals, and customers.
4. Provides required resources and appropriate budget for the project.
5. Forms cross-functional teams.
6. Appoints team members dedicated to SS implementation.
7. Facilitates leadership behavior to create an organizational favorable for SS application.
8. Effectively communicates the importance of SS project and its potential benefits to the team members and Staff.
9. Assigns role of Project Champion, Master Black Belts, Black Belts and Green Belts to key employees and define their roles.
10. Prepares training curriculum and provides necessary training through tutor lead or online-self place training curriculum.
11. Recognizes and regularly update customer requirements and market needs.
12. Measures project performance by evaluating the success of SS implementation and through Balanced Score Cards.
13. Rewards team members in case of successful SS applications.
14. Ensures that team members understand all the steps of DMAIC and DMODV methodologies and associated tools used for Six Sigma Implementation.
15. Develops project management skills in the team members; ensures that the Six Sigma project objectives align to Corporate Strategy.
16. Motivates team members and staff for participation in Six Sigma project

Apart from this, team-building, project planning, proper resource allocation, superior leadership, shared vision, optimal scheduling, organizing and project control are the success factors of SS project (Badiru, Badiru, Badiru, 2007),

However, research conducted by Chakrovorty (2010) concluded that 60% of 100 Six Sigma projects implemented in an Aerospace company failed as the team members after starting the project very passionately later lost the motivation to carry out the implementation and started following the old processes and methods. Failures happened when the project leader and the Six

Sigma expert moved on to another project in the middle of an implementation project and started giving attention to another project. Because of lack of leadership and lack of Six Sigma expert, the team member lost their objectives and failed to receive any guidance as well as training from the expert, which demotivated and discouraged them from making any improvements which led the project to be a failure. Therefore, it is important the Six Sigma expert, and project leadership should always motivate and mentor. They should provide continuous learning to their team to excel and register gains, however in the case of absence or cost implications for deploying a Sigma expert and project leader for each group, the company can appoint an improvement expert on part-time for two years, and simultaneously impart training to the managers.

3.4.6 Lean Six Sigma Project Management

Lean Six Sigma (LSS) Project Management, a business improvement approach (Pamfilie, Petcu, & Draghici, 2012) is an integration of two distinctive management philosophies Lean Principles and Six Sigma Methodologies (Pepper & Spedding, 2010). These two views complement each other to improve enterprises processes and results through process improvement by elimination of waste (Zhang, et.al., 2012). These two aspects are integrated through the unification of their methods and principles (George, 2003) using the DMAIC (define, measure, analyze, improve, control) cycle. Through conjoint continuous improvement framework (Cheng & Chang, 2012) and conjoint efforts, the reduction results in production defects, and process variability along with process simplification and standardization and waste reduction (Qu, Ma, & Zhang, 2011). Research by Akbulut-Bailey, Motwani, & Smedley (2012) demonstrated that Lean Six Sigma implemented successfully in an aerospace company (Spector, 2006).

The objective of an LSS project is to identify the Critical-to-Quality process factors (CTQs), as per customer requirements as the client is regarded as a top priority as per LSS philosophy. Therefore, Project Leader must reflect on opinions and needs of the clients in the final product or service. It is, therefore, important that Project Leader takes customer satisfaction surveys in the closing phase of every project. Through this exercise, the project leader identifies key customer requirements and detects the Voice of the customer (VOC) on the DMAIC approach. Process improvements can be brought in project management by following LSS proposed methodology leading to stable processes through continuous identification and assessment of improvement opportunities in PM procedures and decisions. If stable project management systems are in use, consistent application of traditional LSS tools improves project management processes in an organization (Tenera & Pinto, 19 March 2014).

3.4.6.1 Description of DMAIC Phases

Define Phase: DMAIC phases starts with this step. In this phase, Project Leader detects problems and issues concerning customer expectations. Project Leader also identifies Critical to Quality (CTQ) process factors, maps processes, and describes challenges and goals in Project Charter (Tenera & Pinto, 19 March 2014). It is important that Project Leader uses SIPOC (Supplier, Input, Process, Output and Customer) diagram in the Process Mapping phase to focus on identified processes and all stakeholders associated to the identified CTQs for the achievement of the improvement target.

Measure Phase measures process performance through the definition of metrics, a gathering of process related data, calculation of Six Sigma value, and later redefining of the target.

In Analysis Phase, Project Leader performs value Stream Mapping for process improvement and uses Affinity diagrams and Ishikawa diagrams for cause identification.

In Improve Phase, Project Leader identifies potential solutions for each cause and prioritizes resolution of root causes through the application of tools such as Prioritization Root-causes matrix (Pereira & Requeijo, 2008), and root-causes tiering through Pugh matrix.

In the Control Phase, Project Leader uses control procedures and monitoring tools for sustaining continuous improvements in a systematic way (Tenera & Pinto, 19 March 2014).

3.5 Project Methodologies for New Product Development Projects (NPD)

Project Leader can apply different methodologies in NPD projects such as Stage-Gate Product Development (SGPD), Toyota Product Development System (TPDS) and IDEO product development process. Nevertheless, we will discuss Stage gate product development, as the same approach is applicable for managing the project.

3.5.1 Stage-Gate Product Development

Developed by Cooper (2001), Stage-Gate Product Development (SGPD) is a model widely used in Project Portfolio mainly for decision making (Christianson & Varnes, 2006), and for accelerating the projects from Idea to launch. SGPD can handle various sizes and types of projects. Project Leaders collect information in different design phases called "Stages," and further evaluates, and takes decisions at points known as "Gates" at set intervals between the phases (Cooper 2008). Project Leader assesses against "should meet Criteria" and "must comply with Criteria" at the gates. Project Leader discards not meeting the criteria, and prioritize projects meeting the criteria through scoring (Cooper, Edgett, & Kleinschmidt, 2000), (Cooper, Edgett, & Kleinschmidt, 2001), (PMI, 2008).

In a portfolio, Project Leader compares projects with each other and then takes a decision on either continuation or halting of project and programs. This ensures selection of right projects (Cooper, Edgett, & Kleinschmidt, 2000). Through this, Project Leader maximizes the value of projects; maintains the right balance of projects in the portfolio; and links portfolio to the business strategy through Stage-Gate (Cooper, Edgett, & Kleinshmidt, 1997a) (Cooper, Edgett, & Kleinschmidt, 1997b).

Stage-Gate process provides structure to Project Management and provides standardization in planning, scheduling, and control through application of forms, checklists, and guidelines. It allows project leaders to make structured decisions. However, Project Leaders should not only appoint gatekeepers but also empower them to take decisions. They should avoid selecting those gatekeepers who lack the courage to terminate a project. However, it is important that Project Leader sets right criteria, and ensure that gatekeepers are sensible, competent and experienced and maintain some flexibility in assessment. Failure to do some may lead to rejection of potentially profitable projects. Moreover, project leaders should avoid project team to concentrate more on Gates rather than on stages. Furthermore, Stage-gate process is one of a process, and neither a conclusion nor a self-sufficing methodology.

However, Project Leaders can customize Stage-gate process, an essential part of project management, for every project to enable decision-making and risk management (Kerzner, 2009).

3.5.1.1 Best Practices for NPD projects

Table 3.3 lists some Best Practices for NPD projects.

Researched by	Sample data	Best Practices
(Johnson & Luo, 2008)	Research conducted on 62 projects at 62 NPD projects in a plastic printing corporation.	Engineering efforts in early product development process and involvement of customer has a positive impact on project timeliness.
(Kandemir, Calantone, & Garcia, 2006)	Research conducted on 2010 biochemistry companies in USA, Germany.	Identification of resources of the firm that stimulate NPD success.
(Simpson, Kollmannberger, Schmalen, & Berkowitz, 2002)	Research conducted on US and German High Technology companies.	Proficiency of the project team in product development is a critical success factor in Germany. However, no relationship was found between product development and competence of project team in the US.
(Fact Finders, Inc., 1996)	Research conducted by 134 respondents and seven industries.	57% employed formal process, 58% reduced cycle time, and 80% considered team membership as a part-time responsibility.
(Group EFO, 1995)	Research conducted on 103 marketers from 83 firms consumer packaged goods.	The absence of NPD commitment.

(Todd & McGrath, 1995)	Research conducted on over 200 participants in many high-tech industries	• Measurement of development effectiveness and project performance. • Use multi-functional teams. • Reduction of cycle time by 9.5%. • Action oriented phase reviews. • Management of product strategy and NPD pipeline.

Table 3.3: Best Practises for NPD Projects.

3.6. Summary

Most of the organizations, today, use PMI's PMBoK project management processes (Initiation, Planning, Execution, Monitoring and Control, and Closing) as base processes and then customize these processes to align with the organizational, operational and business needs. PMBoK processes were followed by the maximum of the respondents while working on IT projects. Agile PM approach is a standard method practiced in IT projects. However, application of agile in the aerospace projects is very challenging, but Agile can be applied in Aerospace Projects as it reduces cost with an active schedule, improves quality, increases responsiveness, and is readily adaptable to any situation. Furthermore, Agile PM approach has following features:

- It advocates a rigid organization structure, strong cross-functional communication through meetings.
- Fosters Agile leadership.
- Agile PM encourages an improved decision-making process.
- Recommends just the right level of documentation.
- Proposes better reward and recognition system for project teams

Correspondingly, Project Leader need to

- Unremittingly focus on the development of an active culture.
- Perpetually monitor team performance measures.
- Build up collaboration between the team.

For that reason, the project leader must be trained in agile project management (DoD, 2012). Research has also revealed that Project Leader must apply direct communication practices, SWOT and FMEA tools, and rapid prototyping in Agile project management process in Aerospace projects.

Numerous factors and management related technologies are associated with a traditional mode of philosophy about project management for, e.g., in PMBOK. PMBOK concentrates on activities and resources and on-time and budget delivery. Critical Chain (Goldratt, 1997) focuses on bottlenecks in key resources. PRINCE2, significantly similar to PMBoK, centers on product-based planning with a Product Breakdown Structure (Office of Government Commerce, 2009).

Different project management methodologies such Agile, Lean Six Sigma, Critical Chain project management, were reviewed in this chapter. Each of this approach has different application and can result in project success if applied in a disciplined way by a dynamic project leader.

4. Project Risk Management

4.1 Introduction

Project risk is a possible event in a project by which the viability of the project is negatively affected (Pinto, 2010).

Risk = (Probability of Event) (Consequences of Event)

Risk management aims to evade and reduce risks, thereby increases the likelihood of the accomplishing the project objectives (Brown & Grundy, 2011).

4.2 Risk Management Practises

The financial effect of risks is required to be quantified against risk register implying that quantitative and qualitative risk as defined by PMBOK are not sufficient and impact of all the risks need to be analyzed.

A formal risk management program delivers a comprehensive base for decision-making on projects to meet all demands of project schedule, scope, and budget as per stakeholder requirements for achieving project objectives (Fontaine, 2016). Risk management is a continuous process in which each risk goes through subsequent phases serially and independently. Project Risk Management (PRM) consists of three phases (Buchan, 1994.): Risk Identification, Risk Assessment, and Risk response. For managing risks in IT projects, Software Engineering Institute (SEI), (Van Scoy, 1992) formulated risk management model based on PDCA cycle (Williams, Walker, & Dorofee, 1997). Conventional risk management processes and management practices adopted in the industry (Kwan & Leung, Improving Risk Management Practices for IT Projects, 2007) mapped to SEI model are discussed below.

4.2.1 Identify Risk

In Risk identification process, Project Leaders identifies and documents risks. Project Leader identifies risk by

- Examining the crucial areas of a project through team-based assessments (Pinto, 2010).
- Interviewing, brainstorming, expert opinion (Delphi Technique).
- Checklists and diagramming techniques such as Cause and Effects diagram.
- Through risks analysis in previous projects.
- Through the application of analytical tools and technologies (PMI, 2008), (SEI, Aug. 2006), (AMS, 2003).

However, this approach recognizes and manages events independently and furthermore identifies risks rather than opportunities; therefore, it is important that Project Leader gives preference to techniques such as SWOT Analysis, Constraints and Assumptions Analysis, and Force Field Analysis (Hillson, 2011). Project Leader should identify risks or probable responses stored in the Risk register and update them on a regular basis (PMI, 2008).

4.2.2 Evaluate and Priorities Risk

In Risk assessment process, Project Leader performs qualitative risk analysis and quantitative risk analysis by finding the probability of occurrence and significance of its occurrence (Pinto, 2010), (PMI, 2008) (COSO, 2004). Failure Mode Effect Analysis (FMEA) and Failure Mode Effect and Criticality Analysis (FMECA) (Lock, 2007) are the approaches applied in the project risk analysis. FMEA identifies risks and their related effects. Project Leader ranks risk according to their criticality and their probability through FMECA (Bouti & Kadi, 1994).

4.2.3 Develop Risk Responses Plans

Table 4.1 depicts the risk response strategies which organization should implement for developing response plans and actions.

Severity Risk	Probability	Impact	Purpose of Response Actions	Description
Risk (I>0)				
High	High	High	Reduce Impact & Probability	The action is required either to decrease the risk severity level (by reducing the risk likelihood and risk effect) or by removing the risk.
Medium	High	Low	Reduce Probability	The action is required to lessen the risk likelihood.
Medium	Low	High	Reduce Impact	Action needed to alleviate the risk effect.
Low	Low	Low	Monitor Risk	No action is necessary, except monitoring.
Opportunity (I<0)				
High	High	High	Exploit Opportunity	The action is required to realize the opportunity.
Medium	High	Low	Enhance Impact	Action needed to enhance the positive effect of the opportunity.
Medium	Low	High	Enhance Probability	The action is required to reinforce the possibility of the opportunity.

Low	Low	Low	Ignore Opportunity	No action.

Table 4.1 Risk Responses. Adapted from (Kwan & Leung, 2011)

Risk response plays an active part in mitigating the negative influence of project risks (Miller & Lessard, 2001). After identification and analysis of project risks, Project Leader selects appropriate risk response strategies to reduce global risk exposure in project implementation (Zou, Zhang, & Wang, 2007). Risk response analysis is hence considered a critical subject in PRM (Ben-David & Raz, 2001).

For correctly analyzing risk responses, Project Leader must analyze risk interdependencies as project risks are not independent (Adner, 2006), (Kwan & Leung, 2011), (Zhang, 2016). Therefore, it is vital that Project Leader comprehends interdependencies amongst project and their risks for project portfolio success (Teller & Kock, 2013).

4.2.4 Monitor Status of Risk and Associated Risk Response Actions

Project Leader must continuously monitor risks all the way through the project life cycle, and should regularly monitor the changes in the identified risks, the effectiveness of risk responses, and performance of the implementation of risk management.

4.2.5 Control Risk Responses Actions

Risk control is a continuous process throughout the project lifecycle. Project Leader follows following procedures:

1. Reassess the risks, and decides on alternative risk response actions.
2. Evaluates existing risks and identifies news risks.
3. Alters risk priorities.
4. Decide response actions for a particular risk.
5. Based on the results, Project Leaders evaluates and restructures risk response plans.

4.3 Other Risk Management Practises

Project Leader undertakes few methods for managing risk

1. Risk avoidance (eliminates the cause).
2. Risk mitigation (reduces the impact of the risk).
3. Risk acceptance (assumes the risk and considers that all risks must have a contingency plan).
4. Risk transfer (assigns the risk to another entity to reduce the risk) (Brown & Grundy, 2011).

Brown & Grundy (2011) recommend steps for managing risk:

1. Determine the likelihood of risks.
2. Calculate and find out the impact of the project goal.
3. Prioritize risks using risk matrix.
4. Assign each response risk activity a risk owner.
5. Consider organization attitude toward risk.

Project Leader should monitor risks by continuously tracking and evaluating the performance of risk response actions, taking corrective actions when required, and implementing a contingency plan in response to risk event triggers (Brown & Grundy, 2011). However, it is important that Project Leader should:

1. Have competency in concepts of risk management.
2. Assign ownership of risks through organization's process.
3. Maintain risks register mandatorily.
4. Update risk management plans on a regular basis.

Risks differ as per project type. Project Leader classifies projects as per the intensity of risk. Risk management techniques employed listed below

1. Shape and Mitigate: When risks are definite and controllable, reduce risks.
2. Shift and Allocate: When risks are definite and uncontrollable, move or allocate risks using contracts or financial markets.

3. Influence and Transformation institutions: When risks are undefined and uncontrollable, transform risks through influence for gaining control.

4. Diversify through portfolios. When risk is unclear, significant but controllable, diversify risks through portfolios and projects with support from sponsors.

CHAPTER 5

5. Change Management

In projects, changes in the project are inevitable. Therefore, there is a need for change management. Any alteration in the project scope that increases or decreases the cost, schedule or, quality is a change. These changes affect the progress and performance of the project (Hwang & Low, 2012). However, the changes happen due to delays in project, increase in project cost overruns or variance in agreed quality (Isaac & Navon, 2008). Changes in aerospace or other technological projects are more. Therefore, change management is essential (CII, 1995).

Regarded as most active practice (Motawa et.al, 2007), Change Management is done to resolve the problems to reduce the changes, and the impact of changes on the project progress (Zou & Lee, 2008). Principles of change management are to identify changes, to evaluate changes, to implement changes and to learn from past mistakes (Hwang & Low, 2012).

Through change management, Project Leader anticipates any likely changes, recognizes changes already occurred, plans preventive measures, and coordinates modifications across the entire project. Time, effective change management program also takes cost and quality care. Project Leader should resolve differences through a formal change management process; otherwise, it might lead to disputes and project failure (Hwang & Low, 2012). Project Leader manages the changes in projects through customer changes request upon approval from shift control board (PMI, 2008). Organizations running projects appoint change agent to manage changes. Project Leaders should implement Change Management Plan to find and analyze variations between planned vs. actually budgeted cost (Nasina & Nallam, 2016). The Project Leader should allow any changes in the project scope only after getting consent from Change Control Board and manage those changes through Change Control Process.

CHAPTER 6

6. Project Innovation

Leadership is also considered for bringing change and influencing innovation within the organization (Chandler, 1962), (Kanter, 1984), (Peters & Waterman, 1984). Elenkov, Judge, & Wright (2005) describe alternatives ways through which leaders can influence innovation within an organization. Leaders also promote management innovation through reduction of ambiguity and complexity within the project (Birkinshaw, Hamel, & Mol, 2008) by communicating a collective vision and developing a distinct culture.

Innovation and Project Management are integrated, and innovation activities happen in a project framework (Midler, Killen, & Kock, 2016). However, innovation in complex one-off projects seems to be a major problem (Flyvbjerg B., 2014). It is important that Project Leader selects right type of management approach for successful innovation project management (Midler, Killen, & Kock, 2016).

Project Leaders should classify the project as complexity, pace, technology, novelty and pace (Shenhar & Dvir, 2004), (Shenhar & Dvir, 2007) as per project type in the Initiation Phase only. They should not come under pressure from top management to adopt traditional rational approaches for all projects and must apply an appropriate Project Management methodology model (Lenfle S., 2008), (Lenfle & Loch, 2010). In complex integrated product development projects, the level of concurrency in innovation projects should increase (Akkermans & Oorschot, May 2016), (Clark & Fujimoto, T., 1991), (Midler & Navarre, 2004). Speed, quality, and cost improve in the concurrent process through the overlap of innovation processes, and through enhancement of communication by facilitating consideration of new information in planning even before the close of the previous phase. However, there can be a risk in concurrency, and significant delays can occur in major and extremely innovative complex systems.

Although downstream phases may require more rework due to flaws in the initial information released in a concurrent process, the benefits of enabling feedback loopbacks between project phases in complex and large innovation projects reduce risks and, and overall an average level of concurrency minimize project delays (Akkermans & Oorschot, May 2016).

Project Leaders implementing these innovative projects should:

- Develop the content of radical innovations.
- Stimulate creativity for the projects.
- Meet time, cost and quality performance levels.
- Manage the project group dynamics internally as well as externally with the key stakeholders.

Sicotte, Drouin, & Delerue, (2014) suggested a set of six critical capabilities for innovative companies managing successful projects. Biedenbach & Muller, (2012) studied the relationship between innovative capacity and long-term project success.

Classification of projects based on degree of information available to the project teams

- Instructions projects: Most information is available. The project team has a good understanding of the best policy to be implemented. Planning focusses on the critical path and risk management. This project exploits known information and does not deal with high degrees of ambiguity.
- Selections project is a project where there is not enough information to design an optimal policy. Project tame faces with a higher level of uncertainty, and it cannot accurately anticipate the results of the actions. The team is encouraged to explore new knowledge rather than exploiting existing knowledge. Plan multiple trials and prototypes while executing them simultaneously, and then selected the best performing solution.

- Learning project: These projects are susceptible to unforeseen events that might influence its course. There is little benefit in detailed planning of the entire project because the unexpected might alter its course and force the team to learn and continuously readjust the plan. While each project needs a clear vision, its detailed planning can only be done for the nearest tasks and must be updated with progress.

The diamond of innovation (Shenhar & Dvir, 2004), (Shenhar & Dvir, Reinventing Project Management, 2007) provide a possible framework for analyzing innovation at the project level by integrating project management and innovation management. A high-tech project must include at least three cycles of design, build, and test. Such project needs to allocate about 305 of the time and budget as a contingent resource beyond a typical traditional plan (Shenhar, Holzmann, Melamed, & Zhao, 2006).

There is no single comprehensive model to understand and analyze the entire spectrum of innovation challenges in highly complex projects. Companies should rely on a combination of models to comprehend the extent of innovation in a project and find the optimal ways of managing them, Moreover, using several models of analysis may shed different lights of understanding the challenges of a complex project (Shenhar, Holzmann, Melamed, & Zhao, 2006).

7. Management of Complex Global Projects

7.1 Complex Global Projects

Complex Global project faces challenges such as

1.   Lack of stakeholder involvement.
2.   Trust-deficiency amidst outsourcing partners.
3.   Hidden costs
4.   Statutory and regulatory issues.
5.   Lack of knowledge transfer.
6.   Uncertainty in project controls.
7.   Remoteness.
8.   Poor communication.
9.   Absence of coordination (Daim, et al., 2012), (Damian, Izquierdo, Singer, & Kwan, 2007), (Khan & Niazi, 2012), (McLaughlin, May-June 2003), (Miyamoto, 2015), (Nidhraa, Yanamadalaa, Afzalb, & Torkara, 2013), (Parka, Lee, Lee, & Truexb, 2012), (Yang, Kherbachi, Hong, & Shan, 2015).

Nowadays companies are using Global Software Development (GSD) model for developing high-quality and low-cost software in short span (Bush, Tiwana, & Tsuji, 2008), (Niazi, et.al, 2016). Through the application of GSD model, Project Leader engage in software development by geographically distributed teams across the world (Ali-Babar, Verner, & Nguyen, 2007) leading to a reduction in development time and project life cycle via 24/7 development model. However, the concern is that clients endorse global contracts with their suppliers before testing their project management preparedness for a global activity (Carmel & Abbott, 2006). Therefore, it is vital that project leader must comprehend and address cultural, coordinative and communicative issues for successful project management and maintain long lasting relations with all stakeholders located across the globe (Minevich & Richter, 2005). Inter-organizational processes at cooperating development sites must be synchronized and aligned through a common language understood by everyone, through templates for gathering requirements, test scenarios and functional designs enabling better insight of project progress to project leader (Smite, Wohlin, & Feldt, 2010).

Zhang et al. (2008) highlighted some vital factors Global Project Success

- Engagement of remote virtual teams from other operational centers or subsidiaries in various phases of project execution.
- The process that can be described as global project execution for enhanced cooperation between distributed teams.
- Application of VPM (Virtual Project Execution).
- The splitting scope of work as sub-projects.
- Multicenter project execution.
- CBC (Cross-Border Cooperation).
- Virtual integration by CMC (Computer Mediated Collaboration) using GVT (Global Virtual Teams).
- Use of formal procedures and structured processes.

Complex projects require the involvement of numerous participating organizations (Schwab & Miner, 2008), (Jones & Lichtenstein, 2008). It is thought-provoking for companies to employ personnel with right skill-sets and knowledge for each project while preserving the collective knowledge base, resources and skills required for managing current and future multiple projects and programs. The Extraordinary level of managerial experience, knowledge, expertise in individuals and project teams is vital for handling large, complex, global, urgent, innovative and uncertain projects; however, these traits are lost when the project is dissolved (Morris & Hough, 1987). Moreover, broad and complex projects have to complete regular, monotonous and predictable project routines when circumstances are unchanging and foreseeable, while together promote innovation to deal with unforeseen, fast changing and novel situations

(Brady, Davies, & Nightingale, 2012). Complex projects are an amalgamation of different tasks; it is, therefore, important that Project Leader must employ innovative procedures for the first time, and apply highly standardized and the repetitive tasks applied to earlier projects (Engwall, 2003). As these complex projects are predictive as well as highly uncertain, Project Leader must balance instability, and makes changes in these complex projects (Davies & Mackenzie, 2014). Nevertheless, it might be challenging (Brady & Davies, 2014), (Davies & Mackenzie, 2014), (Davies, Gann, & Douglas, 2009), (Lenfle & Loch, 2010), (Sapolsky, 1972), (Sayles & Chandler, 1971). Therefore, Project Leaders have to maintain limited flexibility while executing these complex projects. They should follow a fixed or predefined project routines and processes when circumstances and risks are predictable, and adjust and modify only certain processes and methods when conditions are unpredictable (Sapolsky, 1972) to enhance dynamic capability (Davies & Brady, 2015).

For complex projects, waterfall methodology is recommended as agile methods are not a good option for non-functional requirements of a project. It is also found that agile methodology is not fit for security and real time projects and system critical middleware projects i.e. project wherein there is limited functionality but lot of technicality. For technical and integration, waterfall methodology is recommended. Amalgamation of agile and waterfall methods can be suitable for complex projects. However, certain challenges can also arise. Those problems need to be adequately addressed and taken into account while implementing these approaches together. Agile does not favor producing too much documentation. Therefore, waterfall approaches need to be used for complex and large scale projects. However, close coordination as per Agile Philosophy is helpful to gather feedback as close collaboration with customers is required for large scale projects. Close coordination with client enables necessary improvement. Complex and Large scale projects require more structured approaches which are found in waterfall methods but lacking in agile methodologies (Siddique & Hussein, June 2014).

8. Why Project Fails

8.1 Project Success Factors

Project Success factors are defined in the table below:

1. Organizational responsibilities of each personnel on the project should be documented and regularly updated.
2. Overall Project duration should be kept below three years as possible.
3. Project Trackers should be maintained for decision making, particularly for the change request. Project tracking is a continuous management process through which project management process can be enriched, and operations performance can be enhanced (Nasina & Nallam, 2016).
4. Measurement of project performance baselines must be maintained with integrity.
5. An efficient management process for ensuring benefits of delivery should be existent. This necessitates shared collaboration of project administration and production.
6. Only those projects should be selected by the organization, through Portfolio- and program management practices, that aligns and complements to company strategy and business objectives.
7. Balanced Scorecard (Kaplan & Norton, 1996) should be used to measure Performance and success metrics, which reflect true picture and give insight on the current performance of the project, program, and portfolio. From that feedback, the future course of decisions and

actions should be taken, and the link between project success and corporate success is devised.

8. Comprehensive and well-defined work breakdown structure should be developed for improved estimation, and logical and effectual scheduling for enhanced control on project cost (Nasina & Nallam, 2016).

8.2 Root Causes of Failure

Risks in software project cost overrun increase with the involvement of too many people (Moløkken-Østvold & Jørgensen, 2005). Conflicts with stakeholders and poor communications are usual causes of failure (May, 1988).

Factors for project failure:

1. The absence of concurrence on project goals.
2. Application of a wrong project management methodology.
3. Dissimilarity to previous projects.
4. Requirements volatility.

8.2.1 Why project fails or go into loss

8.2.1.1 Estimation

1. Wrong estimates in time delivery and cost.
2. No CFT while estimating a project. The operational team is not involved in the evaluation.
3. Project Leader randomly reduces the estimates for either obtaining the contract or for making a project attractive.
4. Project Leader or Sales team or the customer compels the project team to make unrealistic deadlines. Project Leaders gives estimates without analyzing project scope.
5. Project Leader does not validate or documents assumptions used while estimating.
6. Project Leader prepares estimates without taking in notice what went wrong in previous projects

7.   Project Leader does not use better estimation tools and techniques in projects (Emam & Koru, 2008).
8.   Inaccurate rough estimates lead to project failures due to insufficient budget provisions, or wrong time calculations (Masticola, 2007).

8.2.1.2 Risk Management

1.   Risks not identified properly.
2.   Risk aversion not done properly. Not much work subcontracted with stringent contractual obligations. No Adherence to one-time delivery, quality, and on a budget. The leader should follow rulebook wherein it should be mentioned that contracts to be competitive apart from other factors such as trust.

8.2.1.3 Project Leadership

1.   People not competent to complete the tasks on time. Right people not selected for task completion. People not empowered.
2.   Lack of training and skills assessment.
3.   Processes not established or not fully worked out and planned.
4.   Unstable processes. Special causes not identified, and route causes not analyzed earlier.
5.   People not empowered to face all troubles, obstacles, etc. and achieve goals i.e. poor leadership.
6.   No emphasis on speed and efficiency.
7.   Not attaining desired results the first time. First pass yield not monitored.
8.   Project Leader not inspiring.
9.   Expertise within the team not developed.
10. If anything goes wrong, no hunt for scapegoats but solutions.
11. Deadlines and budgets not realistic and achievable. Targets are altered again and again to suit circumstances.
12. Project Leader does not ask right and straightforward questions.
13. Project Leader lacks PM skills. More of a technical person rather than a business person.

14. Project goals and objectives not aligned with the strategic business goals and operational requirements.
15. Project Leader doesn't consider ideas, suggestions from all individuals from all levels and takes it seriously.
16. Not open to new ideas.
17. No extraordinary procedures. No bureaucracy
18. People not convinced/ motivated to accept change and evolve on the modification.
19. Untimely monitoring procedure or mechanism. No automation in monitoring.
20. Unethical work or corruption ignored
21. Too many overheads.
22. No Annual Review of actual and budgeted cost, schedule variance, delivery variance.
23. No action to reduce overhead costs.
24. Project Leader selects the wrong project and fails to ask why the project is required, and what will be achieved from the project.
25. Lack of role of PMO to handle multiple projects. It might result in projects misaligned and conflicting with each other.
26. Lack of governance structure to manage the project.
27. Lack of commitment of top management towards the project.
28. Lack of ownership of project sponsor towards the project.
29. Not many initiatives were taken by project leadership for team development.
30. Failure to develop an effective business, technical and an organizational leader.
31. Project Leader is devoid of the social or cultural skills required for building strong project team for effective project execution.
32. Project Leader's failure to regularly and diligently track project progression letting the project to fail.
33. Inability to identify and engage stakeholders.
34. Not ensuring that demands/requirements of each stakeholder are met.
35. Lack of communication modes between team members and stakeholders.
36. There is the absence of well-defined roles and responsibilities leading to chaos, failures, and lapses.

37. There are insufficient team members deployed for executing projects tasks to abide by the commitments given to the customer. This makes team members overloaded.

38. It is expected from project team members to perform full-time operational jobs while also adhering to project milestones.

39. Apart from carrying out round-the-clock operational jobs, Project Leader expects team members adhere to project milestones.

40. In the team, there is the absence of Subject Matter Expertise required to finish the project successfully.

41. Haste showed by Project Leader to appoint the first available personnel for a project role instead of waiting for the talent.

42. No feedback mechanism creates discontent in the team.

43. Project Leader fails to coach and handle non-performing team member or control poor group dynamics resulting in disengagement of remaining team members.

44. Project Leader performs actions that sabotage team motivation.

45. Project Leader being biased or favoring a particular team member for political reasons.

46. Project Leader is compelling the group, which is at present exhausted to do additional overtime.

47. Project Leader adds extra resources to an already delayed project. This leads to excessive stress on the team resulting in lower than expected team performance (Brooks law).

48. Poor scope definition or poor understanding of requirements.

49. Unclear job responsibilities.

50. Inability to handle the increase in project scope work as scope not freezes. The scope of work is increased without following formal change management process.

51. Project Leader fails to comprehend the end application of the product being produced when the project completes.

52. Project Leader shows an inability to plan and instead directly starts project execution without applying any thought.

53. Project Leader fails to understand the complexity of tasks/operation.

54. Project Leader fails to create WBS.

55. Project Leader at no time prioritizes requirements resulting in team concentrating on lesser priority tasks rather than high priority tasks.

56. Project Leader fails to consider suitable culture change tasks in the project plan.
57. Project Leader fails to allocate time and budget required for team development training and team building activities.
58. Project Leader fails to control change requests offhandedly without evaluating their repercussions or without approving changes in budget and schedule.
59. Project Leader fails to plan for future, anticipate and resolve potential problems.
60. Project management regard risk management as an autonomous process instead of an integral part of the planning process.
61. Project teams start developing discrete components without considering overall system integration resulting in gaps, unanticipated integration costs, and related wastefulness.
62. Project Leader fails to consider non-functional requirements while designing a product or service leading to an impracticable deliverable.
63. Project Leader fails to set a system, which ensures that team members are informed of future project tasks and activities.
64. Scope creep.
65. Ignoring project warning signs.
66. Team weakness.
67. Project requirements are not studied in detail and identified what is needed to ensure that requirements can be delivered. Assumptions are not explored thoroughly. Similar projects not reviewed to avoid forgetting major items.
68. The business case, which Project is going to accomplish not thoroughly, considered and scrutinized. Gaps or areas wherein details required are not identified.
69. Benefits management approach is not followed leading to reduced focus on delivering the ultimate advantages of the project.
70. Changes in environment not monitored closely.
71. Poor project implementation.
72. Untimely communication to stakeholders about project future if change found in project requirements.
73. Unaligned expectations.

74. Inadequate systems in case of the global project team cannot access things or update project progress as systems and inadequate.
75. Team conflicts.
76. Project Leader implements the projects before the project is approved leading to out of scope and out of budget projects.
77. Inaccessible systems leading project team not understanding the milestones or targets.
78. Project leader and stakeholders do not have access to a schedule or reports. Due to this, the project leader is neither able to give timely direction to the team nor able to cancel the project. This leads to schedule and cost overruns.
79. Switching priorities.
80. Inexperienced and new resources delays projects schedule as more time is required for task completion.
81. Lack of visibility on the part of Project Leaders to understand on which projects project team members are employed on.
82. Project priorities are not clearly set. This will increase the probability of the organization to take up multiple projects simultaneously and force an average team member to complete more work in a day to complete that job.
83. Project Leaders have no centralized view of the project history.
84. Project Leader do not have access to centralized information related to project and task communication due to the absence of any web-based collaborative or project systems.
85. Taking shortcuts.
86. Not asking simple questions.
87. Disorganizing information.
88. Not recording knowledge base and incorporating the same in the processes.
89. Organization creates a Superficial Quality assurance system only to get certifications.
90. Organization with convoluted management structure wherein Managers acted to protect their former constituency and made political rather than economic decisions (Gauthier-Villars. & Michaels, 2007), (Matlack, 2006).

91. Control issues, not resolved before the project was undertaken, not after (Shore, 2008).
92. Each silo is focusing only on its immediate task, with apparently little effort directed at integrating their role with that of others; there was no suggestion of a strategic relationship with vendors and agencies (Shore, 2008).
93. The Recency effect.
94. Conservatism can be the reason if senior managers largely ignore data from past results/recent projects; they ruined to review their previous conviction that the system was operating properly. There was also evidence of overconfidence.
95. Lack of senior management involvement.
96. Cultural problems, together with financial pressures, create a propagation ground for the occurrence of systematic biases.
97. Management falls prey to the sunk cost trap and carries on delivering defected product.
98. Groupthink.
99. Not assuring close coordination between users and the IT organization.(Mumford, 1981).
100. No re-engineering business process before implementing IT projects (Hammer & Champy, 1993).
101. Underestimating the cost of training and support.(Summer, 99)
102. Non-standardization of data.
103. Project Leader is lacking Business acumen.
104. Not putting a steering committee in charge.
105. Adding people to a project when it is already behind schedule.
106. Lack of discipline.
107. Reassessment and handling of risks not done throughout the project.
108. Stakeholders lose vision of the project goals, and rather emphases on managing temporary tasks and handle the project in an unplanned way (Janssen, van der Voort, & van Veenstra, 2014).

8.2.1.4 Schedule

1. Buffers not added in estimation as well as project schedules.

8.2.1.5 Contract Management

1.   Tenders were not broken into smaller contracts rather kept as big ones, so the organization never had full control.

8.2.1.6 Procurement

1.   No penalty for contractors for not obligating as per requirement.

8.2.1.7 Finance

1.   Money received at high finance rates.
2.   No zero based HR structure.
3.   Inflexible management and administrative system.
4.   Leadership not visionary.
5.   Meeting with no agenda.

8.2.1.8 IT

1.   Poor IT system or support system

8.2.1.9 Team

1.   Constantly working persistently and under extreme schedule pressure.
2.   Not able to conform to customer expectations.
3.   The planning process is comprehended as a responsibility of the Project Leader rather than a team action.
4.   Project Leaders makes certain team members overburdened leading them to poor performance in vital areas of the project while underutilizes other team members.
5.   The work of one team may be incompatible with the work of another.

8.3 Critical Success Factors of a Project

Project success and impact of Project Leader on project success has been debated, however seldom agreed upon (Pinto & Slevin,1988a). Earlier in 1970, Project success was measured through time, cost (on a budget), and developments done in functionality but later shifted to quality-based focus in the 1980s to 1990s, however nowadays project success is determined through CSF. Moreover, project success today embraces satisfaction of the stakeholders, the success of the product, team development and benefits attained by business and organization (Atkinson, 1999), (Baccarini, 1999), (Nixon, Harrington, & Parker, 2012).

Nokes & Kelly (2007) theorized that an organization implements projects to bring a change faster than the speed at which the organization naturally progresses and changes. These projects, therefore, are associated with risks. For management and assessment of those risks, the project leader should involve team member right from the initiation of the project. This helps in building trust, and maximizing communications within the project team (Kloppenborg, Shriberg, & Venkatraman,2003). As projects are supposed to accomplish something novel, it is vital to develop new approaches (Nokes & Kelly, 2007, pp14) and follow best practices of project management.

Pinto & Slevin (1988b) identified ten critical success factors for project success and emphasized communication as a vital factor. Turner's (1999) seven forces model recognized project team management, leadership, teamwork and industrial relations vital for project success. Research conducted by Cooke-Davies (2002) quantified that despite vast research and immense experience gathered in project management, project results are still a reason for frustration for stakeholders. Cooke-Davies (2002) concentrated on time, cost and quality as vital factors for successfully implementing project success, however, ignored individual team member and performance of the team. Certain literature considers Time, budget and quality as critical success factors (Blaney, 1989), (Duncan, 1987), (Globerson & Zwikael, 2002), (Redmill, 1987), (Thomsett, 2002). However these dimensions are not sufficient (Nixon, Harrington, & Parker, 2012), and quality of project management process, the performance of the leadership, and satisfaction of the stakeholders by meeting their expectations is essential (Baccarini, 1999), (Schwalbe, 2004). Therefore, it is important to consider these dimensions along with time, budget and quantity for project success (Nixon, Harrington, & Parker, 2012). Belassi & Tukel (1996) suggested a framework for grouping above dimensions into four interrelated areas viz. project, project management and team members, organization, and external environment. Research done by DeLone & McLean (2003) on measuring success in projects in Information Systems (IS) found limitations in success/

failure criteria and therefore proposed a model with six dimensions (Table 8.1) for measuring success in IS projects, however, model lacked provision to measure the influence of project leadership and measurement of leadership performance on the project (Nixon, Harrington, & Parker, 2012).

System Quality	Information processing system is measured.
Information Quality	Information system is measured.
Information use	Recipient's consumption of the output of an information system is measured.
User satisfaction	Recipient's response to the use of the output of an information system is measured.
Service Quality	The quality of service itself is measured.
Net Benefits	Effect of information on the recipient, and measure of the effect of information on organisational performance is measured.

Table 8.1: Dimensions for measuring success in IS projects. Adapted from (DeLone & McLean, 2003)

Research by Jugdev & Muller (2005) determined followings factors critical for project success:

- Identification of key project stakeholders at project initiation in order to map their requirements and expectations for determining the success category they fit it.
- Building collaborative relations and effective communication between the project sponsor and Project Leader.
- An empowered Project Leader to deal with project issues; and active involvement of project sponsor in project performance are vital factors for project success.

However, research by Turner & Muller (2005) concluded that project leader, his leadership style and his/her competence are also vital for project success.

Research conducted by Kuen & Zailani (2012) regarding projects in Malaysia concludes that 75% of business improvement and transformation projects failed due to incompetencies of the project personnel, and undefined project mission, which are otherwise all-important for the success of NPD projects. They further deduced that well-defined project mission and involvement of top management as crucial success factors for Non-NPD projects.

Murphy, Baker, & Fisher, (1974), identified 31 managerial factors related to project success. Pinto & Slevin (1987) and Schultz, Slevin, & Pinto (1987) defined factors for project success:

- Support from Top management.
- The presence of experienced Project Leader and staff.
- Usage of appropriate control mechanisms.
- An effective communication channels, and being responsive to customer demands.

Research by Fisher (2011) concluded that project success relies on:

- Organizational structure.
- The level of authority is lying with the Project Leader.
- The size of the lean manufacturing, lean thinking, and lean construction into the scope of the project.

Moreover, Fisher (2011) construed that project success is also dependent on measures such as meeting the delivery schedules, meeting the allocated budget, and achieving the desired technical performance.

8.4 Critical processes while managing projects

8.4.1 Communication

Communication is the essential and crucial part of project management.

Communication is paramount. 99% of project management is communication.

In the global project, collaboration is essential. Communication is vital.

Communication is essential to project management (Ara & Al-Mudimigh, 2011), (Kerzner, 2009, p.p. 233), (Nokes & Kelly, 2007). Without effective, well-timed and accurate communication, project leader won't be able to build a project team and its morale (Meredith & Mantel, 2012), coordinate with team, delegate tasks to them, monitor their performance, and resolve their issues and problems (Verzuh, 2005). This can lead to confusion and increase conflicts in the project teams due to increased confusion and can halt the progress of the project due to lack of urgency in the team members to understand the status of the project (Barnett, 2009). For that reason, the project leader should improve communication within project teams as well as with stakeholders (Ashworth et al., 2012) through productive and focused meetings (Pinto, 2010, p.p. 132) with clear agenda and objectives involving at least one cross-functional team member. However, duration of these meetings needs to be controlled. "Obeya" systems or big room practiced by Toyota and Boeing (Barnett, 2009) can be applied where the strength of the team and power of the team members can be unified to improve communication and coordination between cross-functional teams (Liker & Morgan, 2006). This will lead to effective problem-solving, generation of new ideas for increasing capabilities of the team members, minimization of organizational barriers, and recognition of future actions for achieving project objectives. Additionally, Obeya process will allow project leader to act proactively rather than reactively (Barnett, 2009). For global projects, some ground rules should be set for communication (Thompsen, 2000). More in-person interactions are recommended through initial visits to the project location, however as meetings are critical means through which Project Leaders can communicate (Pinto, 2010, p.p. 132), short duration meetings approximately 30 minutes, usually twice or thrice a week, should be encouraged but daily meetings should be avoided.

8.4.2 Maintaining Interaction with customer

The project leader should maintain regular interaction with the customers. During the implementation of IT implementation project at the client side, Project Leader has to explain and convince the client about the reason for making changes in the customer process, get client's acceptance through negotiation, attain client's support in execution and obtain final acceptance from the client after the completion of the project. All this requires active communication.

We have to explain to the customer why we are using the process and why this is important for this process to be implemented in their environment. It is tough to convince the client that his method is not as good as IBM is providing. As they have taken IBM as their service provider, it becomes a mandate for them to follow IBM process. Therefore, I think execution and then being accepted of the deliverables requires many communication skills with the customer.

8.4.3 Project Initiation and Project Planning

Project Initiation and Project Planning phases are the critical phases during the implementation of a project, and in those phases, apart from creating plans to meet the end dates, the decision is also taken for selecting right manufacturing process methodology. Project Leader sets proper process controls to check whether the processes are stable and whether the required facilities and resources are available. During these phases, most of the project planning work should be completed including finalization of scope which is done after consulting the stakeholders; market analysis, and buy/make analysis should be done in order to check whether the selected project management process is correct and is aligned with organizational strategy and organization objectives.

One of the most important factors will be project-planning side because raw material and assemblies need to be released to the shop floor depending upon the customer requirement. You have some end dates; therefore, to meet those end dates, planning and method for planning are more important. In project planning, you have to consider the manufacturing process methodologies, and the process control to understand whatever processes we are implementing is very well controlled, whether the facilities are in place and whether the production processes are stable. These things should be thought from the Project Planning side.

For any project to be successful, we need to start with the initiation. An initiation is a place where you can set boundaries. You can set up the scope. Most of the planning work has to happen in the initiation and the planning side. Before you enter the planning side, you need to have a clear idea of whether the work you will do is real, what the sponsored has asked. However, as a professional responsibility, you have to go out and do some work and analyze whether the work you are opting to do is required to be done in that way. Maybe there are some options to do that. One option may be to go and do market research and analysis and prepare to make/buy analysis, look at the organization strategy and organization objectives. After that, you do the scope direction and come up with the documentation requirement. At this stage, missing out any details can break the project.

Initiation phase is considered as a critical phase as most of the projects fail due to incorrect activities done in Initiation phase such as the improper definition of business and systems requirements, inappropriate requirement gathering. It is recommended for bringing all people together and conducting route cause analysis for the avoidance of above-mentioned problems in future.

"Something that I think the most critical is the ability to define good business and system requirements. This is felt that the most projects fail during the implementation phase, look at the cause and analyze the problem occurred during the requirements phase. Once the requirements are gathered, all came together and did an excellent job in requirement gathering.

8.4.3.1 Project Initiation

Project initiation is a critical project management process, and the literature supports the same. Main activities done in the Project Initiation Phase are listed hereunder.

- Identification of key stakeholders, either internal or external (Cleland, 1986).
- Gathering of project requirements from the customer and the stakeholders.
- Understanding those requirements in depth.

Attention should be given to this phase since the lack of consideration to stakeholder's expectations can lead to project failure (Legris & Collerette, 2006). Cost overruns, project delays, or the project stoppages due to clashes arising from product design and implementation (Olanders & Landin, 2005) might also occur due to stakeholder's negative attitude for the project. Conversely, in IT projects, unrealistic stakeholder expectation is also a major identified risk (Baccarini, Salm, & Love, 2004). Therefore, Project Leader should give foremost attention in this stage; inability to do this may result in failure to meet a project deadline, cost, and quality.

8.4.3.2 Project Planning

Project planning is deemed as a critical process in project management, and the literature supports that project planning is essential in IT projects (Grover, et.al., 1995) and project lifecycle. In this phase, Project Leader decides the mission of the project, schedules, budgets, goals and milestones, and type of stakeholder relationships. Moreover, Project Leader performs tactical planning including evaluation of technical capabilities of the project, human resource allocation, selection and training of the team members and, deployment of a control system for monitoring, and generating feedback (PMI, 2008), (Pinto & Prescott, May 1990). Pre-project planning done in this phase is also vital for project success.

Risk planning should be done in this phase (Walker & Shen, 2002) as risk and uncertainty are serious threats designing a precise, elaborate, chiseled and well-formulated project plan. This also necessitates making the complex Aerospace or IT projects less complex and straightforward (Giezen, 2012) through work breakdown wherein the project is divided into small tasks, subtasks, and work packages in an hierarchal order with a view to managing the scope. This work is also done in project planning along with managing scope changes (Meredith & Mantel, 2012). However, there must be flexibility in the planning process to take more agile and quick decisions. Moreover, a project leader must plan for a process for implementing and the customers in IT and Aerospace projects (Walker & Shen, 2002) request handling change requests in the project since countless changes.

Being a critical process, it is essential that quality gates or checkpoints are put at predetermined milestones of the project planning process which will allow problems and issues related to project planning to be resolved and allow halting any further work on the project until project objectives are aligned with customer requirements (Meredith & Mantel, 2012). Gates will give stakeholders and team members an opportunity to participate and contribute through their unified consensus, feedback and suggestions to any planning issues, and allow room for improvements at the early stages of the project. Application of Lean Six Sigma tools such 5Whys; Cause and Effects Analysis is vital for bringing process improvements through cause analysis. Integration of these tools with quality project management will promote agility and innovation, and allow project leader to monitor risks, monitor project timeline, cost and schedule and overall project performance.

8.4.4 Requirements Gathering

Requirement gathering is a critical process, and any problem in the same will result in the failure of the program.

> *Requirement gathering is the part of the execution phase. Everybody knows how to do that and if you have not done any requirement gathering, then you are in real trouble. That is even worse than not planning.*

> *Requirement gathering and documenting it and agreeing upon that is the most critical factors for project success.*

Requirement gathering is a critical project management process, and the literature supports that project leader should gather complete and consistent requirements through the proper methodology for project success (Verner & Cerpa, 2005), (Wysocki & Rafeq, 2007). Incomplete requirements can lead to inaccurate estimation, late schedules and cost underestimates due to the late addition of team members in the team (Verner & Cerpa, 2005). It is, therefore, crucial that project leader should gather all requirement through requirement gathering sessions (Nadeem, Qureshia, Asim, Nadeem, & Mehmood, 2012) before proceeding to next stage.

8.4.5 Risk Management

Risk Management is considered as one of the critical element of project management.

Risk management is the key focus area for any Project Leader.

Risk management is also one of the key sectors.

Risk management is a critical project management process, and the literature supports that effective project risk management is the vital for project success and is regarded as a competitive advantage (Kwak & Stoddard, 2004), critical strategic and operational precedence (Shimizu, Park, & Hong, 2012), and stresses the role of project leader in risk management (Kleindorfer & Saad, 2005), (Tang, 2006), (Ahmed, Kayis, & Amornsawadwatana, 2007), (Dillon & Tinsley, 2008), (Keizer & Halman, 2009), (Eckhause, Hughes, & Gabriel, 2009), (Geraldi, Lee-Kelley, & Kutsch, 2010), (Jani, 2011), (Steffey & Anantatmula, 2011), (Shimizu, Park, & Hong, 2012), however it is perceived as an expense and additional work (Kwak & Stoddard, 2004) which means that project leader should handle project risks.

8.5 Best Practices in Project Management

Best practice is a technique or methodology delivers results effectively, efficiently, consistently and in a standardized way (Kerzner, 2010, p.p. 18-19). It is a proven way of accomplishing an objective. Application of best practices leads to project success. Project Management best Practices are listed hereunder as researched by Kerzner (2010).

- Project Leader must take consent of stakeholder in project and program charter for documentation of business objectives.
- Project Leader should discuss purpose and scope of the project with the stakeholders, and key members should be present at the Kick-off meeting.
- Project Leader should properly define management and financial processes for standardization to increase efficiency.
- Project Leader should distribute work among team members after proper analysis.
- Project Leader should create project maps, procedures, policies, workflow and templates for critical processes.

- Project Leader should schedule and conduct meetings to discuss the milestones.
- Project Leader should evaluate the project performance and must discuss with other team members after completion of the project.
- Project Leader should not be replaced and change project manager even if the project is in bad condition.
- Project Leader should facilitate project management training throughout the lifecycle of the project.
- Project Leader should apply methodologies and techniques of project management across the whole enterprise.
- Project Leader should properly structure each project.
- Project Leader should regularly update project plans.
- Project Leader should create a list for the project to register the issues encountered during the execution of the project.

According to Bresnena, et.al. (2003, p.p. 213), knowledge capturing, transfer and learning in projects depends on upon social practices and processes, and therefore Project Leader should follow community-based approach (the social process of learning) along with application of technological mechanisms for capturing project based learning, and adopting best practices.

PM best practices in Canadian Organisations as explored by Loo, (2002) are listed below:

- Effective scope management of projects.
- Integrated project management system.
- Effective project planning, scheduling and controlling.
- Effective contract management.
- High competent project teams.
- Involvement of stakeholders.
- Effective communication across the organization and with teams.
- Effective human resource management.
- Project documentation and project preplanning.
- Effective control of budgets.
- Effective meetings and customer satisfaction.

Empirical research by Visitacion (2003) derived that failures in the project take place because of poor planning and unclear requirements, which further led to poor productivity. As per the Pareto rule, 20% improvement in project management processes through proper planning and dynamic project management leads to 80% increase in productivity. Nevertheless, Visitacion, (2003) considers that best practices Project Management lies in the execution.

Research by Ling, Low, Wang, & Lim, (2009) on project management practices in China extrapolated that for high performance in large global projects:-

- Project Leader should break the project work in small packages.
- Project Leader should fully define contracts.
- Project Leader should discuss project objectives with the employees.
- Project Leader should prepare project schedule in detail and should update it regularly.
- Project leadership should accept and approve and commit to the schedule early.
- The project leader should apply high-quality cost control techniques and quality management plans.
- Project Leader should provide adequate resources for executing project work.
- Project Leader should properly resolve labor issues and should manage risk effectively.
- Project Leader should effectively manage health and safety matters in the project.
- Project Leader should give a high degree of response to perceived variations.
- Project Leader should concentrate to control the language barrier in case of the global project through more and more face-to-face communications between team members.
- Project Leader should increase relationships between global team for better team engagement in the future.
- The project leader should also concentrate to manage public image and public relationships.

Research on project management practices in China revealed that in project management, among the triple objectives of time, schedule, and technical performance, technical performance is stated as the most vital objective than financial results or cost and schedule (Yan, 2012).

Table 8.1 list out the Best Practices and Bad Practices for project success and failure respectively in India and Global Arena as researched through literature by various authors and scholars.

Best Practices	Authors Name
• The emphasis on client results (outcomes) rather than deliverables (output). • Clear and well-communicated expectations and outcomes. • Investment up-front in learning the client's environmental. • Incremental success.	(Appelbaum, 2004).
• Adequate project planning. • Regular plan reviews and troubleshooting.	(Boadle, 2004), (Pinot & Slevin, 1987), (Frese & Sauter, 2003).
• Managers to inspire a shared vision. • Communicate with all team members and client, and lead with enthusiasm and demonstrate exceptional energy level. • Demonstrate integrity by embracing ethical practices. • Display consideration towards team members. • Result driver, and phenomenal political skills. • Honest feedback and communication. • Espouse goal commitment from the project team.	(Boadle, 2004), (Pinot & Slevin, 1987), (Morris, 1986), (Morris & High, 1987).

• Effective project leader. • Competent and experienced managers with necessary technical and leadership skills, with team building and problem-saving skills. • Experienced, hardworking, motivated, focused and enthusiastic project team members with necessary capabilities and management skills. • Appropriate team.	(Boadle, 2004), (Pinot & Slevin, 1987), (Frese & Sauter, 2003), (Morris, 1986), (Sturdivant, 2004), (CERF, 2004), (Belassi & Tukul, 1996), (Pinto & Kharbanda, 1995), (Sayles & Chandler, 1971), (Martin C., 1979).
• Applying best practices in schedule and cost control.	(CERF, 2004).
• Regular and periodic project reviews by internal and external parties, as well by peers. • Proper tracking.	(CERF, 2004).
• Developing a procurement strategy with the risk management program at the conceptual design stage of the project. • Robust front-end planning and risk assessment.	(CERF, 2004), (Mengesha, 2004:45).
• Tailor procurement approaches to project.	(CERF, 2004).
• Use of performance metrics and incentives.	(CERF, 2004).
• Phase funding by linking to the critical decision points.	(CERF, 2004).
• Establish and control the performance of the contractors and link contractor performance to desired business results.	(Kanter & Walsh, 2004), (CERF, 2004).

• Have a proper, adequate, realistic and appropriate level of project planning in regards to detail and precision and, have control process in place.	(Mengesha, 2004:45), (Baker, Murphty & Fisher, 1983), (Morris, 1986), (Frese & Sauter, 2003), (Boadle, 2004).
• Stakeholder management; ensuring that the technology being implemented works well; having an objective management orientation; suitable project organization.	(Mengesha, 2004:45).
• Top management support.	(Mengesha, 2004:45), (Sturdivant, 2004), (Frese & Sauter, 2003), (Tukel & Rom, 1995), (Pinto & Kharbanda, 1995), (Pinto & Slevin, 1987), (Appelbaum, 2004).
• Interface with surrounding projects.	(Mengesha, 2004:45).
• Management of the design process.	(Mengesha, 2004:45).
• A clear statement of requirements, vision, projects objectives, responsibility, and accountability and defined goals. • Deliverables that meet the business needs and business objectives. • Financial contract to avoid legal problems; clear project goals. • Portfolio and program management practices matched to corporate strategy and business objectives.	(Sturdivant, 2004), (Frese & Sauter, 2003), (Morris & High, 1987), (Pinto & Slevin, 1987), (Baker, Murphty & Fisher, 1983), (Boadle, 2004), (Cooke-Davies., 2002).
• User involvement. • Realistic expectations. • Project ownership.	(Sturdivant, 2004).
• Smaller project milestones.	(Sturdivant, 2004).
• User involvement.	(Frese & Sauter, 2003).

• Adequate schedule control and project scheduling with the proper control mechanism in place.	(Frese & Sauter, 2003), (Cleland and King, 1983, (Cleland & King, 1983), (Sayles & Chandler, 1971), (Pinto & Kharbanda, 1995).

Table 8.1: Best Practises and Bad Practices in Project Management

Apart from above, Project Leader should focus on project management process, concentrate on aspects of project leadership, project team along with the impact of culture on project success.

8.5.1 Standardization of Project Management Methodology

In global projects, Project Leader should standardize project management methodology in order to have a joint project management framework. Each country has different methodology influenced due to cultural differences existing between the countries. A common methodology will enable team members and customers located in various countries across the globe to work in sync with the organization and follow common processes and practices.

Standardization is essential for global projects as we are working in different countries and each country has an own way of doing things. When you take your project to these countries, they should be following the same standard for your project. Reporting, creation of schedules and various formats should be kept in a standard way. That means your job as the Project Leader or the program director become simpler as they are following your direction, and you get the information. You can feed that information to your stakeholders.

One is having a global methodology operative. My previous company was into this. Just the fact that you are all working the same way against the same structure, the same framework is one of the most important things. Because customers come to these clients and us are global organizations so they cannot expect us to work in the same way. They do not expect us to sign up for a project as for the people in America are working in a different way to the people working in Italy, different to the people working in China. Customers do not want that. Therefore, the first thing is to have a standard project framework and methodology.

We followed the standard project management methodology of SAP practice, which is known as Accelerated SAP implementation wherein we have few phases. In any project, we do the analysis.

I think the standardization of some project management methodology. You got PMBOK, you got Prince2, you got IPMA, ASAP all these places but for global teams, it should be clubbed in one project management framework.

Standardization of Project Management methodology in the global project is a best practice, and the literature supports that standardized methodology in project management provides project leader with single project management framework integrated with industry best practices and organization's experience (Kerzner, 2010). Standardization of Project Management methodology brings consistency across projects, tightens controls (Liu, et.al. 2008), establishes standards (Nidumolu, 1996), lays procedures and processes (Dietrich & Lehtonen, 2005), and brings coherence to single process (Payne & Turner, 1999). This leads to quicker process implementation and better process quality through the definition and implementation of standard tools (Milosevic & Patanakul, 2010), however for standardisation, the project leader must be competent, must identify industry best practises, and have a capable organisation for executing project related activities (Milosevic & Patanakul, 2004).

8.5.2 Communication

Communication was referred to a vital part of project management. It is significant that Project Leader prepares a robust communication plan, and emphasizes largely to written communication.

Key enablers for better communication:

- Project Leader should pre-plan and schedule meetings.

- Project Leader should ensure recording and circulation of Minutes of Meetings (MOM).
- Project Leader should encourage open houses wherein every team member is free to share his/her opinion and share project objectives.
- Project Leader should conduct team training sessions in common language.
- Project Leader should educate team members for developing awareness on technical and non-technical aspects of the project.
- Project Leader should set high-tech communication systems enabling file sharing, remote access and data sharing over a cloud with high levels of privacy and security restrictions.
- Project Leader should set multiple communication channels.
- Project Leader should appoint a single point of contact (SPOC) in each geographically co-located team.
- Project Leader should promote team interactions through frequent catch-ups.
- Project Leader should continuously assess project's communication requirements.

8.5.2.1 Two-way stream / Parallel communication

Two-way communication is regarded as one of the best practice in project management. Two-way communication enables:-

- Team members to get engaged in the project.
- Allow Allow to update project progress or relate issues for reporting to each stakeholder.
- Share information allowing team members to see the bigger picture.
- Allow team members to connect with each other for better mutual understanding.
- Increase their motivation and commitment towards the project.

Once the project is started, communication is one of the critical factors. Communication should be flowing from both sides. They should be getting enough information to see the bigger picture and the impact they are going to make in your organization. They should see the benefits of the project so that they can connect with your project. People should be engaged in the project. This will increase their motivation and increase their commitment towards the projects.

Moreover, then after execution, we ensure that parallel communication is maintained, and any issue is rightly communicated to every stakeholder. We have sign-off for each phase.

In the global project, collaboration is essential. Communication is paramount. Parallel communication is required.

Collaboration between team members increases:

- Through the application of voice-based technologies and improved bandwidth technologies.
- Using stringent protocols of collaboration.
- Through the application of accurate and adequate collaboration tools with a clear definition of the roles and responsibilities of team members.
- Building a shared company-wide communication platform for recording and monitoring all communication events.
- By application of collaborative tools including meeting and reporting tools through which geographically co-located team members can concurrently engage in project execution and monitoring.

8.5.2.2 Frequent Focused Meetings with clear agenda and objective

Project Leader should arrange focused meetings within the project team members to improve communication and should spend time with the team members through periodical review meetings, group meetings, and technical meetings.

There might be regular status review meetings, group meetings, and technical meeting. These meetings are essential to improve communication.

8.5.2.3 Right communication at right time

Project Leader must maintain proper, frequent and good communication between the project leader, project team members, and stakeholders at the right time.

> *This is crucial. Unless they provide proper communication at the right times, they cannot be a good leader.*

> *Whenever we do a global project, it is crucial to have an exquisite communication and a very frequent communication.*

8.5.2. 4 Use of latest communication technologies

Project Leader should maintain communication using the phone and use latest Internet technologies such as email, video conferencing, video calling, and conference call. However, Project Leader should give more preference to face-to-face meetings than web conferencing.

> *The communication mode can be through phone, through emails, through VC because otherwise, it is tough to maintain such a large team when you are working globally.*

> *I believe in face to face meetings as they are more fruitful than VC or conference call.*

8.5.2.5 Need of Communication Model and Communication Plan

Communication model should be present in the organization to decide what to communicate and how to communicate with the team members. Communication model defines the communication rules and records the artifacts emerging out of the communication. Creation of a communication plan increases stakeholder engagements and improves conversation with community, team members, and with people who are most impacted by the project.

> *Communication model in place when you decide your project i.e. how you want to communicate, what you want to communicate,*

what are the documents, what are the artifacts should come out of those communications. These are vital.

For that, you must have many stakeholder engagements. You not only need to talk to your key stakeholders but also speak to those people who are going to be impacted by that. As a professional responsibility, you have to go to talk to other community and people as well. Prepare a communication plan, meeting and engaging them can make your project very successful.

For improving communication, Project Leader should initiate parallel communication between team members, start right communication at the appropriate time, use latest communication technologies, and a prepare communication channel and plan. Literature supports that clear and efficient two-way communication channels (Armstrong, 2008), appropriate clear and effective, open and direct communication should be maintained (Adnan, et.al, 2012) which exemplifies that project leader should promote two-way communication channels.

Parallel or two-way communication between team members will enhance employee participation in the project (Silva & Rocha, 2012), foster collaboration (Lyons & Wilker, 2012), and will allow team members jointly to address critical project issues (Edmondson & Nembhard, 2009). therefore Project Leader should arrange frequent project team and stakeholder review meetings, consistent milestone presentation meetings (McFarlan, 1981) and status review meetings for discussing, evaluating project progress, identifying discrepancies, non-conformances and future problems, and later for taking corrective and preventive actions (Cleland & King, 1968), (PMI, 2008), (Mignerat & Rivard, 2012), (Tsai, et.al., 2012). Besides, project leader should openly communicate right, consistent, clear and accurate messages (Meredith & Mantel, 2012, p.p. 105) to team members and stakeholders, at appropriate time through suitable medium (PMI, 2008) such as meeting, phone or by using latest communication technologies such as Email, Skype, Video Conferencing and Conference call, MS SharePoint, which improves team collaboration (Jamison, Cardarelli, & Hanley, 2007), (Lyons & Wilker, 2012). Nevertheless, after meeting, the project leader should send follow-up email containing the summary of the meeting to all team members and should communicate any project changes, which will increase mutual understanding between team members (Lyons

& Wilker, 2012). The communication plan should be prepared early in project planning phase by the project leader to document the method for communicating efficaciously with stakeholders and should allow the provision of time and budget to communication activities. Likewise, the project should review and revise the plan on a continuous basis (PMI, 2008).

8.5.3 Conduct Stakeholder Analysis

Identification of key stakeholders and analysis for understanding customer and stakeholder requirements along with proper planning is significantly important for Project Leader. Only after getting proper consensus from all stakeholders, the project should be initiated.

> *First and the foremost thing where we all make mistakes is that we do not understand our stakeholders. There are seven key areas where we concentrate on, we do not get interested parties, and we do not understand the requirements. Therefore understanding the requirement is the first and important. You should also know who your key stakeholders are. If you don't get it and take requirements from the stakeholders who are different and is not related to the ultimate goals you are looking at, you have already lost.*

> *Moreover, Project Leaders start with execution before they have any agreement on what they are going to do.*

> *Be prepared. Do all the planning understanding the context you are working within*

Literature supports that Project Leader should conduct stakeholder analysis for identification of interested parties through brainstorming (Calvert, 1995), understanding their roles and needs for improving contact and realizing their needs while contemplating cultural differences (Armstrong, 2008), (Kochan & Rubinstein, 2000).

Project leader should perform proper planning in identifying what information is required to whom, when and in which format (Armstrong, 2008), and further suggest various approaches for greater understanding the stakeholder such as mapping stakeholders according to their impact on organisational objectives (Mitchell, Agle, & Wood, 1997), classification of interested parties as per roles (Kochan & Rubinstein, 2000), and laying importance on stakeholder analysis and level of support required (Turner, Kristoffer., & Thurloway, 2002). This means that project leader should perform stakeholder analysis for project success (Olander & Landin, 2005) and should further engage in identifying difficulties and possibilities in the project in the early stage in the project allowing the project leader time and chance for maneuvering (McElroy & Mills C., 2003), (Elias & Cavana, 2006), (Karlse, 2002), (Andersen, et.al, 2004.). Stakeholder management is vital for project management, and therefore essential to recognize the stakeholder's interests. Stakeholders can surge the operating costs of the project through various fees, and their actions can pose a negative impact on the position of the companies involved in the project (Aaltonena, Jaakkob, & Tuomasa, 2008).

8.5.4 Cultural Awareness

Cultural awareness as regarded as one of the best practice. Project Leaders must be aware of the diverse cultures of different countries when managing global or local projects.

> *Cultural understanding is also vital. If you are not aware of the different cultures, you will not be mindful of the fact that for example in some countries, people will not say no. They will always say yes even if they mean no.*

For improving cultural awareness:-

- Project Leader should develop training curriculum and imparting training for comprehending client's culture.
- Project Leader should conduct employee orientation and exchange programs for improving awareness on cultural issues.
- Project Leader should increase interaction among offshore and onshore team through events, teleconference and team meetings.
- Project Leader should arrange team's visit to diverse places in order to meet other team members and for learning and understanding team member's cultures.
- Project Leader should hire team members with international experience.
- Project Leader should exchange resources on a rotational basis.

However, it is essential that Project Leader ensures that team members avoid the use of expressions, words that disgrace the cultural value of others.

8.5.4.1 Understand Cultural background of Team Members

Project Leader and team members must understand the cultural background of the team members while working on global projects, and should adapt to the local culture of that country after appreciating the local culture. Project Leader, thereafter, should mold its solution according to the culture of that country for sustaining globally and for an effective team communication.

> *You also need to understand the cultural background. If I have a group of different people from different countries, I would like to research for understanding the culture of the teammates before meeting them, and try to understand their background, what type of things they have done, what their interests are, what are their likes and dislikes. Then, based on that, I aim to communicate effectually with the different team members from different regions.*

> *Companies that have a strategy and ensuring that have a local understanding to sustain globally. So global projects in the way are implemented globally have a global employee employed locally. Therefore, at that point, you have people on the ground and the countries. You have to mold your solution to a particular country considering its culture. You need to be prepared to go in, look for people you can trust upon, and find what are the issues in the environment. Therefore, being prepared to understand the constructs of the local culture and cultural background of the project team members is imperative.*

Project leader should have cultural awareness, and the literature supports that culture awareness of the team will allow Project Leader to build closer personal relationship with the cross-cultural team members, build trust between them, and enable them to be aware of the cultural differences through cultural sensitivity programs or face-to-face meetings (Barczak, McDonough, & Athanassiou, 2006) during shift work using video-conferencing.

Nevertheless, the skill of working with cross-cultural team members comes through experience, and while working on the job. Therefore, those team members should be selected who have some kind of experience of working with cross-cultural teams and have some cultural awareness (Lee-Kelley & Sankey, 2007) which depicts that cultural awareness is a best practice.

8.5.5 Proper Risk Management

Project Leader must perform Risk Management Analysis, Planning for successful projects.

8.5.5.1 Perform Risk Analysis and Risk Mitigation Planning

Risk mitigation planning is considered as one of the best practices. Detailed risk analysis should be done to understand the implications of risks followed by risk reduction planning during the planning phase to create risk reduction plans. Thereafter, risk-related reports should be attached along with status report while reporting project status to the management. Project Leader may recruit a separate risk analyst for the task of dealing with risks associated with different customers through creation of proper risk mitigation mechanism.

> *The Project Leader needs to assess the risk to be taken, what the implication of the risk will be and how to mitigate that chance.*

> *We have risk mitigation analysis during the handover phase. There is an engagement handover. We have a risk analyst, and we have a risk mitigation plan because some customers are tough, and some customers are easy going. Risk analysis and mitigation planning should be done in detail once you enter in a planning phase. The risk is a constant thing. You can do a project when you are doing a status report. Risk has to be attached along with the status report.*

8.5.5.2 Need for a Risk Management and Assessment System

Risk assessment is also regarded as a critical part of project management. Project Leader should properly classify the risks and must deploy a proper risk management system and risk evaluation system for assessing risk scenarios in project and programs, and techniques for capturing risks.

You need to understand what your systematic risks are, what are your risks are. If you cannot classify your risks properly, you cannot find solutions for your risk. Moreover, for the solution for your risk, you need to have a proper risk management system in place. You need to have an organizational risk assessment system so that any projects that you take or undertake or any think that you go for using in your portfolio, as a portfolio manager should very much go ahead and assess the risk scenario for those risks. There are approximately 15 risk areas into which risks can be broadly classified. We have got and techniques for capturing those risks.

The Project Leader needs to assess the risk to be taken. There must be a proper Risk assessment system.

It is important to link intensity of risks in projects with the selection of project management methodology. In the case of low-risk projects, straightforward or a standard project management process might work, but for high-risk projects, it is necessary to have a proper methodology to avoid missing any detail.

In case the project is a low-risk project or it is a straightforward process, then it is not necessary to have anything available, as most people will be able to do that. In case the project is a high-risk project, or you have much complexity due to geographical locations, then you need a methodology again to make sure that you do not miss anything

The project leader must prepare proper risk analysis and risk mitigation plan and must have a risk management and assessment system for assessing risk (Boehm & Turner, 2003).

Risk analysis should be done by identifying the risk through a formal process of creating a list where all the risk are categorized according to the type of project being planned. Through this process of identifying risk, enough information will be generated for the team. This will enable project leader in transforming company culture through better teamwork and reducing blame culture (Vose, 2008). Project Leader should perform risk mitigation planning in project planning stage to minimize the impact of the risk (PMI, 2008).

Regular reviews or risk assessment are necessary in order to re-examine the validity and utility of the risk register where the potential project risks were listed according to its priority. The project leader should regularly update the risk register and evaluate new potential hazards (Nokes & Kelly, 2007). This establishes that conducting risk analysis and, mitigation planning is project management best practice.

8.5.6 Well defined Change Management Process

Organization must have a well-defined change management including change request and change control process in order to meet any adjustment in the system as requested by the customer and to appropriately evaluate the impact of the change in project scope schedule and cost.

> *While you are implementing, some changes are requested or something new comes in due to which scope increase. For that, you must have well-defined change management process. Anything that is coming or any change that is being proposed should be well evaluated. The impact of the modification should be assessed.*

> *Without modification request process, you are going to be a failure. If you are not following the change request process, sponsor or client will keep asking new functionality. As you have been given a finite number of days and fixed budget, you cannot complete your budget on time and with high quality. That is where change request will come into play. This is very critical.*

The project leader must have a well-defined change management process to manage and control changes in project scope. Project change management allows the project leader to handle the customer and foresee the effect of the modification on project schedule, cost and technical performance (Kerzner, 2010), yet project leader should involve customer and should submit proposed change requests to change control board for approval (Yeh, Wei, & Wei, 2012). Project Leader should document the change if approved (PMI, 2008) and instantaneously communicate the customer in case change is not possible (Kerzner, 2010), (Nokes & Kelly, 2007). An integrated change control process is a critical process where all change request are reviewed for approval and managedIt safeguards the project leader from scope creeps and adds to the handling of stakeholder expectations (Kerzner, 2010). The project leader should create change management plan for outlining the process of handling change in the project (PMI, 2008). This establishes that the change management process can be regarded as a best practice, and the project leader should give due attention to it.

8.5.7 Regular Project Monitoring

Project Leader should frequently monitor project execution through meetings on a weekly basis or twice a week.

> *Regular monitoring is essential. In case the project deadline is very close, I will have weekly meetings or meetings twice a week.*

8.5.7.1 Use Balanced Scorecard

Project Leader should monitor the performance of the project using balanced scorecards at project as well as program management level.

> *Therefore, the eye view has to be different for a different size. There are dashboards at different levels. Some of the dashboards which are at governance level are called balanced scorecards. Some of the dashboards which are at program management level or project management level or account management level are seven key parameters we monitor. This is how we do the monitoring. Projects should be measured through Balanced Scorecard through project leader's performance can be measured.*

8.5.7.2 Keep track of Scope, Time, Quality and Cost (STQC)

The project leader should constantly monitor Scope, Time, Quality and Cost of the project while performing the risk assessment.

> *Keep track of scope, time, cost and quality. PM should be active in monitoring these four things.*

> *So, scope, time, quality and cost are being considered right on, and they are also part of the risk assessment. At the end of the*

day, risk assessment forms are used as center points for scope, time, quality and cost.

The project leader must perform regular project monitoring by using the balanced scorecard and by tracking Scope, Cost, Schedule and Quality which is known as Project Management Triangle or Iron Triangle. Project Leader should measure Scope, Cost, Schedule and Quality (Atkinson, 1999), (Westerveld, 2003), (Kerzner, 2009) and should also measure the project risks against the project plan (Nokes & Kelly, 2007). Project Leader should measure the project performance through balanced scorecard (Keyes, 2010).

8.5.8 Select skilled, experienced and trusted team members

Project Leader should select those team members who have technical expertise and multi skills, have relevant expertise in the field of project management with proven record of accomplishment and those who can be trusted for realizing the project.

Pick the people whom you trust and those who are technically excellent

They all choose their people very carefully, but people also trusted them as they inspired confidence in what they were doing.

In today's project environment, project leaders are working with very smart people (team members) where they need to get their trust. Once you got that, you can achieve amazing things.

A mixed blend of team members should be selected depending upon their previous assignments, their next assignments, and all those factors. That is one of the key factors.

Project Leader should be one who already has experience in this field because it is good to have people with hands-on experience in this kind of projects

The project leader should select skilled, experienced and trusted team members relevant to their role in the project. The team should be competent

(Hunter & Peters, 2012). Project Leader should select team members who have both knowledge and prior experience related to the project along with technical skills (Brinkkemper & Jansen, 2012), (Tsai, Moskowitz, 2003). Team members must have acquaintance and understanding of their co-team members working on the global or local project (Cohen & Thias, 2009), (Leinonen, 2005). They must demonstrate a sense of ownership to the project, especially global projects which means that team members should be well-composed (Cohen & Thias, 2009) especially for globally distributed projects (Brinkkemper & Jansen, 2012).

8.5.9 Put a Governance Structure

There must be a management structure at the top level to take high-level decisions on certain criteria such as project prioritization.

> *Once we have agreement with the stakeholder or the sponsor, then we talk about the governance structure, the key resources, key stakeholders and key risks, what we see as a risk and what organisation sees as a risk for the project, funding, resource side, and marketability side, etc. decisions are taken and discussed in details.*
>
> *Primarily the aim out here to put the governance model in place at the topmost level.*

The project leader should put a governance model to take high-level project decisions. Presence of project governance model is important to ensure that projects are aligned with company-wide strategy; projects are stable in reference to corporate policies, and projects flourish by instituting a well-defined approach that all stakeholders can understand and agree to, and through which progress of the projects and programs executed by the organisation can be measured proactively (Dinsmore & Rocha, 2012).

8.6 Customer Satisfaction

Customer satisfaction in project management is typically measured at the end of a project after the client has committed most of their money. Torbica & Stroh, (2001)argue that by measuring satisfaction only in the later stages of project management, relevant information might be lost (Lia, Nga, & Skitmo, January 2013). They contend that customer satisfaction should be measured during the early stages as well as at the end of the project. This total measurement gives companies more information and knowledge how to improve their customers' satisfaction index (Lia, Nga, & Skitmo, January 2013). Project Leader should conduct client survey which will aid in improving customer satisfaction as well as help in identifying and rectifying weaknesses in the company's project management process (Torbica & Stroh, 2001). Improvement in customer quality index correspondingly arguments product quality which translates into future projects for the enterprise resulting in positive implications such as increased revenue and profit (Kärnä, 2014).

8.7 Summary

This chapter reviewed the critical success factors and best practices of project management.

8.7.1 Summary of Critical Processes in Project Management

Critical Process in Project Management in IT and Aerospace Projects			
	Final Results	**Result Triangulated Yes or No**	**Supported by**
1	Communication.	No	
	• Maintain regular communication with customer	No	
2	Project Initiation.	No	
3	Project Planning.	Yes	Case Study 7
4	Requirement Gathering.	No	
5	Risk Management.	Yes	Case Study 7 and Case Study 4

Table 8.2: Critical Processes in Project Management

The results listed in Table 8.2 and Table 8.3 are supported by Interview results and Literature; however, Communication (Visual communication) was considered critical in Case Study 5 (Lean Six Sigma). Correspondingly, Project Planning and Risk Management were regarded as imperative in Case Study 7 (ERP Implementation). In addition to this, Case Study 4 regarded Risk management as a vital process. Thus, three of these results are triangulated which means these are fundamental processes in IT and Aerospace Projects. However, project initiation and requirement gathering are also significant in IT, and Aerospace Projects as any failure to collect detailed requirements while Requirement Gathering or any failure to identify Key Stakeholders in Project Initiation phase can prove to be a very costly mistake, and undoubtedly can lead to project collapse.

8.7.2 Summary of Best Practices in Project Management

Best Practices in Project Management in IT and Aerospace Projects			
	Final Results	**Result Triangulated Yes or No**	**Supported by**
1	Standardization of Project Management Process.	Yes	Case Study 4
2	Communication.	No	
	• Two-way stream / Parallel communication.	No	
	• Frequent focused meetings with clear agenda and objective.	Yes	Case Study 7
	• Right communication at the right time.	No	
	• Use latest communication technologies.	No	
	• The need of communication model and communication plan.	Yes	Case Study 7
3	Stakeholder Analysis.	No	
4	Cultural awareness.	No	

5	Proper Risk Management.	Yes	Case Study 4
	• Perform Risk Analysis and Risk Mitigation Planning.	Yes	Case Study 5
	• Need for a Risk Management and Assessment System.	No	
6	Well-defined Change Management Process.	Yes	Case Study 7
7	Regular Project Monitoring.	Yes	Case Study 6
	• Use Balanced Scorecard.	No	
	• Keep track of Scope, Time, Quality and Cost (STQC).	No	
8	Select Skilled, Experienced and Trusted Team member.	Yes	Case Study 3
9	Put a Governance Model.	No	

**Table 8.3: Best Practices in Project Management
in IT and Aerospace Projects**

Table 8.3 lists the Best practices in Project Management in IT and Aerospace projects. The triangulated results are also shown in the table along with the supporting Case study.

The project leader should be aware of these practices, however, for application of these practices, the Project Leader must have expertise in project management methodologies and approaches. In the next chapter, we will discuss project leadership.

CHAPTER 9

9. Project Leadership

9.1 Introduction

Leadership is an essential part of project management, affecting the performance of the project (Shenhar, et.al, 2002). Leaders influence organizational results by improving performance (Finkelstein & Hambrick, 1990), choice (Finkelstein, 1992), and encouraging innovative thinking (Zhou & George, 2003).

Leadership empowers employees to voice ideas for bringing improvement in the organization and processes (Detert & Burris, 2007). Research conducted by Burns (1978) and Bass (1985) on leadership behaviour, transformational and transactional leadership demonstrated up to what point leaders engaged their subordinates by inspiring them to accomplish organisational goals, and later define the rewards after the accomplishment of those aims (Rubin, Munz, & Bommer, 2005), (Yammarino, et.al., 1997), (Yammarino, Spangler, & Dubinsky, 1998). Additionally, transaction and transformational leadership encourage management innovation (Atwater & Bass, 1994), (Bass, 1990), (Howell & Avolio, 1993), (Podsakoff, Bommer, & Podsakoff, 2006), (Vaccaro, et.al, 2012). Leadership is also regarded as an important factor for project excellence (Kerzner, 1987), and an influence of project culture (Shore, 2008), and a medium for mustering individuals for change (Patterson, 2010). Project leaders must maintain equilibrium between project schedule and cost, tangible and intangible benefits (Murphy, 2002), (Phillips, Bothell, & Snead, 2002).

This chapter will identify the qualities and traits of project leader, and the role project leader should play to deliver successful IT and Aerospace projects locally and at the Global Arena.

9.1.1 Cultural Awareness

The project leader must have certain leadership style to align with the culture of the country where the project is being implemented. Project Leader should have a cultural awareness of the team members and have an understanding of the cultural difference between countries and organization, and that they should be enough broad minded not to act as a hierarchical boss of the geographically distributed project team members in order to just command them but should rather enable them to achieve success.

> *Cultural differences between the two countries or two organizations need to be properly understood. It becomes very hard to make decisions when it is a critical time. This is because he will not take a decision now. Moreover, people at the remote site might not be ready to accept your decision or your commanding order or accept you are providing leadership from a remote location. Cultural awareness enables decision-making.*

> *However, on top of that, for global projects, cultural awareness, which means somebody needs to be broad, minded enough if my understanding of the successful Project Leader is somebody who enables the team to achieve results. So a Project Leader is not a hierarchical boss that tells people what to do. He is more somebody that says, "I need these things to be completed. "What can I do to have this thing happen?" Moreover, you need to be aware of your team members, their strengths, and weaknesses. Working globally is even more important to know these things.*

> *It is based on the cultures. Therefore, you have to be aware of the culture and have a certain leadership style to work with those team members or teams.*

> *If it is a small project where you do not want two resources, a half-time Project Leader, and a technical half-time person because you now have two people in the meetings and everything, then, it makes sense to have one Project Leader who is a hybrid Project Leader. The other issue, of course, is that when you ask for a*

technical Project Leader, it is a different skill set from a Project Leader. Project Leaders if they are magnificent, they are excellent in communication. People without technical knowledge would be more into fixing than problem-solving. You would very rarely find somebody who is technical as well as useful in communication. So, if you go for hybrid people, you will not get the best of both.

The project leader must have cultural awareness while managing local and geographically distributed teams. Project Leader should be conscious of cultural distinctions of the team members and should demonstrate understanding and awareness of the values and beliefs of other (Fisher, 2011). This entails that cultural awareness is vital for the project leader to transfer concepts, technology and ideas across geographically distributed virtual teams (Moran, Harris, & Moran, 2011). Project Leader while managing people from varied cultures, should develop, demonstrate and apply an awareness of cultural difference of the team members by adjusting to some of the team member's native country behaviours suitable for that situation, express positivity about cultural differences, and communicate messages which endorse that cultural diversity is cherished as an improvement to own beliefs and values, however, while managing geographically distributed teams, leader should realise when not to act commandingly, and should rather lead to behaviour and demonstrate appropriate degree of capability and self-confidence (Fisher, 2011). But effective communication or collaboration is not resultant of diversity and requires that team members be willing to collaborate, ready for any change and keen for interdependence.

9.2 Project Manager versus Project Leader

Project leadership and leadership traits are associated with each other when contrasted with project management (Yanga, Huang, & Wu, 2011). Planning and organizing of project tasks through the decision-making process for enhancing the efficiency and effectiveness of a project is called project management, however, guiding, promoting, and motivating people for the attainment of project objectives through the realization of their potential is called Leadership (Anantatmula, 2010). Successful project manager persuades the staff for bringing change; stimulate novel methods of thinking and problem solving, and boosts them to work collectively for accomplishing project objectives in challenging work environments (Keller, 1992), (Anantatmula, 2010). Project leaders mentor and guide the team members to develop together as professionals, while simultaneously implementing the project responsibilities (Anantatmula, 2010).

Despite the fact that project leader and project manager denote different attributes and responsibilities, overlap exists between the two since effective project management involves effective leadership (Nixon, Harrington, & Parker, 2012) for project success. Nicholas & Steyn (2008) described Leadership as a management function, and divided the duties of the manager into five operates as illustrated in Table 9.1.

Duties of the Manager	
Planning	• Takes the decision about how to execute a task.
Organizing	• Completes preparatory work first and then plans for an arrangement for the work.
	• Hires, trains, mentor people, allocates roles and responsibilities, allocates resources.
	• Project Manager creates organization structure, policies, and procedures.
Leadership	• Mentors employees, directs and motivates team members upon accomplishment of project goals.
	• Builds teams and their performance, and focuses on behavioral traits.
Control	• Project Manager evaluates the performance of the employees with respect to the goal.
Change	• Project Manager assesses all the above functions to understand their functioning and checks whether any change is required.

Table 9.1: Duties of the Manager. Source: Adapted from Nicholas & Steyn (2008).

The project sponsor should select a high-ranking member of the project team as project manager. Selection should not only be based on their competency in project management, but importance should be given to behavior skills and leadership skills as done by GE (West, 2010).

		Leader	
		Poor	**Good**
Manager	**Poor**	Fail	Dysfunctional; short-term appearance of success; long-term failure
	Good	Sustained but only moderate success	Sustained and high success

Table 9.2. Combining Management and Leadership for success. Source: Adapted from Parry (2004)

Both management and leadership competencies are required for sustainable success in a management position. As per Henry Mintzberg, direction and management are inseparable, and both are dysfunctional. Those project leaders who do not know how to manage fail to understand what is going on. In the same way, management devoid of leadership is misdirecting. Table 9.2 illustrates that people having good leadership skills but poor management skills can achieve short-term success but long-term failure. In the same way, people with poor leadership but sound management skills can attain sustainably but only moderate success. The combination of right direction and administration skills can lead to strong and high success (Muller & Turner, 2010).

Concerns	Manager	Leader
Creation of Purpose	• Manager concentrates on planning and budgeting activity.	• Leaders institutes direction for the team and develops a vision and the required strategies

Developing a network for achieving the agenda	• Manager arranges the staff and constructs a structure for the realizing plan.	• Project Leader aligns team members to attain the objective.
	• Manager assigns responsibility and authority.	• Project Leader communicates direction through discussion.
	• Manager develops procedures for guiding behavior.	• Project Leader builds collaboration.
	• Manager develops monitoring systems.	• Build teams that comprehend and share project's vision.
Execution	• Controls and resolves issues.	• Encourages and motivates.
	• Manager monitors result and execute corrective actions.	• Leader rejuvenates people to overcome obstacles.
	• The manager does the things right.	• Project Leader takes personal initiative.
		• A leader does the right thing.
Outcomes	• Creates a degree of expectedness and order	• A leader creates change.
	• Manager pursues to sustain the current situation.	• Leader challenges the current situation.
	• The manager asks how and when.	• The leader asks what and why.

	• The manager focuses on the efficiency of operations.	• The leader focuses on the effectiveness of outcomes.
	• Manager prepares short-term plans	• Leader prepares long-term plans.
Focus timeframe	• Manager evades risks.	• A leader takes the risk.
	• Upholds and emulates.	• Transforms innovates and creates.
	• The manager has eyes on bottom-line.	• The leader has eyes on the horizon.
	• The manager focuses on systems.	• The leader focuses on people.

Table 9.3: Difference between Leader and Manager.
Source: Adapted from DuBrin (2011), Kotler (1990),
Lussier & Achua (2001), Pinto(2007), Bennis (1989).

Table 9.3 describes the attribute wise difference between Project Leader and Project Manager. Project Manager takes decisions about tasks and organization whereas Project Leader, who are pioneering, zealous and competent to overcome difficulties and challenges, incorporates overall vision and dedication to the team (Bull, 2010). Therefore, for project success, the project manager must have the qualities of a leader (West, 2010) since true leaders inspire and empower team members to execute project tasks efficiently and enthusiastically and work with them rather than above them or through them (Bull, 2010).

Leadership is equated to maintaining a supervisory or managerial position. In other words, possession of definite personal qualities is an essential trait of leadership (Judge, et.al. 2002). Leadership depicts a class of behavior where individual performs in a certain manner thereby persuading others to comply (Koene, Vogelaar, & Soeters, 2002). Research conducted by Zaleznik (1977) established that manager and leader have difference attitude towards their work, have different concepts towards works, and have difference relationships with other. Nevertheless, efforts put into developing a manager might hinder the development of a leader. Kotler (1990) said that although managers compliment management leaders, they could not substitute it. Research by Follet (1927, p.p.

235) concluded that best leaders have no followers but individuals working with them.

The three perspectives of Leadership		
Perspective	**Description**	**Author**
Leadership = Management	Leadership involves selecting talented subordinates, providing them with goals and direction, and establishing follower's trust by backing up one's work with action; the management functions of planning, organizing, and controlling represent critical components of the leader's job.	Drucker (1988)
Leadership and Management are a separate but complementary process.	The primary function of leadership is to produce constructive or adaptive changes; in contrast, the primary function of management is to ensure that an organization achieves its goals on time and on a budget. Both processes are needed for an organization to prosper	R. Quinn (1988), Kotler(1990), Bass (1985)
Leadership is not equal to management.	Leaders and manager have fundamentally different temperaments. Managers perceive work as an enabling process; management is an orderly and stabilizing process. Leaders risk disorder and instability as they seek out opportunities for change; leadership is a creative force.	Zaleznik (1977)

Table 9.4: Leadership and Management. Source: Adapted from Gardner & Schermerhorn (1992), Taylora, et.al. (2011).

Figure 9.4 describes the perspectives when the leadership and management are equal; when they are separate but have a parallel process; and when leadership is not equal to management.

9.3 Different types of Leadership

Leadership and Personality are both interrelated. Project Leader should first understand the structure of the project and then select the leadership style that matches with his/her personality (Kerzner, 2010). Leadership styles as researched by Hersey, Blanchard, & Johnson (1988) and Ryan (2008) are described here under.

9.3.1 Directing Leadership Style

o   This style is effective when the project team members are inexperienced and require quick decisions.

9.3.2 Coaching Leadership Style

o   This style is effective when the confidence of project team members are beginning to grow, or their enthusiasm is declining.

9.3.3 Supporting Leadership Style

o   This style is effective used when project team members are competent and when team members are eager to contribute to the project.

9.3.4 Delegating Leadership Style

o   This style is effective when project team members are top performers and ready to be self-sufficient.

9.3.5 Cohesive Leadership Style

o   By using this style, project leader expects team members do the way as told by the head. This leadership style has short-term benefits which result in low motivation level and bottom results.

9.3.6 Visionary Leadership Style

o   By using this style, project leaders take the people along with them to the pathways of success, share ideas, create plans, maintain communication at all levels and act as a role model.

9.3.7 Affiliative Leadership Style

o   In this Leadership style, project leader gives priority in building personal relationships rather than on completion of the task. This encourages sharing among team members which further increase motivation level, team collaboration and loyalty. This leadership style is beneficial in teamwork, however not effective in highlighting benefits when used in standalone mode and is therefore used more efficiently with visionary style.

9.3.8 Democratic Leadership Style

o   In this Leadership style, project leader builds commitments through people participation and values those commitments. This leadership style is of great importance and vital especially in the case of mergers and acquisitions when people have different cultural values and beliefs. Leaders spend a lot of time on making a decision and reach a consensus; however, there are many buy-ins once a decision is made. This leadership style also works best with the visionary style of leadership.

9.3.9 Pacesetting Leadership style

o   In this Leadership style, leaders instruct every team member to perform better and faster.

9.3.10 Coaching Leadership Style

o   In this Leadership style, Leaders mentor to team members to increase their performance and develop them for future by building long-term capabilities. Leader concentrates on day-to-day activities for improving project performance. Apart from increasing motivation and improving people skills, this leadership style promotes value creation for the organization. This leadership style results in long-term benefits; however, its takes a long time to accomplish.

Hersy & Blanchard, (2001) believed that leader who knows how to use power are looked upon more competent and efficient as compared to those leaders who do not or will not use power. An effective leader gathers several bases and sources of authority and then selects them for their application in suitable situations. An effective leader seldom rests on merely one source or base of authority (Ehsani, Koozechian, & Mora, June 2012). Leaders who apply their power effectively are able to successfully realize tasks in the organization irrespective of their designation in the organization and without any dependence on their subordinates (Fuqua, Paynex, & Cangemi, 1998).

9.4 Summary

The project leader should show flexibility in their management style after analyzing the experience and commitment level of their team members since the effectiveness of each of these styles is highly dependent on those factors. As leaders have to manage team member with different abilities and competencies, they must have tractability in their management styles because new team members will require a lot of mentoring and direction whereas leader can delegate tasks to team members with high experience and high skills. However, great leaders can be very dissimilar and have very diverse yet successful styles (West, 2010).

9.5 Theories of Leadership

Leadership is a process through which project leader guides, explains and influences team members to perform certain tasks and later motivates and coordinates to deliver the required deliverables successfully in the form of product or service in the context of the project (Morris & Pinto, 2007). Leadership Theories and the role of the project leader practicing those theories are described hereunder as researched by Bass (1985), Keegan & Den Hartog (2004), Morris & Pinto (2007).

9.5.1 Situational Leadership Model:

- Leaders employ relationship-oriented behavior in certain situations
- Leaders employ task-oriented behavior in other circumstances.
- The leader delegates authority when a team member is proficient as well as motivated.
- Leader adopts participative approach when a team member is proficiency but lacks motivation.

- The leader provides guidance, advice on decision-making.
- The leader provides necessary instructions in case team members are motivated but lacks experience.

9.5.2 Path-Goal Theory

- Explains satisfactions and performance of subordinates are influenced by the behaviors of the leader.
- Leader consistently rewards the team members for work-goal attainment.
- The leader gives clear directions, removes roadblocks and increases opportunities for increasing the satisfaction of the team member.

9.5.3 Leadership Substitutes Theory

- Experienced, trained, professional team members substitute leaders.
- A leader understands that selecting the right set of team members can decrease the load on them, and led to the creation of an efficient work system.

9.5.4 Charismatic Leadership Theory

- Team members perceive Leader to be charismatic if the leader is confident and articulates a vision that is different from the existing state of affairs but socially acceptable.
- Performances in an exceptional way to achieve that vision, and persuades team members to aligns with his vision rather than being authoritative; take risks, make personal sacrifices and even pay prices to attain that vision.

9.5.5 Transformational Leadership Theory

- Transformational leadership distinguishes between transformational and transactional leadership. Leaders motivate others by creating awareness in the team members about the importance of their work, persuading them to act for the sake of the team without taking care of the self-interest, and encouraging them to attain goals.

- Leaders believe in exchanging rewards for task performance but do not inspire other people or build long-term commitments.
- Leaders build a mutual vision and strong identification with team members, which is based on more than the just rewarding accomplishment of project activities.

9.5.6 Future-oriented Project Leaders

- Leader envisages the positive view of the future and is most effective when project environment is dynamic and varying.
- Leader challenges the existing systems and looks for opportunities for improvement.
- Best suited for flexible projects with open management styles.
- Leader fails to recognize the past endeavors and make frequent changes without consulting the teams, which can frustrate the team members.
- Leaders are useful at evaluating team performance and give appraisals.
- As these leaders are focused on the future, they fail to connect with the team cognitively.

9.5.7 Present-Oriented Project Leaders

- Leader deals with day-to-day issues, lives in present and addresses problems as they come.
- Leaders are cognitively available to the project team and are excellent in problem-solving.
- Leaders are good in leading projects similar to ones they have implemented in the past, and are a responsibility to provide project information to team members.

9.5.8 Transformational Leaders

Research by Hur, Berg, & Wilderom (2011) in a South Korean organization concluded that transformational leadership facilitates the relationship between emotional intelligence and leader effectiveness, and between emotional intelligence and service climate, however not between emotional intelligence and team effectiveness. The role of Transformational Leaders as researched by Morris & Pinto, (2007) described hereunder.

1. Transformational leader influences team members encourages and provides them support for improved performance.
2. A transformational leader inspires the team member by communicating a positive future vision.
3. Transformational leader intellectually stimulates team members to be aware of potential problems and reviews the issue from a different perspective.
4. Transformational leaders can bring change in an organization.
5. Transformational leader constantly looks for a new opportunity for exploring others.
6. They create a vision that appeals to the values, goals, and interest of followers.
7. They empower other to make decisions and encourage other to innovate.
8. They model the behavior they value and want other to practice.
9. They reward and recognize the followers publicly.
10. Transformational leaders also involve in creation and communication of vision across the organization to drive organizational behavior.
11. At the project level, the transformational leaders identify potential barriers to achieving the vision, convince followers to stay committed, select project team member with similar values, set a goal for the project and the team, communicate the vision to the team members and provide feedback to team members regarding their performance.

Further to this, different types of leadership styles such as transformational (Bass, 1985), distributed (Gibb, 1954) and complexity (Uhl-Bien, Marion, & McKelvey, 2007) should be followed by project champions (Taylora et.al, 2011) during different phases of the project. Project champions should use transformational leadership behavior during the Initiation phase; occurrences of coordinated forms of distributed leadership during the endorsement and Implementation phases; enabling leadership is a constituent of complexity leadership (Uhl-Bien, Marion, & McKelvey, 2007), and is significant to the leadership process. Project champion can create an environment that the facilitate emergence, collaboration, innovation, risk taking and learning for the project champions (Taylora, et.al, 2011).

Research carried out by Keller (1992) revealed that transformational leadership style enhances the performance of project teams, and is associated to project success factors of budget/schedule and project quality. Besides, the project teams directed by strong leadership have a superior sense of mission, intent and significance of the project leading to project success (Keller, 1992). Transformational Leader enhances team performance by:

1. Project Leader should increase awareness among the team members about the importance of the project results.
2. Project Leader should motivate team members to move beyond self –interest for the benefit of the team.
3. Project Leader should meet the set of individual needs on Maslow's hierarchy (Bass, 1985).

9.6 Project Leadership

Organisation should develop those managers as future project leaders who understand their work thoroughly, follow the philosophy and serve as a mentor and coach to others. Those leaders then should develop extraordinary people, and build robust teams that follow the company's philosophy. Strong Leadership is vital for the implementation of Lean and requires long-term commitment as it is a long-term objective (Davis, 2012).

As per Purvanova & Bono, (2009), project leader make use of inspirational motivation techniques to motivate the team members by:-

1. Discussing the purpose of the work and the project with confidence and enthusiasm.
2. Expresses confidence that the project will be successful.
3. Applies intellectual and divergent thinking to create new innovative ideas, and encourages others to come up with new ideas and looks at problems from different angles.
4. Looks for strength in each team member and assigns them a role in the project.
5. Treats team member with respect and provide advice to them.

Integrative leaders are apprehensive about the results either tangible or intangible, and they ensure that the energies lead to sustainable projects and systems contributing to the common good through cross-sector collaborations (Bozeman, 2007), (Crosby & Bryson, 2010, p.p. 209).

Authentic leaders are focussed on the development of strong leader-follower relationship, high ethical values, and integrity. Measurement of authentic leadership is based on five dimensions such as exhibiting self-discipline, leading with heart, instituting long lasting relationship, exercising firm values and passion for the purpose (Tate, 2008), (Wong, Laschinger, & Cummings, 2011). Authentic leaders maintain openness and truthfulness in close relationships, develop mutual intimacy, and trust (Ilies, Morgeson, & Nahrgang, 2005).

9.6.1 Leadership Model

Adair (1988) has demonstrated that Task, Team, and Individual are interrelated. It is essential that the leader should apprehend the requirements of the tasks and needs of the individual, and the team for project success. Main tasks are accomplished through the power of the team. Therefore, the team must have the clear apprehension and understanding of the tasks to be accomplished. The team will collapse if the individual requirements and needs are not fulfilled, and if their role in the team is not properly structured, appreciated, and valued. The Leadership model was further simplified by West (2010).

West (2010) described that vision is the top priority, and without any purpose of the project, clear objectives and apprehension of the tasks to be accomplished, the project will result in failure (West 2010). Project Leadership and Team best practices as recommended by West (2010)

1.   A leader must inspire and persuade team member for achieving project objectives. In other words, Leader should motivate team member after understanding his/her mind and gratifying that need/gap.
2.   Roles and responsibilities should be clear from ambiguity.
3.   Team members should work collectively and efficiently with a team culture; that boosts success.
4.   Teams should have a systematic understanding of the task to accomplish.

5. Teams should have the scheduled timeframe for the duties, and budgets allocated to execute those tasks.
6. Proper project planning is indispensable.
7. Project performance measurement and evaluation of the result is significant to check whether the project is in the right direction.

The project leader should assess requirement, form strategy, create a vision, and inspire team members to deliver the vision, achieve the purpose and deliver the project successfully.

9.6.2 Toyota Leadership Model

Liker (2004) described the Toyota Leadership Model that endorses the Systems Integrator (Builder of Learning Organisation) known as *"Chief Engineer (CE) System"* with a Chief Engineer for integrating and managing product development programs from initiation to end and, acting not only as a Project Leader but also as a guide as well as coach. A matrix organization structure is committed to the CE system. Functional groups have their own General Manager, who supervises the team members, takes decision on their project assignments and evaluates their promotions for promotion however; the overall program is controlled by the Chief Engineer, who instills culture in Toyota that encourages the accomplishment of shared objectives for satisfying customers, and making the company successful (Morgan & Liker, 2006). The types of leadership in Toyota as per Morgan & Liker, 2006 is described hereunder.

Bureaucratic Manager:

o   Coordinates people top down.
o   Do not use his experience but rather depend on standards and rules.
o   Uses Gantt chart to meet deadlines and rules.
o   Targets schedules and delegation.
o   Forces project efficiently.
o   Lacks flexibility in adjusting to the timeline and lacks technical vision beyond routine work.
o   Fails to be creative to move the project beyond initial vision and capabilities of individual engineers.

o   Requires technical and engineers skills to reach the leadership position.

System Designer (Task Master):

o   Exceptional technical skills.
o   Possesses a passion for making a product having technical excellence.
o   Creative thinker and excellent systems engineer, however, lacking skill in managing people and having the patience to coordinate, teach and listen.
o   Uses top-down approach for taking technical decisions, and employs subordinates for detailed work.
o   Lacks flexibility, as everyone is busy executing the detailed work, driven from the top, and therefore less room for following instructions.
o   Teams are incapable of thinking of themselves without any decision from the top.

Group Facilitator:

o   Developed engineering skills and able to take a group of individuals and facilitate their working.
o   Not a great engineer.
o   Rather loves to communicate, facilitate and acts as a catalyst to move a talented team of professionals towards the common goals.
o   Flexible thinker and employs autonomy to organize and reorganize itself.
o   Lacks strong technical vision from the top.

Systems Integrator (Builder of Learning Organization):

o   Strong technically.
o   Employs bottom-up process to generate best ideas from the team members.
o   Leaders have strong visions for the product and drive the technical integration of the project.
o   Leader facilities dynamic team process with great flexibility.

In Toyota, Chief Engineer (CE) or leader not only manages cultural change but also leads it by bringing change which is visible; leads cross-functional teams; implements new processes, and uses Lean Project Methodology to create opportunities for developing real transformational leaders. Leaders in this manner foster in building a learning environment, which drives continuous improvement; takes and studies feedbacks from customers as well as shop floor to improve learning and get rid of rigid bureaucracy. Through this CE system, the project leader manages and administers a small team and concentrates on technical vision and horizontal cross-functional group facilitation. Organization is also benefitted from the top down management to meet strict timelines and targets apart from getting flexibility and creativity from bottom-up style management. Combined with technical as well as strong leadership skills, CE mobilizes the organization and builds a consensus across functions (Morgan & Liker, 2006).

9.7 Key attributes of Project Leader

Key attributes of project leader as researched by Ryan (2008) are described here under

o   The leader should build trust with those who meets him.
o   The leader should be reliable, consistent, good values, shared values, challenging, honest, should put other's interests first, fair, supportive and should maintain the relational psychological contract.
o   The leader should have a high level of patience and persistence and should raise motivation of others. Leaders should not take things personally in case decisions are not taken on their side and should continue to proceed.
o   The leader should create an environment of high energy.

Project leaders' responsibilities toward the team member (Moran & Youngdahl, 2008), (DTI, 2003), (West, 2010) and characteristics of Project Leader (Briner, Hastings, & Gedder 2011) described hereunder:

o   Project Leader should build teams diverse in native cultures, functions, and technical skills, and should endorse every idea from that diversity.

o   Project Leader should acknowledge those requirements of the project team that evolves during the life cycle of the project. Project Leader should allow for shared leadership.

o   Project Leader should recognize project team members for their positive behavior as this leads to performance dividends.

o   The project leader should pause periodically to understand the need of project team members. The Effort-Performance-Rewards-Effectiveness model assists in understanding the roadblocks to performance and motivation.

o   Project Leader should ask "What is in or me?" from the perspective of each project team member from his or her cultural lenses.

o   Project Leader should listen to everyone.

o   Project Leader should show empathy.

o   Project Leader should demonstrate persistence and optimism.

o   Project Leader should provide more attention to globally located virtual team members.

o   Project Leader should comprehend the requirement and expectations of the project sponsor, client, end users and suppliers.

o   Project Leader should ensure that the project team members meet the project targets and learn from their mistakes by using appropriate control systems.

o   Project Leader should create realistic plans; raise necessary resources and required monitoring and reporting systems.

o   Project Leader should further monitor their performance during the execution of the project.

o   Project Leader should manage project lifecycle, manage stakeholders, as well as managed their performance.

o   Project Leaders should perform major task including management of the project, management of the stakeholders, as well as management of their performance.

o   Project Leader should not only integrate, energize, orchestrate and co-ordinate people and processes but should also give more emphasis to managing the organizational context as well as manage the technical delivery.

o   Project Leader should be an integrator who pull together all activities of the project and further analyze and detect broken links.

o   Project Leader should be ready to deal with unexpected events in projects through innovative actions, application of detachment strategies, creating rigorous meeting schedules and negotiating project condition (Soderholm, 2008, p.p. 215).

o   Project Leaders follows value management approach to get vital insights of what being delivered by the team members and whether there is anything else that meets the requirement will help the team members to integrate into the team.

o   Project Leader selects team and assigns roles and responsibilities.

o   Project Leader assesses the risk.

o   Project Leader identifies the details of the deliverables.

o   Project Leader identifies required tools and ensures their compatibility.

o   Project Leaders identify the communication channels to be used.

o   Project Leader completes the plan of action and prepares the roadmap.

o   Project Leader analyses how the project team and people can be developed and aims to increase the reputation market o the company through his project.

o   Project Leader creates a vision and inspires team members by up keeping their needs sincerely, candidly and honestly.

o   Project Leader involves each and everyone in the organization.

o   Project Leader trusts their people, have high listening skills and recognize accomplishments made by the group member.

o   Project Leader concentrates on the development and training of the team members, fostering the next generation of leaders and focuses on building new teams.

o   Project Leader should perform his/her roles with clear vision and objectives, right strategy with right team composition and good teamwork, and diverse ideas and behaviors for delivering successful projects (West, 2010).

o   Ability to lead change, functional competencies such as Technical & human resource management, high achievement, high motivation, persistence are few qualities of a Project Leader (Caudron, 1999).

o   Project leadership qualities include team building skills, communicating skills, demonstrating trust and respect, focusing on results, reinforcing positive behavior, developing team members and empowering team members to perform and setting goals while remaining flexible to respond to the inevitable changes (Zimmerer & Yasin, 1998).

By possessing these traits, and roles and responsibilities, project leader's relationship with the project team members will flourish. Further to this, Project Leader (PL) is responsible for the accomplishment of project goals, which require very dynamic and visible activity. Project Leader executes a high-risk role but has limited authority. However, it is essential that Project Leader negotiates for resources and support from an extensive network of people within and outside the organization. Project Leader should go beyond the organizational boundaries and customs should be unconventional in approach and should deal with resistance or opposition (Briner, Hastings, & Geddes, 2011). Project Leader must look in these six directions as described by Briner, Hastings, & Geddes (2011)

Looking Forward:
   o   Project Leader manages clients, suppliers, and subcontractors for ensuring the project meets their expectations.

Looking Outwards:
   o   Project Leader creates a plan to make sure that teams set realistic targets, and obtains appropriate resources to achieve those objectives.

Looking Downwards:
   o   Project Leader manages the team for optimal performance as well as managing visible and the invisible across disciplines, departments, cultures, and countries.

Looking Inwards:
   o   Project Leader conducts Personal Performance review and management to ensure that team leadership is a positive contribution to the project.

Looking Upwards:
   o   Project Leader monitors progress with appropriate control systems for ensuring that the targets of the projects are met.

Looking Backward:
- o   Project Leader manages project sponsor to achieve organizational commitment

9.7.1 Looking upwards and outwards

Project Leader should "*look upwards and outwards*" and follow following steps

Securing stakeholder's agreement: Project Leader should ask questions from the stakeholders and understand their requirement, build their credibility by clarifying their ideas, and should act as a negotiator to satisfy as many requirements of the stakeholders as possible (Briner, Hastings, & Geddes, 2011).

Building Credibility: Project Leader should build credibility by securing the positive support of the colleagues. Project Leader should demonstrate to the stakeholder that he and the team members have complete insight and analysis of any technical issues and difficulties they might be facing, and must demonstrate their capabilities in understanding the financial impact through in-depth research and analysis of financial costs, benefits, and risk. Project Leader should maintain an effective credibility rating of the project for securing official and unofficial resources (Briner, Hastings, & Geddes, 2011).

Networking: Project Leader should build network of relationships for getting things done, should talk to people informally and should learn what they hear, and use networking to test new ideas, learn formal and informal ways for executing tasks, and spotting new talent for the benefit of the project (Briner, Hastings, & Geddes, 2011).

Marketing the project: Project Leader should communicate the merits, project intentions and ideas, project progress and problems to the target audience through formal and informal presentation, formal reports, newsletters, updates throughout the project lifecycle, and should ensure that enough recognition and attention is received (Briner, Hastings, & Geddes, 2011).

9.7.2 Looking forwards and backward

Project Leader should "*look forward and backward*" and follow following steps

Anticipating: Project Leader should take a step back from daily executions of the project, take an overview of the whole situations, anticipate the future problems, and should conduct SWOT analysis to understand the implications, and plan contingencies (Briner, Hastings, & Geddes, 2011).

Continuous planning and reviewing: Project Leader should ensure continuous planning and reviewing throughout the project lifecycle, and should have complete understanding of the limitations and benefits of the tools employed, should involve those people who have best-quality information, should conduct constructive reviews after planning and, should develop a learning culture where people admit mistakes and poor performance honestly, and are empowered to move on (Briner, Hastings, & Geddes, 2011).

Keeping the team informed: Project Leader should maintain the interest and enthusiasm of the project by keeping the stakeholders informed about the recent happenings, involve the employees, and inform them about their roles and about the tasks supposed to be performed on them (Briner, Hastings, & Geddes, 2011).

Seeking feedback: Project Leader should ask for feedback through questionnaires, which builds the project team's credit within the organization, and should not only ask for feedback but taking appropriate action on the comments (Briner, Hastings, & Geddes, 2011).

9.7.3 Looking inwards and downwards.

Project Leader should "*look inwards and downwards*" and follow following steps

Provide purpose and direction: Project Leader should create a sense of purpose of the project amongst the team members and should explain them about the importance of the project for the organization. This will motivate team members and project leader can get fresh and new ideas from the team members. Project Leader should communicate the team members that the project can help them to achieve their personal visions and aspirations, and should communicate the excitement, conviction, and sense of mission about the project to sustain purpose, direction, and momentum (Briner, Hastings, & Geddes, 2011).

Clarifying individual success criteria: Project Leader should translate the project objectives into clear goals, specified work with defined time, and cost constraints, and should direct the team members how they should discharge their responsibilities which will influence their success (Briner, Hastings, & Geddes, 2011).

Being Tough on Quality: Project Leader should ensure that the high standards of success criteria are set for every individual including himself, and should make sure that those criteria are met. In case an employee is underperforming, the project leader should address that issue promptly and should advise the employee for improvement (Briner, Hastings, & Geddes, 2011).

Creating a supportive culture: Project Leader should develop supportive cultures so that employee can perform to their highest levels, and should support the employees with extra resources when the team member feel inhibited. Additional resources should be provided to the employees to reduce their pressure (Briner, Hastings, & Geddes, 2011).

Reflecting: Project Leader should consciously spend time on reflection, introspection, and self-analysis of the daily activities and concerns, and their performance. This will enable the project leader to discover the tasks that are felt difficult to handle and monitor their personal stress levels (Briner, Hastings, & Geddes, 2011).

Celebrating Success: Project Leader should increase the momentum within the project by recognizing and celebrating the collective and individual achievement of the team members. This can be done by sending felicitations to the team member, or by publically talking about the team members. Project Leader should respect the capabilities and efforts of others in the team (Briner, Hastings, & Geddes, 2011).

However, additional competencies are required to be an effective global project leader as required by leaders of domestic teams (Bird, 2008), (Mendenhall, Osland, Bird, Oddou, & Maznevski, 2008). Leaders must be culturally component (Pusch, 2009) and must be adept at the common leadership styles in diverse regions in the world (Chen & An, Chen, G., & An, R. (2009), (Javidan, Dorfman, Sully de Luque, & House, 2006). The global project leader should be aware of interpersonal cues of the team members from different cultures, and be able to switch leadership style as per team member expectations (Gundling, Hogan., & Cvitkovich, 2011), (Moran, Harris, & Moran, 2010). Apart from managing challenging project requirements of a global project, the global project leader should give foremost importance to above cultural aspects (Wildman & Griffith, 2015). Diversity in their teams can be leveraged by global team leaders through the application of right knowledge and tools for bringing outstanding results beyond those accomplished by traditional homogenous teams. Risks arising from diverse and geographically co-located, virtual and distributed teams can be effectively mitigated through recruitment of right team members, development of appropriate skills, detailed design of work, regular performance management and active team management leading finally to team success (Connaughton & Shuffler, 2007). The global Project leader must continuously respond and accustom to changing circumstance and diverse stakeholders, and should direct and build an atmosphere conducive for the team to flourish and later fine-tune the process as per team performance (Wildman & Griffith, 2015).

9.7.4 Team (People) Management skills

The project leader must have people and team management skills for better project success and should understand project team members, and inspire them to support other team members by first coming out of their functional roles (or silos).

> *They are going to work along with team members, and they are going to understand them a little bit and know each other's strengths and weaknesses and where they can help each other. When I think of a team, team effort does not mean just because you in one area functionally, you cannot help some other team members in another field. Sometimes it is a hard thing if you work in a big company. Sometimes it is a big thing to bring people out of their silos to help other people.*

Literature supports that people and their management, along with leadership and teamwork are some of the forces for successful implementation of projects (Turner, 1999), and the project leader must have this competency (Hoerl, 2001) i.e. that project leader must delegate work to team members, enthuse them for higher performance and encourage them to help fellow team members; develop team members, communicate with people those are working within the team and out of the team, and cooperate with them. Nevertheless, the project leader should not count on his/her existing knowledge but should devote time to developing his/her management skills and avoid using their authority wrongly by requesting the team members to perform a task that is not aligned with the best interest of the organization (MindTools.com, 2012).

9.7.5 Perform Appropriate Team (Workforce) Planning

It is asserted that Project Leaders should select those team members those who can work with the customers and stakeholders properly, have right skills and abilities, and then assign them at the right time for the right task and to the right project.

> *We look for "right people with the right skill at the right time," and everything is built around its skills, ability, and its delivery capabilities.*
>
> *They all choose their people very carefully, but people also trusted them as they inspired confidence in what they were doing.*
>
> *I think the second part is all about having right people for the right project and working with the customers and the stakeholders in a real and efficient way.*
>
> *Therefore, you should have right people for the right j.*
>
> *In project management, it is tough to understand whether the person should fit in the new role or not. Assigning right people to right roles comes through experience. You must have skilled people on your team.*

The project leader must perform appropriate group (workforce) planning and the literature support this. The project leader must assign team member with right skills to the right task in the project at the right time (Stokker & Hallam, 2009). Project leader should concentrate on what project work to be done, how it will be organised and then how to plan systematically for aligning the best configuration of the competency and the quantity of team members for performing projects tasks, and meetings customer needs for effective, efficient and measurable results and outcomes with least spending of money, time and effort (Rothwell, Graber, & McCormick, 2012, p.p. 12). Conversely, the project leader should look to all people in the team and fit them in the project as per project requirements rather than the concentrating on the best team members. In other words, the team should be Lean but Agile.

By Lean, it is meant the project leader should undertake calculated and systematic effort for planning work resulting in the realization of customer wants, and should plan team members needed for the work in a timely way for optimizing productivity, quality, and cost-effectiveness. By Agile, it is meant that workforce to be nimble and pace, ready to deal with dynamic changes (Rothwell, Graber, & McCormick, 2012, p.p. 12).

9.7.6 Able to take project decisions

It is advocated that decision-making is a major task for project leaders. The project leader should have relevant knowledge and experience with proper skills sets, and confidence to make decisions, document those designs, defend those decisions and should be answerable for them.

> *The leader has to be the focal point and can take decisions. This is another thing with the communication. People can make a decision on the fly, and be able to document those decisions and defend those decisions. I think decision-making is really after communication.*

> *I make many decisions myself. It is teamwork. We are accountable and enabled to take our decisions.*

> *Decision-making is also an important factor. Projects are exclusively dependent on decision-making, and the decision comes from experience, skill sets, and confidence. In case you do not have these three, you cannot take decisions.*

The project leader should be able to take project decisions, and the literature supports that Critical project decisions should be made by Project Leader after thoroughly understanding the complete status and issues of the project (Fui-Hoon Nah, Lee-Shang Lau, & Kuang, 2001). The project leader should practice participative decision-making by taking project related information and inputs from project team members to make sound and practical decisions (Dinur, 2012). Project Leader should engage in problem solving (Druskat & Wheeler, 2003) that will encourage team members to give their feedback and voice their opinions (Locke, Alavi, & Wagner, 1997) which improves employee satisfaction (Miller & Monge, 1986) and strengthens their commitment to the decision (Barge, 2004). However, the project leader should take a decision and bear responsibility for the decision (Caroll, 2012). Furthermore, decisions in India are made at the top level, and there in reluctance to take accountability for project related tasks, and disinclination to take bold decisions (Bharat, 2012).

9.7.7 Effective communicator

The Project Leader should be an effective communicator and must be consistent in communication, as he/she has to deal with locally and globally distributed teams.

> *Some leaders lead by examples, some are an excellent communicator, I think; communication will be stressed enough as I believe that excellent leaders find it tough to communicate, be consistent in the manner of communication.*

> *The most important factor that the project leader must have is effective communication as teams are located globally in different time zones.*

Project Leader must be an effective communicator, and the literature supports that Project Leader must endorse competent behavior that is consistent and correct to his/her settings(Jablin, Cude, House, J., & Roth, 1994). The project leader must engage in open communication, interactive and supportive discussions with all stakeholders and with the project team at all times, (Yoo, et al., 2011) as communicative project leader have more effect on employee attitude, welfare and employee performance (Johansson, D Miller, & Hamrin, 2011). Moreover, communicative leaders are accessible, respectful, demonstrate concern about the team, convey priorities, explain short term objectives and long term goals, establish clear expectations for quality, efficiency and proficiency; involve in dialogue with other team members and use stories and messages for supporting and encouraging sense-making during exchanges that are informal and formal (Johansson, D Miller, & Hamrin, 2011).

9.8 Competency of Project Leader

Competency of the project leader is dependent upon the project size and complexity. Project Leader must have national and international experience and prior domain expertise for executing a project. He/She should be able to associate with the problem of the team members, must be aware of the latest trends, technologies, and future scope. He/She should lead the team collaboratively rather than aggressively. He/She should accept challenges and related criticism and should apply knowledge and skills from PMBOK, ISO standards set for project management, General Management skills and Project Environment Management.

9.8.1 Hybrid Project Leader:

Project leader should not only be technically competent in his/her domain and have complete knowledge about the project, but also must have strong knowledge of the project management methodologies, however it might be suited only for small projects as large projects will require project leader to concentrate more on communication, and other aspects of project management rather than spending time on technical problem-solving. However, in a new project, hybrid project leader might not get respect from the team due to lack of specialized technical skills.

> *They should have the technical knowledge base, not expertise but a knowledge base so that they can make decisions and keep the time, the cost, and the scope moving forward. However, they must have strong knowledge in methodology in project management.*

> *If it is a small project where you do not want two resources, a half-time Project Leader, and a technical half-time person because you now have two people in the meetings and everything, then, it makes sense to have one Project Leader who is a hybrid Project Leader. The other issue, of course, is that when you ask for a technical Project Leader, it is a different skill set from a Project Leader. Project Leaders if they are excellent, they are splendid in communication. People without technical would be more into fixing than problem-solving. You would very rarely find somebody*

who is technical as well as useful in communication. So, if you go for hybrid people, you will not get the best of both.

9.8.2 Competency in Project Management skills

For large projects, project leaders need be competent in project management skills to manage the project properly rather than concentrating on technical problems.

If your project is big enough, then the answer would be no because, in the case of technical difficulties, you will focus on solving those technical difficulties. Not only that, you would probably be doing half project management and half technical things.

9.8.3 Leader must have hands-on Skills (Participative)

The Project Leader must have hands-on skills, and should actively participate in project activities.

"The able one that already has experience in this field because it is good to have people with hands-on expertise in this kind of projects."

I want to say is that a Project Leader although it should not be technical as he should be actively participating (hands-on) in the project. This is my opinion although I am often hands-on in the project I do not think that is a right thing to do. Sometimes, that is required.

The project leader must be competent enough to deliver projects, and the competence of the Project Leader is dependent upon the size of the project and complexity. Literature supports that irrespective of the project size, Project Leader must have technical and people management skills (Fisher, 2011) along with project management techniques (Morris, 2004) for delivering successful projects which mean that project leader must have problem-solving expertise, related knowledge of the domain, analytical and leadership skills, and expertise in people and communication skills in addition to project management expertise (i.e. creating and managing scope, timelines and budget), (Brill, Bishop, &

Walker, 2006). Project Leader should concentrate on building leadership competencies apart from technical and project management skills (Mu¨ller & Turner, 2010) which support the notion that project leader should be a hybrid (skilled in all areas). However, as the size of the project increases, complexities in the project also increases due to increase in stakeholders, partners, virtual teams, and the new applicable technologies emerge due to the long timeframe of these projects. Project leader needs to thrive in this constant change of technology, business strategies, organization policies and project's stakeholders and needs to reevaluate the business case continuously. Therefore, the project leader must devote more time in applying project management and people skills of project management such as team building, stakeholder management and leadership rather than problem-solving or performing technical work (Kerzner & Belack, 2010), (Goodwin, 1993). Hence, the project leader should concentrate more on project management and people management for large projects. Moreover, more projects fail due to improper application of good project management rather than technical reasons (Jurison, 1999). Literature also supports that project leader should be participative which means that Project Leader should actively participate with the project team in project activities.

9.8.4 Excellent Leadership Skills and Qualities

Project Leader must have leadership skills traits and qualities to manage teams, and it is one of the factors on which their performance is measured.

> *It comes back to a lot of excellent leadership skills and how you manage your team to keep those conflicts at the minimum.*

> *I think the project leader or Project Leader both must have excellent leadership skills because he is going to manage a team.*

> *The Project Leader needs to show the leadership qualities to various stakeholders.*

> *You should have hands-on experience, external environment, and some leadership qualities.*

The project leader must have excellent leadership skills, and the leadership qualities are associated with project results and are the measures of project success, success in problem-solving, and project delivery within allocated budget, and literature supports that. By having good leadership skills, project leader has an enormous impact on project teams. Project team guided by good project leader has a strong feeling of project work, aim, and the importance of the project, and it is the Project Leader's leadership style which influences project success (Nixon, 2012). This establishes that good leadership skills can be considered an important trait of the project leader.

9.8.5 Good Political sense

The project leader has political sense to understand the needs and the motives of the team members, being tactful at situations to bond with people to make people believe in him/her.

> *Right political sense, ability to not get upset, ability to be very intuitive and understand the motive and what people really need, ability to keep your mouth shut when people around you not making any sense but you don't want to tell them that, being able to allocate a large sections of your time at critical periods of project, being able to people believe what you are doing, create a good bonding with the team members.*

The project leader must have a good political sense while managing teams and the literature supports that. Political skills in Project Leader are one of the vital skills critical to leadership effectiveness (Ahearn, Ferris, Hochwarter, Douglas, & Ammeter, 2004). The project leader cannot ignore to give their attention to organizational politics, and that majority of work performed by them is reliant on their capability to effectively manage not only the technical side of things but behaviors aspects of the team members as well (Pinto, 1996). The project leader should identify and manage the interaction between the project political concerns associated with the project and the Project Leader (Sense, 2003), develop the ability to convince, encourage, inspire and control others (Mintzberg, 1985), and facilitate performance of the team rather than just empowering team member.

9.8.6 Right Attitude

Project Leader must have a good attitude toward problem-solving and make the project successful.

> *However, if the leader has the right attitudes toward work, then there is no problem.*
>
> *Above all, he should have a right attitude to make the project successful.*

The project leader must have the right attitude to managing projects, and the literature supports that. Project Leader must have an attitude which boasts excellent communication through project documentation, project management systems, and a Project Management Office; an attitude which increases project awareness, exert extra energy in planning, challenge workers and provide them freedom for performing tasks (Cioffi, 2001). This corroborates that project leader must have the correct extent of determination, confidence (Madsen, 2012, p.p. 153) and positive and helpful (Bartram, 2012) attitude to push and lead the team towards success (Madsen, 2012, p.p. 153).

9.8.7 Vision of the Objectives

The project leader must have the clear understanding of the project objectives and should motivate the team members for the attainment of project objectives of completing the project within allocated time, cost and schedule.

> *I will look for someone who has a clear vision of the objectives, they communicate it, and they recognize the people efforts towards it. The Project Leader should cultivate the vision for the project and be a source of motivation for the team members to achieve project objectives.*

9.8.8 Business Acumen

Project leaders must have knowledge, awareness and understanding of the competition, business and customer requirements, and business strategy. Project leaders should build a business portfolio and link project strategy with business strategy with continuous evaluation for achieving business goals and objectives.

> *"Management in business, and make sure that they know about the operational requirements and the strategy outside. They should tie the business, strategy, projects, programs together and review that at least twice a year."*

> *They should have proper processes in place to be able to look into projects and programs and decide and check whether we will be able to achieve their business goals and objectives through these projects and programs.*

> *All these leaders need to understand the complete business portfolio and build up a portfolio based on the customer requirement, business requirements and how we can target those customers based on our skills, ability and capacity.*

The project leader must have business acumen with an understanding of the competition, business strategies, customer requirements and market, (Soliman, 2011), (Mathur, 2009), (Lo, 2011). This attests that project leader must have the business acumen for effective leadership.

9.8.9 Good Negotiator

The project leader should have excellent negotiation skills, and should be adept at negotiating price and other project terms with the customers while dealing with their project change requests, and while dealing with stakeholders to accommodate that changes.

> *Those projects are successful where project leader understands to negotiate well.*

> *The problem is the execution where you nearly have to negotiate with the customer.*

The project leader must be good negotiator while negotiating terms with their clients during change requests, and while dealing with stakeholders.

Negotiating skills coupled with communication skills are essential as the project leaders should engage in two-way discussion to negotiate with the contractors, suppliers and consultants for achieving interests of the firm and therefore develop these skills to evade any adverse consequence on the project (Gushgar, Francis, & Saklou, 1997), (Goodwin, 1993).

9.8.10 Give constructive and authentic feedback

Project Leader should provide constructive and genuine feedback to the team members on their performances and the tasks executed by them.

> *We do give feedback to our individuals on their performances. We are straight in saying what is right and what is wrong.*

> *The constructive feedback mechanism can be given for improvement.*

The project leader must provide constructive and authentic feedback to the team, and the literature supports the same. The project leader should (Blomkvist & Uppvall, 2012) give continuous, meaningful and constructive feedback to the team members about their performance and allow them to improve their skills (Walter, Humphrey, & Cole, 2012). The project leader should enable coactive learning by providing vital performance feedbacks to team members and encourage them to jointly reflect upon the group process (Zaccaro, Rittman, & Marks, 2001). Moreover, Project Leader should give feedbacks to developing capabilities in the team members. However, Project Leader should avoid giving person-oriented feedbacks, and should give task-oriented feedbacks (S. I., Smith-Jentsch, & Behson, 1998) along with specific constructive feedbacks and suggestions according to their experience (Brinkkemper & Jansen, 2012).

9.8.11 Listen and take feedback

The project leader should listen to team members and customers, and take their feedback for suggestions, problem resolution and bringing change.

> *They should share their experience and their current tasks and receive review and comments about his work and ask for suggestions.*

Moreover, thenI can sound pretty much from their feedback if they are going to be capable of change because sometimes.

The project leader must take their feedback for the suggestion and bring change, and the literature supports the same. Project Leader should take feedback during project reviews from team members, employ Agile and iterative methods for potential plans and scope changes, meet stakeholder and document those changes and furtherr modify project objectives and engage in re-planning the project (Kendrick, 2012). The project leader should ask questions, listen actively to them, be open to ideas (Singh, 2012) and take advice from team members. Project Leader should employ engagement feedback forms for gathering specific feedback on current projects to make an alteration to the service or product delivery, and use constructive feedback form for bringing improvement in existing or potential projects (Brinkkemper & Jansen, 2012). However, the project must accept feedback and ideas from others (Zaccaro, Rittman, & Marks, 2001).

9.8.12 Emotional Intelligence

Research conducted by Goleman (1998) concluded that project leaders lacked soft skills and traits through which successful results can be attained. The project leader must have typical traits such as intelligence, strength, fortitude, vision, and soft traits such as self-cognizance, self-regulation, motivation, compassion and social skills. Therefore, the project leader must have emotional intelligence, which is considered as pre-requisite of leadership (Goleman, 1998). Table 9.1 illustrates the traits of emotional unintelligent people.

Components	Definition	Hallmarks
Lack of self-awareness	The incompetence to identify and comprehend attitudes, feelings, and drivers, as well as their effect on others.	No confidence.
		Unrealistic self-assessment.
		Directs humor at others, never at self.

No-regulation	The inability to control or convey disrupting impulses and moods; no propensity to suspend judgment and think before acting.	Non-trustworthy.
		Uncomfortable with ambiguity.
		Unwilling in change.
Lack of motivation	Not demonstrating a passion for working for reasons outside money or status; requiring a drive to pursue goals with energy and persistence.	No drive to change.
		Pessimistic.
		No organizational commitment.
No empathy	The inability to comprehend the emotions of others; lack of skills in handling others according to their emotional reactions.	Cannot build or retain talent.
		Cross-cultural insensitivity.
		Disservice to clients and customers.
Lack of social skills	Incompetent of managing relationships and building network; unable to find common ground and build a relationship	Ineffective in leading change.
		Not believable or persuasive.
		Fails in building and leading teams.

Table 9.1: Traits of Emotional Unintelligent people. Source: Adapted from Nixon, Harrington, & Parker (2012)

Emotional Intelligence is also classified as the major six schools of leadership (Dulewicz & Higgs, 2005). Additionally, there is a strong connection between emotional intelligence and different styles of leadership particularly transformational leadership, which further influences the project results (Clarke, 2010). However, poor level of emotional intelligence can directly contribute to poor leadership (Nixon, Harrington, & Parker, 2012).

High levels of emotional intelligence breed a work culture and environment, which improves, trust, information sharing, risk-taking, and learning. In contrast to this, low levels of intelligence breed an environment full of fear and anxiety leading to terrified and tense employees who are productive for short term leading to excellent but short-lived organizational results (Goleman, Boyatzis, & McKee, 2001).

9.9 Summary

This chapter reviewed the different leadership style used for project leadership.

Qualities of a Project Leader are listed in Table 9.2

Qualities of a Project Leader		
Final Results	**Result Triangulated Yes or No**	**Supported By**
1	Team (Project Management Skills)	Yes	Case Study 3
2	Perform Appropriate team (Workforce) Planning.	No	
3	Able to take decisions.	No	
4	Effective communicator.	No	
5	Cultural awareness.	Yes	Case Study 5
6	Competency of a Project Leader. * Hybrid Project Leader * Leader must have hands-on Skills (Participative)	No	
7	Good Leadership Skills and Qualities.	Yes	Case Study 3
8	Good Political Sense.	No	
9	Right Attitude.	No	
10	Business Acumen.	No	
11	Good Negotiator.	No	

12	Gives constructive and authentic feedback.	Yes	Case Study 5
13	Listen and Take feedback	Yes	Case Study 5

Table 9.2: Qualities of a Project Leader

Table 9.2 illustrates the qualities and traits for Project leader. The project leader must have these qualities and traits for executing successful IT and Aerospace projects and globally. Triangulated results are also shown. The project leader should play a collaborative and as well as directive leadership style for managing aerospace projects, as same styles were successful in IT projects. (See Case Study 6).

Project leader needs to apply this leadership style according to the project phases and should switch and combine different styles according to the situation.

10. Project Teams and Team Building

This chapter explores what team building practices are applied in projects for building innovative and collaborative teams.

10.1 Project team

For completion of project work in time, project work is distributed and shared among the project team. These project teams bring together complementary skills, talents, and responsibilities required for completion of the project tasks. These multi-disciplines teams allow fast tracking of product and development tasks. Creative ideas and possible solutions are developed and generated by these teams through stimulation of team synergy, and through brainstorming, leading to better, collective decision-making, and even riskier decision. Moreover, project team enhances motivation; reduce frustration among team members and increase productivity. Furthermore, planning and controlling the work becomes easier through project teamwork, and interpersonal conflicts are resolved through group discussions. Information flow also improves through communication and leads to job satisfaction (Burke & Barron, 2007).

10.1.1 Team Roles

Various Team roles as researched by Bilbin (1981) are discussed here under:

Executive:
- Initiates the project and provides motivation for completion of the tasks.

Chair:
- Ensures the process is observed and that all the team members can participate and give their opinion.

Ideas Person:
- Those people come up with innovative ideas creative thinking. However, support is required from the team for its implementation.

Worker:
- Implements the ideas.

Detailer:
- Provides attention to the details.

Procurer:
- Buys raw materials, machines and other items required for the execution of the task.

Critic:
- Recognize the fault in the idea.

Human Resources:
- Play a role in conflict resolution.

It is important the project leader assigns clear role and responsibility to each team member meeting his/her personality, skills, and attributes for generating maximum performance and building high performing team. Timely progress assessment of all team members is carried out for determining project status and monitor deviation in actual plan.

Figure 10.1 illustrates the Team Building Models as articulated by Tuckman (1965).

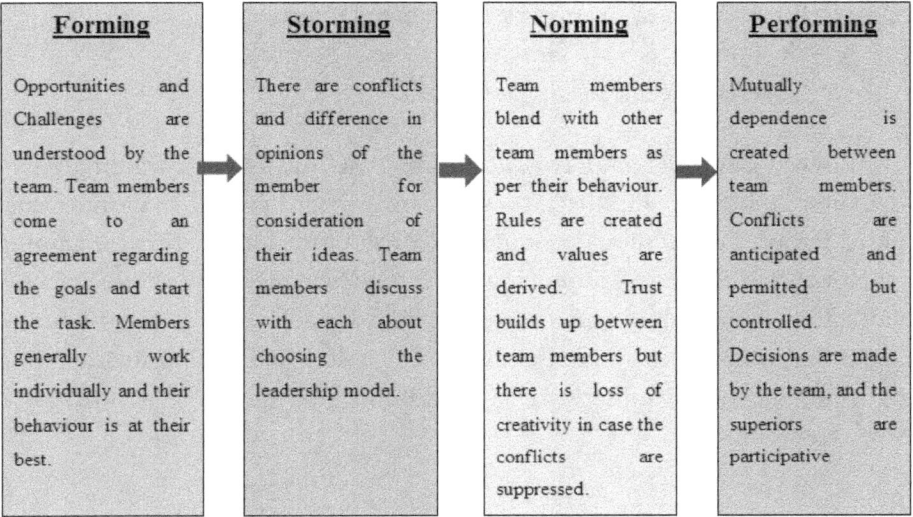

Forming	Storming	Norming	Performing
Opportunities and Challenges are understood by the team. Team members come to an agreement regarding the goals and start the task. Members generally work individually and their behaviour is at their best.	There are conflicts and difference in opinions of the member for consideration of their ideas. Team members discuss with each about choosing the leadership model.	Team members blend with other team members as per their behaviour. Rules are created and values are derived. Trust builds up between team members but there is loss of creativity in case the conflicts are suppressed.	Mutually dependence is created between team members. Conflicts are anticipated and permitted but controlled. Decisions are made by the team, and the superiors are participative

Figure 10.1: Tuchman's Team Building Model.
Source: Adapted from Tuckman (1965).

The team should get through the forming, storming and norming stages of the project, and reach the stage of performing as soon as possible to accelerate the progress of the project. There is another stage after performing i.e. adjourning which is a formal split of the team. However, the project can decelerate in case the Project Leader is changed in between the project. Finally, successful projects can be delivered by good teamwork. Strong leadership providing clear objectives, direction and the application of the right strategy delivers good teamwork (West, 2010).

10.2 Cross functional team

A cross-functional team is a diverse group composed of different members of various cultures where success is regarded as the success for the team, rewards as team rewards and blames are shared among the team. The team is tied by a commitment towards the completion of the goals (Young, 2010). Benefits of Cross-functional teams are listed below:

- Time of Project development is reduced.
- Complex problems are solved by increasing abilities.

- Inter and Intra- teamwork is promoted effectively.
- Customer needs are satisfied by focusing on resources.
- New technical skills are developed.

Project Leader should enhance team dynamics since combination of dynamics and leadership increases the team strength greater than individual parts. Project Leader should minimize the risk of job termination for gaining employee confidence and improving efficiency. Enactment of a robust dynamic work structure enables team members to adjust to project requirements. Team-building games and exercises should be designed for improving group dynamic and improve productivity, and build a cohesive and well-disposed work environment.

Requisites for enhancing Team Dynamics are described below:

- The team leader should have requisite team management Skills.
- The Project Leader should be clear and consistent with team's responsibilities.
- Team members should participate in important decisions.
- High priority and should be given in developing relationship with Key stakeholders.
- Satisfaction of the needs of the stakeholders and customers should be the primary focus of the team.

However, there are certain obstacles on the way to team success, which is described hereunder as adapted from Young (2010).

Limitation of team leadership

A leader must have extensive technical knowledge, skill for managing the new team members, and apart from focusing on project team process and technological progress, the leader should concentrate on dealing team problems such as unproductive meetings, resolution of conflict and involvement of everyone in the group decision.

Unclear team authority

Mostly project team lacks clarity about their authority leading to confusion, resulting in inconsistency. The leader should give assurance to the team and provide them necessary powers, engage them with the key stakeholders and proceed in the interest of the project.

Ambiguous or unclear objectives and goals

Project team suffers from a lack of vision of where they want to go or what to accomplish; have short term planning tools and action plans but have no clarity of how the efforts will fit into the whole projects. Project Leader and the entire team should establish team goals for ensuring understanding, acceptance, and commitment.

Managing the Boundaries

Leaders fail to give attention to the teamwork, which results in project failure.

Performance Appraisal

Performance is not properly evaluated in the fulfillment reviews, and the functional manager and the Project Leader often miss to give credit to the team member resulting in demotivation and aggravation of member. The functional manager should give team members due to credit for their work, and their job should be appraised appropriately.

Team Dynamics

Team members fail to work in a team without any conflicts due to bring ingrained work style and practices. Leaders should provide a lack of cross-functional training and maintain opened door policy; give time to understand each member to avoid conflict.

Lack of Management Support

Due to high dependency of the cross-functional team on senior management and functional support, senior management should help the team.

10.3 Teams Development

The project leader should ascertain if his team is a team or a group. The project leader must endorse horizontal and vertical growth in the company. The organizational hierarchy should be transparent in accordance with creativity and seniority of the team member. Project Leader must appoint experienced people in higher positions and should appoint skilled and certified team members at each level for superior process yield. The understanding between team members improves through informal events and gatherings.

Research by Lencioni (2005) concluded that team members should share common goals along with rewards and responsibilities for achieving them, and should leave their personal and individual needs for achieving better results for the group.

Listed are the activities to be performed by Project Leader for developing Team Member's group activity as researched by Bull (2010, pp 39-41), Nokes & Kelly, (2007).

- Engage in team building exercise by pulling team members out of their comfort zone.
- Encourage team members to get familiarized with each other on personal as well as a professional front by allowing team members to work with each other. Promote inter- group communication by setting internal and external communication strategies.
- Run formal and informal ad-hoc coaching sessions; arranging weekly team meetings; set standards for acceptable behavior from each team member; set ground rules and ensure each team members share responsibilities of enforcing them.
- Assess needs and capabilities of each before team building exercise.
- Analyse strengths and weakness of the individual, what team members bring to the team.
- Analyse team member's personal interest, the primary source of motivation.
- Assign the team member the task which the team member understands.
- Assess whether the team member can achieve the required results in the designated period.
- Evaluate the current strength of the team.
- Analyze whether team member can engage with each other, understand and respect each other.

10.4 Global Project Teams

Today, global work teams are a necessity for a business to be competitive in global business (Cascio, 2014), (Salazar & Salas, 2013), (Wildman & Griffith, 2015). Owing to increase in diplomatic pressure, and the urge to be cost-effective, focus in organizations has today shifted from individual work to team-based work (Lawler, Mohrman, & Ledford, 1995). Team-based structures give organizations ability to adapt to any opportunity available (Cohen & Bailey, 1997). Global teams, distributed across geographical, time and organization boundaries are connected through IT technologies (Wildman & Griffith, 2015), (Powell, Piccoli, & Ives, 2004).

In Global projects, Project leader should allow flexible working hours that overlap different time zones. Project Leader should encourage the use of email, follow 24-hr development cycle when sites are geographically spread across the globe and should ensure on-time delivery using RAD tools, organize meetings at a time suited to all and respect vacations and weekends in other countries.

Challenges of Global teams as identified by Jarvenpaa & Leidner, (1999) are a lack of clarity, counterproductive work behaviors, social loafing, cultural differences, communication and behaviors across cultures, diversity in cultural values (Hofstede, 1980), the difference in social norms, goals, and role overload. Because of these challenges, the multicultural team fails to appreciate their potential (Adler, 1997). It also increases the potential for misunderstandings, which can create additional barriers to communication and can trigger negative conflicts.

However, global teams allow organizations to build a lean structure, which is vital for adapting to the needs of customers through reduced operational overhead costs and lower bureaucratic costs (Gibson. & Cohen, 2003). Moreover, global teams allow amalgamation of a talented team member with diverse skills and background (Alexander, 2000) to create functioning teams that are linked across geographical boundaries through technological channels (Jarvenpaa & Leidner, 1999).

Although active communication is a vital component of any team, it can be a key element of project success, and failure since distant team members cannot regularly interact with each other due to geographical distance or due to communication and language barriers leading to misunderstandings. Team Conflicts can be either positive being a change or destructive for the team.

Therefore, conflicts management is a vital element of effective communication defining an organization's capability and performance (Wildman & Griffith, 2015). It is important that team members should frequently and persistently communicate with each other (Connaughton & Shuffler, 2007) in-order to build strong interpersonal relations, build trust (Jarvenpaa, Knoll, & Leidner, 1998), and reduce conflicts (Hinds & Mortensen, 2005) between global team members.

Geographical distribution along with cultural diversity has a diverse impact on global teams. However, diversity can bring positive outcome and acts as a catalyst in building an effective team (Shachaf, 2008). Furthermore, cultural factors influence the success of any Global Project (Gurung & Prater, 2006). Project Leader can measure team member's cultural tendency towards teamwork and cooperation through individualism–collectivism dimension (Paul, Samarah, Seetharaman, & Mykytyn, 2005) however; this tool fails to describe dynamic aspects of culture (Connaughton & Shuffler, 2007).

10.5 Global Team Integration

60 to 95% of knowledge workers across the USA and Europe are members of multiple project teams at one point in time, maybe five, ten, or twelve or more teams at a time (Martin & Bal, 2006), (Zika-Viktorsson, Sundström, & Engwall, 2006). Organizations embrace this approach for organizing work for maximizing productive resources utilization, and to encourage knowledge transfer for boosting productivity and learning (Milgrom & Roberts, 1992). However, procedures introduced to enhance productivity often impede practices that promote learning (Adler et al., 2009), (Benner & Tushman, 2003) since learning and team performance increases while working with cross-functional teams (Benner & Tushman, 2003), (Singer & Edmondson., 2008).

Today, in large corporate operate in an ever changing global environment flexibility and advanced communication technologies are required. Therefore, team members need to collaborate for the entire project (Cummings & Haas, 2012). Knowledge-intensive work is required during the project work, which therefore requires expertise and experience of the team members for project success irrespective of their location (Argote, McEvily, & Reagans, 2003), (Kozlowski & Ilgen, 2006). Members are brought together through knowledge-intensive teams for undertaking complex and uncertain projects so that project can be effortlessly managed by a single individual (Cross, et.al., 2008), (Rulke & Galaskiewicz, 2000). These teams bring together members with diverse skills, experience, and functional expertise because of which these teams can handle the challenges of knowledge intensive work (Bunderson, 2003), (Dahlin, Weingart, & Hinds, 2005). In contrast to conventional team where team members work together head-on with each other for providing solutions, and decision making, (Cohen & Bailey, 1997), (Hackman, 1987), (McGrath, 1984), (Steiner, 1972), knowledge intensive teams are reluctant to work in solo team in the one place (Barkema, Baum, Mannix, 2002). On the other hand, the teams progressively devote a portion of their time on the central team, work on other teams simultaneously at different geographical locations (O'Leary, Mortensen, & Woolley, 2011). However, challenges and opportunities are faced by the organizations due to globalization, and there is a need to apportion time for the team members properly, specifically when the project teams are distributed geographically (Boh, et.al, 2007).

The project team should be encouraged to record learning from their experience from the past and current projects i.e. combination of explicit knowledge and tacit knowledge, and build a knowledge base, and apply that knowledge to the continuous improvement of project management processes and practices since continuous improvement signifies the entire stage of project management maturity in an organization. (Cooke-Davies T., 2002).

Efficient project teams should be built with mastery in optimal utilization of resources, and competent in prioritizing projects tasks and activities enabling cost saving and optimum use of project funds (Nasina & Nallam, 2016).

Low level of motivation is found in team members if the team is not rewarded for long working hours resulting in increased risk of project failure (Verner, Sampson, & Cerpa, 2008). Kappelmana, McKeemanb, & Zhan, (2006) found that lack of subject matter experts and unskillful team members is a usual cause of project failure (Evgenia, Torchiano, & Morisio, October 2010). This corroborates the fact that mutual collaboration amongst diverse stakeholders is vital, and assistance from other team members is still required even if a team member is an expert in one's field (Emam & Koru, A.G, 2008).

10.6 Cross-Cultural Values

It is important that cross-cultural factors are given due consideration in global projects (Hofstede, 1980), (Shimizu, et.al, 2004). Hofstede described the dimensions between UK and India.

Dimensions	India	UK	Gap in culture
Power Distance (PDI)	77	35	High
Individualism Versus Collectivism (IDV)	48	89	High
Masculinity Versus Femininity (MAS)	56	66	Some difference
Uncertainty avoidance (UAI)	40	35	Less
Long-term Versus Short-Term orientation (LTO)	61	25	High

Table 10.1: Cultural Difference between India and UK.
Source: Adapted from Geert-hofstede.com, (2012)

Table 10.1 list out the cultural differences between India and UK for illustrating an example of how the culture of the countries are different and what impact the culture of a country has on management style in that country. Each cultural dimension is explained hereunder.

Power Distance (PI): High power distance is found between India which demonstrations that managers in India accept that they are ready to be managed by people in higher authority. These people accept the hierarchical order with their place and need no justification. On the contrary, managers in the UK strive to be more involved and expect more participation in decision making (Geert-hofstede.com, 2012).

Individualism versus Collectivism (IDV): Individualistic is found in the UK which demonstrations that entrepreneurship, success, and individual drive is valued in the UK. On the contrary, Collectivism culture is found in India which demonstrations that planning is essential before any taking any action, and after that analysis is performed afterward between the team members to reach consensus (Geert-hofstede.com, 2012).

Masculinity versus Femininity (MAS): UK's culture is slightly feminine which demonstrates that quality of life, collaboration, concern for others and humility is valued. On the other hand, India's culture is masculine which proves that aggressiveness, material rewards, and achievements are rewarded. Women are usually posted in the organizations at junior positions (Geert-hofstede.com, 2012).

Uncertainty avoidance (UAI): Minute variance lies between India and UK in this dimension. There will be more tolerance for risk taking, equivocalness and uncertainty in India as compared to the UK. People in both countries are tolerant of different behavior and adopt a less structured approach to work (Geert-hofstede.com, 2012).

Long-Term versus Short-term orientation (LTO): Long-Term orientation is found in India whereas short-term orientation is found in the UK. In India, people have more preference for investing and saving, and demonstrate continuous determination in achieving results, and frugality in the expenditure of money or resources, however, in the UK, people follow norms and pertain to directives or rules in their thinking, and focus on attaining quick results (Geert-hofstede.com, 2012).

10.7 Team Building Practises

10.7.1 Awards and Appreciation

The project leader should build a personal and professional relationship with team members located locally as well as globally, reward team member for any small success accomplished during the project either verbally through weekly appreciation emails or monthly awards or through emails. Project Leader should celebrate small success by immediately acknowledging it and appreciating their performance to the team member's direct supervisor in order to promote team building.

> *Along with that, we award recognition. I think it is crucial not only monetary by just verbally or by email. Recognition is good*

> *As projects are of short duration, there is not much left for team building. However, we used to have weekly awards. However, this is not done to show the other team that they are not doing good, but there is a motivation for them that one team is doing right, and the other team can also do good. You have a weekly*

appreciation mail or a monthly award. Even I personally go to my customer for the appreciation if he has felt that someone has done some good.

The project leader should reward team members for their good work and appreciate their performance, and the literature supports that. In order to provide positive support for their desired performance, the project leader should reward and praise the good performance of the team members, Apart from providing rewards intrinsic to the project, the project leader should create challenging jobs, shape future work assignments, assign responsibility to team members, and allow them to improve their performance themselves.(Burke & Barron, 2007). The project leader should set an equitable system of reward (Rajanayakam, 2010) based on positive reinforcement, recognize and reward good behavior which drives the project forward or prevent it from slipping back. Nevertheless, in organizations with blame culture, rewards are given for those successes which are limited and lack innovation. Additionally, the project leader should review reward and appraisal policies for aligning with any change that occurs within the project (Mascia, 2012).

10.7.2 Knowledge Sharing Sessions/Training

For team building, knowledge sharing sessions should be conducted within the unit. Tuckman's team building process (Forming, Storming, Norming, Performing) should be practiced, and corporate or third-party training or training using Webinar (Web Based Seminar) should be conducted which will keep them active and engage all team members in different areas for strengthening the team, and share information.

We also tried to provide training in various parts to all team members and tried to work out that the project is the training

There was technically training within the team. There was corporate level training. Sometimes, the third party was engaged in training. Training always helps. Above that, knowledge-sharing sessions within the group are beneficial as one team member gets to know that the other team member is doing. They have a better feel where overall project is going.

> *They do get together initially to do proper forming, storming, norming and performing style and escalated team building process. So, I think this is the first thing we do. Secondly, we do also try to educate team members. The tool used is Webinar i.e. how you engage people in the webinar, keep them active and solve things.*

The project leader must conduct knowledge sharing sessions and other training for team building process and engage team members, and the literature supports that. On-the-job training, coaching, research around the topic and short courses should be conducted (Burke & Barron, 2007), and knowledge sharing sessions should be carried out to appraise the team members frequently about project status (Gurumoorthy, 2012). Project leader should prepare project team training plan, and encourage project team members to participate in training so that they comprehend the big picture and their supporting role (Crawford, 2011), and engage in distributing knowledge by organising formal and informal knowledge sharing sessions, though, care need to be taken properly to schedule these sessions (Amalia & Nugroho, 2011).

10.7.3 Allocate Time in Schedule for team-building

At the time of project estimation, the project leader should allocate time in the project schedule for team-building activities and knowledge-sharing sessions.

> *From the project management perspective, at the date of estimation, one should keep apart time for training and knowledge sharing sessions*

> *I think it is a challenge. I am not sure if we have any particular guidelines on team building activities other than the fact that this should not be forgotten that it should be included in the schedule. It should be regular, and it should be as inclusive as possible.*

10.7.4 Social Gathering/Socializing

Social gathering should be arranged so that the project leader can socialize with the team members for sharing their views with each other and must have a regular conversation through formal or informal meetings or through outings with team members in order to understand their problems rather than just commanding them for the task. Project Leader should assert of having lunch and dinner together with team members during office hours when projects are of small duration. Project Leader should accompany team members for training or arrange small outdoor offsite trips with team members in case projects are of longer duration.

> *I think some of the biggest things we do for team building is by scheduling trips for small durations for spending much time together.*

> *.obviously lunch and dinner are common while working in an office. You can always hang out with your team. Much motivation is required when you are working with your teams for a minute duration. In case the project is of longer duration i.e. 1 or 2 years, then obviously, for team building, I would like to have 2-3 people going for training together or having a small outdoor offsite gathering. That also helps in team building.*

> *Project team member and project leader should be in touch with each other. They should be having a regular conversation. Informal or formal meetings can be held as communication plays the vital role over here. Project leaders should meet the people who are directly working on the project, talk to them, understand them, rather than just give the command for completion of a particular task. The leader should try to understand their problem and then once it is own to you, and then your command will be well taken by them. That plays a major role in team building. Secondly, you can have HR initiatives such as outing with the team or may be proper yearly increment structure, which analyses the performance of the team members.*

However, team members sometimes may not like the idea of spending their free time with work, and believe that buying free food or drinks does not build good teams but rather being interested in team members as a person.

Therefore, what you do is you take people for drinks after works, or you maybe do lunch with them, or you do an activity, but you are also unaware again. Some people do not like to spend their free time with work. Therefore, it depends on upon a little bit.

The project leader must arrange social gathering and social events for enhancing team building in the project teams, and the literature supports that. Through socialization, coherence with the team members increases as the team members get to understand behavior, attitude, and knowledge (Ahuja & Galvin, 2003), (Goodman & Wilson, 2000) essential for participation in the organisation and, therefore, project leader should promote socialization leading to better communication, high-performance knowledge (Ahuja & Galvin, 2003), (Hinds & Weisband, 2003) and collaboration (H.P., 2002.) through team building (Oshri, Kotlarsky, & P. Willcocks, 2007). An effective project leaders should enhance project team building activities through formal group events; arrange start-up workshops to allow team members to work together in small groups to facilitate team building; arrange at least one socializing event or workshop for projects with short duration; organize some low-impact supporting event for project with longer durations; arrange lunch or meal in a restaurant in order to allow team members to intermingle and familiarize with one another; arrange half-day workshops for promoting informal interaction between team members for increasing their trust and respect for each other, however, leader should ensure that the team members don't become antagonists (Kendrick, 2012) which mean that Project Leader should increase social gathering and socialise for enhancing team building.

10.8 Innovative and Collaborative Teams

10.8.1 Promote brainstorming

Project Leader should act as a facilitator and should follow a process of arranging and planning collective brainstorming sessions between teams at least once a week for sharing experiences and knowledge, taking reviews and feedbacks, allowing team members to give their opinions, and asking for their suggestions in order to build innovation solutions through idea generation and creation of new ideas and then selecting the optimum one.

I think you have to promote idea generation, brainstorming, open forums, open door policy and enhance overall communication. You have to instill upon them that innovation is an important thing and, we need to spread the ideas out here, create ideas and have brainstorming sessions.

They should share their experience and their current tasks, take review and feedback about his work and ask for suggestions. If he is facing any problem, he can bring it to the notice of team members. That is collective brainstorming will be very useful for the developing novel solutions, and find solutions for that.

Yes, I think it works. In another word, you make sure you do not group work but let people speak about their opinions, views and ideas. I think it can be very powerful tool, but still, I conceive it is how it is facilitated and how it is planned out is important. It can be appalling, and it can be superb. I think it depends on upon the leader having a facilitator and having a process, and then explain why they are doing these things. I have seen that it works.

The project team should engage in collective brainstorming at least once a week for new idea generation, and build innovative solutions. Through brainstorming, project teams can develop an array of creative and innovative ideas (Burke & Barron, 2007) which means that innovative solutions can be built through brainstorming however, project leader should act as a facilitator, set aggressive goals, motivate team members to explain ideas, provide feedback, and to make the ideas visible (Wilson, 2006). The presence of a high-ranking person in the team can stifle creativity as their thoughts, inadvertently can take priority, and other team members may be reluctant to contribute their own, diverse ideas (Burke & Barron, 2007). Furthermore, the size of the group should be less for brainstorming as the performance of the team falls as size increases (Cain, 2012).

10.8.2 Use Collaborative tools

Apart from regular short meetings on phones and certain weekly scheduled short meetings, ad-hoc presentations to provide project status, the project leader should use IT collaborative tools such as Instant Messaging, Conference Calls, and E-mails for build cooperation between global teams. Microsoft SharePoint should be used for collaborating and engaging team members, as well storing all project related documentation that can be accessed by any team member across geographically distributed project teams because Microsoft SharePoint is available at low cost, easily customizable and moreover enhances inter-communication between them. However, Project Leader should avoid having daily meetings, as it is not preferred by some team members. Furthermore, coordinating and collaborating is a challenge while working on global projects due to time differences due to which sometimes-virtual meetings are attended from home.

IBM or any other company I have seen that any specific tools for that. IBM is vast, and there are many tools available. Every company is using SharePoint nowadays because it has very low cost and it is very easily customized. We can make the process flow in that way. That is the tool that I normally use for communication. I have many teams spread globally, and IBM itself has its internal tools for developing software or something because they have a big legacy system. Therefore, that communication is taken care already. We have these global things, so Microsoft SharePoint is helpful.

We have meetings on the phone on a regular basis. They can be ad-hoc, and there can be weekly ones scheduled. We have a meeting of short duration so that people do not lose interest. We do it on a regular basis, so there is a regular contact and people will remember to say things. If you want to remember what has happened two weeks ago, probably you do not. Therefore, we do it regularly, and we keep it short. We also do ad-hoc presentations when we provide information on the status of the project. Therefore, that is not about what their specific requirements or questions are but more like generally but the project list to keep an interest overall. We also send email –communication. We have instant messenger. In regular basis when we have questions, we quickly ask them the answers through instant messaging. We use email for conferencing. We use Microsoft SharePoint, a repository where we store all our documentation. Every time, when a document is uploaded, email is sent to the inbox. Therefore, I engage my team members from all the tools that I have. Some people focus on doing meetings of 30 min duration every day. Ido does not want to do that, as some people do not like that. Some people do not talk to their people.

Timing is a big challenge. To get a meeting at one time and coordinating with everyone is a challenge because at one time, a team member at the UK is not available and another time team member at the US is not available. Same kind of meeting has to be set up at all locations once or twice or else we go home and take on conceal. Therefore, I think the timing is a bit challenge on that.

The project team should use collaborative tools for building cooperation and for engaging with team members. Project teams should use collaborative tools such as Meeting and Communication tools such Instant Messaging, Web Based Meeting programs such as Skype, Twitter, Information broadcasting tools such as Blog Software and Podcasts, Information Sharing and Gathering Tools, "Push" technologies such as Email, Faxes and Voice Mails, and newsletters (Brown, Huettner, & Jame, 2006) for increasing knowledge conception, shared intelligence and collaboration, however chosen tools should be easier to use and give rich user experience but should be cost-effective (Lomas, Burke, & Page, 2008).

10.8.3 Allocate time and resources

Project Leader should play a critical role in developing innovative solutions through projects, and should allocate time, cost, enough resources and additional budget for innovation during Project Estimation, interact with team, ask for ideas about implementation and improvement of a particular process, and then combine those ideas for creating a best solution after scoping the project as per customer requirement and bring further improvements or decrease gaps requirements through innovation.

The project leader should also let people know that it is ok to spend a little bit of time in innovation. Again, it depends on upon the project but in general terms; let people know that innovation is the part of their job.

One challenge is time. Depending on the project and what exactly the goals are, you can look at what time is left to complete the project. You cannot get back if you are talking innovation, you must have enough time to able to innovate something. Time is the big thing. Resources play a significant role because if you end up with not enough resources, you will not have enough time. Therefore, proper resources should be provided. Otherwise, it would hamper innovation. Cost is another thing. You need to do budgeting correctly and allocate a little bit of budget for innovation. A Little bit of variant to be planned in the sandbox for additional costs, roles, and development scope. You need to scope your project as per the user requirement and look for improvement or decrease gaps requirements through innovation I speak to my team and ask about their ideas for the particular process to be implemented, what best can be done, and then put together; we can derive solutions which best fits to the requirements of the customer

In the planning phase, the project leader should allocate time and resources for innovation (Loewe & Dominiquini, 2006) during scheduling.

10.9 Motivate Team Members

10.9.1 Engage with team member

Project leader should increase the motivation of the team members by engaging them through their increased involvement and participation in project a activities during office hours, and through recreational activities or engaging in sporting activities after office hours, and providing them the overall information and status of the project, project time frame, their role, benefits of the project, and its impact on them, and further arranging an open forum where they can freely ask questions about project issues that concern them.

They should be getting enough information to see the bigger picture and the impact they are going to make in your organization. They should see the benefits of the project so that they can connect with your project. People should be engaged in the project. This will increase their motivation and increase their commitment towards the projects

I involve with my team members, play sports, and engage with them.

Therefore, I engage my team members from all the tools that I have. Some people focus on doing meetings of 30 min duration every day. I do not want to do that, as some people do not like that. Some people do not talk to their people. We need to do a communication that does not feel too heavy, but that keeps them constantly engaged and aware of the project.

The project leader should engage with team members to motivate team members. Project leader should participate in diverse group behavior for enhancing efficiency of the team, including organising the team, enhancing team member's input towards the team, and function with the team as a whole (Hackman & R., 2005) which build team relationships (Graen, Hui, & Taylor, 2004), (Graen & Uhl-Bien, 1995), and increase team member's exuberance (Gerstner & Day, 1997), (Schriesheim, Castro, & Cogliser, 1999), and motivate them (Bruekelen, et.al 2012). Project leader should engage team member for increasing their motivation (Clark, 2012), (Koonce, Anderson, & Marchant, 1995) and managing change by fostering environments that enhances their commitment such as building a dynamic culture, nurturing real leadership, formulating a compelling strategy, vision, and bringing in line reward and recognition and supplying sufficient resources (Clark, 2012) through behavioral change and performance improvement training programs and worships; education and learning; proactive communication and collaboration; participation and inspiration for innovative, and strategic and imaginative thinking, and (Kravchenko, 2012) through open discussion forums for sharing knowledge (Tu, et.al., 2012).

10.9.2 Support team members

The project leader should motivate project team by supporting the project to achieve success as well to keep their energy level high and should listen to their concerns, and understand the problem faced and supported them with an appropriate solution, which will motivate functions, which can further lead to improving their performance.

> *It is someway else for the Project Leaders to go if they are unhappy going inside in the projects. The So first thing is to try continuously to keep the energy levels high, refresh, etc. Make sure everybody is trying to achieve here because longer the project goes on, the harder that sometimes gets to remember that. Secondly, using the objectives, the PMO in the company should support team members and create a place for Project Leaders to go to. I used to have daily meetings with the team, but he was there on the ground to look after their concerns and support them in performance side and motivation side, and working with the functional managers.*

> *We need to motivate the functions. One needs to contribute to the success of the function or otherwise lose a job. Some projects take away people's jobs, and they are made to work on the project as they are going to lose their job at the end of it. In that case, you should make sure that you help and support people in finding jobs at the end of it, and help them in getting new positions.*

The project leader should help team members to motivate them, and the literature support them (Thamhain, 2004). Project Leader should support team including support groups, suppliers, vendors, partners, government agencies and customers, and support and develop prominent team players who work with others user but who are more experienced and can increase the confidence of the team members; should speak the same language of the team players and understand the problems from their perspective; provide individual training and exchange thoughts about problems and provide helpline support (Briner, Hastings, & Geddes, 2004)which means that motivation of the team members can be increased by supporting team members.

10.10 Manage team conflicts

10.10.1 Deal with conflict directly

The project leader should directly address the dispute, and tell team members what is expected of them, and should encourage them to raise their hands if they feel things are not going correctly.

> *Do not ignore the conflict but deal with it directly. Help the people understand that when the things are not going correctly or when they do not agree with what is happening, then at the point, they should raise their hands and bring up the issue immediately.*

> *Big think I would say communication. Events should be communicated so that everyone knows what is going on and there is no hidden agenda. There is no cheap marketing that the other people are getting. I think having stakeholder assessments and having good stakeholder base helps to avoid those conflicts. If you have functional managers, stakeholders, upper management, and interested parties, they can help things running and moving forward. However, communication is a real big thing at the next level. It is better to figure out these conflicts head on. If your team member is involved in a conflict, you may discuss that in the meeting, but it is better to have one to one conversation with him/ her and figure out the problem. Most things some can do are just to brush it off and do not consider it as an issue and do not care for that. However, again, it comes back to a lot of excellent leadership skills and how you manage your team to keep those conflicts at the minimum. The bottom line is that there will always be conflicts, and we will not be able to go away from this. However, you need to keep that to a minimum. If there are conflicts that you want to better them out, have open discussions early on and do not keep them for a later day until it turns out to be something bigger.*

The project leader should deal with the conflict directly and literature support that. In case of cooperative conflict wherein team members compete to move towards goal attainment, project leader should resolve the dispute by boosting the parties in conflict to convey their ideas and feelings directly taking in consideration the viewpoint of others, and then communicate the need to resolve the dispute for common benefit, and for merging of new ideas for creating new solutions (Tjosvold, 1998). Literature also support that project leader should isolate the people from problem, concentrate on interests and not designations and devise options for shared gain through engagement in open discussions which complements cooperative conflict (Hwang, 1996) and provides a win-win solution which is regarded vital for conflict resolution (Meredith & Mantel, 2012, p.p. 162)(Lacey, 2012, p.p. 51-76). Furthermore, the reoccurrence of effective conflict resolution aids in the development of productive conflict where the team members become assured that they employ their conflict to resolve problems and reinforce their relationships, and further enabling project leader to deliver strategic leadership for innovation (Chen, Liu,& Tjosvold, March 2005).

10.10.2 Identify cause

Project leader should observe the team members, get connected with the team and try to determine the root cause of the team conflicts by listening to the perspectives and pros and cons of the both parties, analyse whether actually a problem exists when a team member is complaining, and then try to reach a win-win situation to resolve the conflict.

> *I think you need to observe what is going on to see where the frictions are in the individuals. You observe at lunchtime, who meets with who. Observe your team. It is all about being connected and being aware of what is going on. You need to understand whether there is some problem in the team when somebody it is complaining, or the person who is complaining is a complainer. Know you team and know your stakeholders well.*

> *You need to bring the concerned party on the phone, listen to both sides, listen separately or may be on the same call and try to understand the viewpoint of the both sides. Moreover, then try to conclude, and try to bring some win-win situation for both the parties. The cause of the conflict should be searched for*

The project leader should identify the cause for conflict resolution, and the literature supports. Project leader should enable mutual sharing amid the parties in conflicts, and emphasize on identification and dealing with the roots so that changes in behavior of the team members and their inter-relationships turn into less hostile and more positive (Mascia, 2012) which means that identifying then cause of the conflict can be regarded as suitable method for managing conflicts.

10.10.3 Counseling from Project Leader

Project Leader should explain to the team members what is incorrect and what is expected from them and should encourage the team members to raise their hands if they feel things are not going correctly; advise them that all jobs are equally important and require equal attention, and the conflict due to priority clashes or first use of resource should be addressed through communication, and understanding of importance of other person's work; in case of conflicts within development team, project leader should encourage the team to resolve conflicts at their level, and for conflicts within the cross-functional team, he/she should act as a mediator by listening to them and finding a win-win situation for both.

Each head should understand that each of their jobs is critical, despite that, the other head is performing well and why he is not performing well. Therefore, some healthy competition can be brought to the team. The team conflicts can be addressed by letting the people know that all the jobs are equally important and require equal attention. Therefore, problems in the particular areas may be time to time formally or informally communicated to the team members. People should be motivated to show some positive energy to solve some problems.

> *As far as possible, the project leader should encourage team members to resolve conflicts at their level. If it is an issue within a development team, then Project Leader should encourage the development team to lead to settle the process. If it is within the cross-functional team, the Project Leader should act as mediator, listen to both sides and then try to find solutions, which are win-win for both parties*

Do not ignore the conflict but deal with it directly. Help the people understand that when the things are not going correctly or when they do not agree with what is happening, then at the point, they should raise their hands and bring up the issue immediately. In case the team member is not performing, at that stage, it is important that you tell them what is incorrect and what is expected from them. If it is in such a role that you cannot help, then, you should come up with a plan. Many times when you are a Project Leader, you are not responsible for the HR type actions of the individuals. However, you can go back to the people that are responsible for and challenge the situation. It all boils down whether you as a person are going to deal that troublesome situation or you are going to sit down and hope if that goes away)

10.11 Evaluation of Team Performance

10.11.1 Performance measurement through KRA

Project leader should set setting KPI's (Key Performance Indicators) through which performance of the team members KRA's (Key Result Area's) are evaluated on the basis of feedback points such as team member's Behaviour, Project Delivery, Cultural sensitivity and Personal Traits, and thereafter a Performance Level is decided for the team members, however, leader should provide the key resources in order to allow him/her to deliver to their potential; and given them increments after analysing their performance after each.

The performance management happens through all these inputs coming from different feedback points. You need to collect those data points. You need to make a scale weight of those and accordingly rate your decisions. They all are relative ratings, they are not individualistic ratings, and you need to see what kind of performance can be considered to be the best performance in this year and what is kind of return that is the best performer and one who is the low performer and then through a relative ranking of your performance. You have five different levels. A person who is performing consistently and exceeding is Level 1. Level 2 +

rating is when a person has done sustainably well but has the scope of improvement. Level 2 is when the person has done the work assigned to him, but he has much scope for improvement. Level 3 is when the person has done badly, and he needs to be removed. We have a proper performance evaluation mechanism, and these are all set using the KRA, which is set at different levels. From the Top level to the bottom level, everything is driven by the KRA. KRA are coming from organization to account sector, and then finally to the Project Leader, project leader, team leader and team members.

KRA's (Key Result areas) should be properly identified, and team members should be provided with the key resources. Difficulties faced by the team members should be summarized quarterly. Increments should be given, or annual promotion should happen after seeing the performance of the team members based on those KRAs. That will give the proper result. If you are not analyzing properly, overseeing the project and giving promotion to a wrong person, then the right person who has the worked on that project will get a wrong sign.

We have something called KPI's. In the case of projects, I have data about each team members in the team. If he is in the organization previously, then I already know about that person from my internal network. I prefer to have something call performance matrix, which is typically done by KPI for measuring performance in team members KRAs. All the delivery measure that I have is quality measures or KPI.

The project leader should gauge the performance of the project team by setting KRAs and the literature also support the same(Liu, Derzsi, Raus, & Kipp, 2008). KRA should be set for project teams members for measuring the KPI's which reflect the team member's performance in the project (Luu, Kim, & Huynh, 2008). Project leader should set KRA for measuring the performance of the team members in relation to project performance.

10.11.2 Performance Management Systems

Project Leader should advocate the use of Enterprise Performance Management Systems under the charge of PMO for Quarterly, Monthly performance evaluation of the team members against set objectives and analyze their reporting working style, how they handle situations and then record project activities and monitor performances.

> *We also use an enterprise project management system as well. However, that's more of the mechanics for reporting and recording the activities of the project. We prefer communication rather than dealing with the source of information and data.*
>
> *We have backend performance systems, so that is another way to evaluate the performance. We go by quarters, every three months, to set up objectives. They have to meet these targets, and that is the easy way to manage their performance. That is an easy way to manage performance. However, I think it always better to check what they are doing, how they are doing; see what's going on, whether they need any resources or costs, or any help. I think that is important.*

Project leader should set up a performance measurement system for performance measurement of the project team members and the literature also support of setting an integrated performance measurement system for measuring the performance of the team members as well the performance of the project (Pillai, Joshi, & Rao, 2002) however, this system will require a lot of initial setup investment in IT systems, and therefore we will be more suited for large organisations running multiple projects.

10.12 Cross project learning

10.12.1 Document Lessons Learnt

Project leader and each team member should document the project learning's, document WWR (What Went Right), WWR (What Went Wrong), project related data and reports, and project related communications after project completion and later indexing that data for future reference and analysis of the problems faced during the project and studied the solution provided at that time in order avoid committing those mistakes in the future.

What I like to see and what I have seen it done well anywhere and I have read about it is that they need to document the Lessons learned more than once a year where they write about what things went right or wrong in the project implementation, that dialogues and that communication. I see things have been drafted that can go fine, but I would like to see open dialogues. I think these are the-the things they can do.

We document the project charter, regulation history, project risks, scope, timelines, planned reports and test data analysis reports. We use devices, so we keep the device history and the device index. All the records are indexed. Everything is indexed.

This is where your Lessons Learned data will come handy. Now, while you are doing projects, a number of things are happening, and this is your top responsibility to record whatever you have learnt, whatever has gone wrong, and whatever went right in the project, who were responsible, what were the actions taken, and what can be done to avoid those future mistakes.

The best practices can also be said as learned lessons. Many people want to follow, but it is not possible because, I always have a practice of whenever the project gets over, it is mandatory that each team member writes down the learned lessons from his project so that whenever I go to the next project, I keep in mind these things. Moreover, in IBM, I think it is mandatory to have these things documented. Because, when we have a something call project management review, which happens every quarter like an audit, we ask for these artifacts.

It is important to create lessons learned after completion of the project and then review those lessons learned so that the people within the project can see what knowledge is gained from the project. There should also be a repository of lessons learned for the organization to refer.

I do not have an ego to that level, but if the analysis of the past projects is done in proper way, for example, a project exceeded the number of days; there might be reasons behind that. If we have a knowledge base of those things, we can learn and apply that knowledge for future projects, and avoid past mistakes. We can also refer the knowledge base in a case similar kind of scenario comes, and refer the knowledge base, and the understand from there that what was the solution applied to the similar problem in the past, so that instead of reinventing the wheel, we always have a solution in place. This type of analysis can be substantial for the companies' profitability and success of the project.

Project Leader should ensure that cross-project learning is done by recording the documenting the lessons learnt, and the literature also support that by documenting lessons learnt, key project experience is stored for future reference and cross-project learning (PMI, 2008), (Schindlera & Epplerb, 2003) which means that this is a best practice.

10.13 Summary

This chapter discussed the various team roles, team building models, cross-functional teams, and how collaboration can be increased within the project teams. Team building practices an organization should follow for building collaborative teams.

Communication		
Final Results	**Result Triangulated Yes or No**	**Supported By**
1	Awards and Appreciation.	Yes	Case Study 1, Case Study 2

2	Knowledge Sharing Sessions/ Training.	Yes	Case Study 5
3	Allocate time in schedule for team-building	No	
4	Social Gathering/ Socializing	No	

Table 10.2 Team Building Practises

Innovative and Collaborative Teams			
	Final Results	**Result Triangulated Yes or No**	**Supported By**
1	Promote Brainstorming	Yes	Case Study 3
2	Use collaborative tools	Yes	Case Study 6
3	Allocate time and resources	No	

Table 10.3: Innovative and Collaborative Teams

The results for this objective are listed in Table 10.2, and Table 10.3 contains the team building practices applied in global projects around the world for building innovative and collaborative teams. However, these results were collected from a small sample of respondents, and therefore applicability of the above findings is limited to the aerospace organization in India.

CHAPTER 11

11. Communication

The role of communication in Global Aerospace and IT projects and identify methods it can be improved.

Communication			
	Final Results	**Result Triangulated Yes or No**	**Supported By**
1	Two-way Communication/Parallel Communication.	No	
2	Frequent and focused meetings with clear agenda and objective.	Yes	Case Study 3
3	Right communication at the right time.	No	
4	Latest communication technologies must be used	No	
5	The need of communication model and communication Plan.	Yes	Case Study 7

Table 11.1: Methods for improving Project Communication

Communication plays a critical role in Global Aerospace and IT projects and is considered as an essential activity in project management (See 11.1). The methods through which project communication can be improved as listed in Table 11.1. Moreover, it is important to follow a decentralised decision-making approach across global projects which will empower team members to take decisions, increase team loyalty, improve information flow within the organisation through bottom-up information flow which will promote collaboration between the team members, boost innovation and problem-solving, will reduce unnecessary communication channels, increase flexibility, reduce non-value added time by reducing in time waiting for decision, and above all reduce long-distance communication costs. However, enough information needs to be available to the team leadership and team member to take right decisions, which can be accomplished through focused meetings.

CHAPTER 12

12. Measuring Project Performance

Major three performance indicators in an industry are Cost, time, and quality. Other indicators gathering attention are safety, functionality, and satisfaction. Qualitative and Quantitative measures are used to set KPI's. KPI's are good indicators of project performance through which all relevant project information is furnished to stakeholders. Through KPI's project performance can be measured and compared in a structured way (Chan & Chan, 2004). However it is important to have limited KPIs as having numerous KPI's can be resource consuming, however for effective performance measurement, KPI's must be accepted by all stakeholders and top management.

KPIs are subjective and can be different for various projects. KPIs for a construction project may be different for KPIs for a manufacturing project.

The set of 75 KPIs developed by Bernard Marr is listed below.

Financial Performance:

1. Net Profit.
2. Net Profit Margin.
3. Gross Profit Margin.
4. Operating Profit Margin.
5. EBITDA.
6. Revenue Growth Rate.
7. Total Shareholder Return (TSR).
8. Economic Value Added (EVA).

9. Return on Investment (ROI).
10. Return on Capital Employed (ROCE).
11. Return on Assets (ROA).
12. Return on Equity (ROE).
13. Debt-to-Equity (D/E) Ratio.
14. Cash Conversion Cycle (CCC).
15. Working Capital Ratio.
16. Operating Expense Ratio (OER).
17. CAPEX to Sales Ratio.
18. Price Earnings Ratio (P/E Ratio).

Customers:

19. Net Promoter Score (NPS).
20. Customer Retention Rate.
21. Customer Satisfaction Index.
22. Customer Profitability Score.
23. Customer Lifetime Value.
24. Customer Turnover Rate.
25. Customer Engagement.
26. Customer Complaints.

Market and marketing efforts:

27. Market Growth Rate.
28. Market Share.
29. Brand Equity.
30. Cost per Lead.
31. Conversion Rate.
32. Search Engine Rankings (by keyword) and click-through rate.
33. Page Views and Bounce Rate.
34. Customer Online Engagement Level
35. Online Share of Voice (OSOV).
36. Social Networking Footprint.
37. Klout Score.

Operational Performance:

38. Six Sigma Level.
39. Capacity Utilization Rate (CUR).
40. Process Waste Level.
41. Order Fulfillment Cycle Time.
42. Delivery In Full, On Time (DIFOT) Rate.
43. Inventory Shrinkage Rate (ISR).
44. Project Schedule Variance (PSV).
45. Project Cost Variance (PCV).
46. Earned Value (EV) Metric.
47. Innovation Pipeline Strength (IPS).
48. Return on Innovation Investment (ROI2).
49. Time to Market.
50. First Pass Yield (FPY).
51. Rework Level.
52. Quality Index.
53. Overall Equipment Effectiveness (OEE).
54. Process or Machine Downtime Level.
55. First Contact Resolution (FCR).

Employees and Their Performance:

56. Human Capital Value Added (HCVA).
57. Revenue per Employee.
58. Employee Satisfaction Index.
59. Employee Engagement Level.
60. Staff Advocacy Score.
61. Employee Churn Rate.
62. Average Employee Tenure.
63. Absenteeism Bradford Factor.
64. 360-Degree Feedback Score.
65. Salary Competitiveness Ratio (SCR).
66. Time to Hire.
67. Training Return on Investment.

Environmental and Social Sustainability Performance:

68. Carbon Footprint.
69. Water Footprint.
70. Energy Consumption.
71. Saving Levels Due to Conservation and Improvement Efforts.
72. Supply Chain Miles.
73. Waste Reduction Rate.
74. Waste Recycling Rate.
75. Product Recycling Rate.

12.1 Earned value management

Earned value Management is a systematic project management process, which assists the project team in the measurement of project performance by finding variances in projects based on work performed and work planned.

Project baseline is a vital component of EVM. It is a reference point for all EVM activities It indicates future performance by using trend data for monitoring project plan, actual work, and work completion value. This also predicts the outcome of projects in terms of time of completion, the cost to completion and expected final costs. It further analyzes whether the project is on track and that the budget and time spent is in regards to the amount of work completed

Earned value analysis is a trend analysis technique through we can predict results and measure project performance by analysis of the amount of work performed on the project and by forecasting cost and expected date of completion of a project. It measures planned expenditure, actual expenditure and technical performance achieved to date.

The method depends on EV (Earned value) or budgeted cost of work. Performance indicators for cost and schedule depict project progress relative to its original plans, and it's future forecasts.

Monitoring and controlling the project without adherence to project scheduled time and budgeted cost is difficult. It is necessary that planning is done at the start of the project and during execution to complete the project in given a time frame and available resources.

12.1.1 EVM Terminology

1. Planned value (PV) or budgeted cost of work (BCWS): estimated value of work planned to be spent during a given period. It comprises a summation of the budgeted cost for work packages scheduled to be accomplished in a specified period. It is found by calculating total budgeted cost up to the analysis date.
2. Earned value (EV) or budgeted cost of work performed (BCWP): estimated value of work completed in a given timeframe. It is the cost originally budgeted to complete the work that has been completed as of the analysis date.
3. Actual cost (AC) or actual cost of work performed: Actual costs are the total costs incurred in completing work on the activity during a given period. It comprises what it costs to complete all the work completed as of on the analysis date.

12.1.2 Measurement of cost

1. Schedule Variance (SV) = EV (BCWP) - PV (BCWS)

   Work actually performed (EV) or BCWP minus the work scheduled (PV) or BCWS is equal to Schedule Variance (SV). The calculation of the same is the difference in dollar value of the amount of work that should have been finished in a specified time and the work actually completed. If the value is zero, it shows that project is right on schedule. If the value is in negative, its shows that the project is behind schedule or over budget. In this case, Project Leader need to increase project budget or accept reduced profit margins. If the value is in positive, it shows the project is ahead of schedule or under budget.

2. Cost Variance (CV) = EV (BCWP) – AC (ACWP)

   Planned cost of work performed EV (BCWP minus actual cost incurred for the work AC (ACWP) is equal to Cost Variance (CV). The calculation of the same is the difference in dollar value of the by which a project is either over-running or under-running its estimated cost. If the value is zero, it shows that project is right on schedule. If the value is in negative, its shows that the project is behind schedule or over budget. In this case, Project Leader need to increase project budget or accept reduced profit margins. If the value is in positive, it shows the project is ahead of schedule or under budget, and Project Leader needs to be reallocating money and resources from projects with positive variances to projects with negative variances.

3.   Schedule Performance Index (SPI) =PV(BCWS)/EV(BCWP)

This ratio is calculated by dividing the Work accomplished EV or (BCWP) by work planned PV or (BCWS) for a specific time. This ratio depicts the speed at which the project is being executed. If the value of SPI is one, this means the project is right on schedule. If the value of SPI is less than one, means the project is behind the schedule or over budget. If the value of SPI is greater than one, it shows that project ahead of schedule or under budget.

4.   Cost Performance Index (CPI) = EV(BCWP)/AC(ACWP)

This ratio is calculated by dividing the cost of work performed EV (BCWP) with actual cost AC (ACWP). This ratio indicates the cost-efficiency of the project and is employed for the forecasting cost of the project at completion. If the value of CPI is one, it indicates that actual cost matches the estimated cost and is on a budget. If the value of CPI is more than one, it indicates that work completed in a lower cost than planned or budgeted cost. If the value of CPI is less than one, it indicates that work completed in a higher cost than planned or is over budget.

5.   Critical Ratio (CR) = CPI x SPI

This ratio is calculated by multiplying the Cost Performance Index (CPI) with schedule performance index (SPI). This ratio is used to forecast the project completion estimates and signifies the overall status of the project.

CHAPTER 13

13. Case Studies

13.1 Aerospace Organisation: Case Study 1 and 2

13.1.1 About the Organization

Organisation is into manufacturing of Aerospace Components and Assemblies, engaged in Aerospace research and development, state-owned aircraft manufacturing companies, and Tier 1 International and Global Aerospace Companies. Organisation is handling execution of major Aerospace projects involving Precision Machining, Fabrication, Integration, Testing &supply of intricate and Airworthy systems.

Organisation has taken initiatives such as TPM (Total Productivity Maintenance) and Lean practices such as Kaizen and 5S. Organisation is certified in AS9100 Rev C, and ISO 140001, OSHAS 18001. Special processes are also NADCAP approved.

13.1.2 Executive Summary

Organisation is headed by the Vice President (VP). He is well supported by General Manager - Projects, General Manager – Finance, General Manager –Purchase, Head - Human Resources (HR), Head - Marketing, Head- Estimation, and Head - Quality Control (QC) and Quality Assurance (QA), and Head - Special Processes.

13.1.3 PM Process

Projects are handled by GM (General Manager) – Projects, who is well supported by Assistant General Managers and SBU (Strategic Business Unit) Heads. There are multiple SBUs currently handling different strategic projects. These SBUs are assigned single or multiple projects after analyzing the type of customer, project scope, and expertise of the SBU's project team members, resource availability, business requirement, available capacity or similarity in different customer needs. All SBUs operate under one roof with some dedicated as well as some shared resources. Each SBU is assigned dedicated Project and Process Planners for handling their respective projects. In some instances, a dedicated Machine Shop In-charge is also allocated to the SBU to monitor and handle the respective SBU's machine shop related activities.

Case Study1 will concentrate on "SBU1", the one of the largest SBU in the organization and Case Study 2 shall focus on "SBU2", the SBU dealing with Aircraft manufacturers.

SBU1 is handling projects related to manufacturing, integration, and testing of Airworthy assemblies which needs to be completed in a designated timeframe to meet Business targets. Out of multiple projects, a couple of projects will be discussed in Case Study 1 and Case Study 2 respectively.

13.1.4 Case Study 1: Projects with Local customers

13.1.4.1 Project Definition

13.1.4.1.1 Objectives

*   Successful development & Integration of Airworthy Systems.

13.1.4.2 Project Description and Issues

Two types of projects are executed in SBU 1. The first type of project *"Build to Print"* involves manufacturing, testing, and integration of aerospace components and assemblies. These projects can also be classified as High-Tech projects (Dvir, Lipovetsky, Shenhar, & Tishler, 1998). Other projects, classified as internal projects involve design and development of tooling, jigs and fixtures as machining aids, and for bringing process improvement for reduction of cycle time. The case study will give an insight into the administration of the first type of project.

13.1.4.3 Project Management Methodology

No formal project management methodology is followed for managing projects. For example, some of the line managers functioned as Project Leaders because of which they were focussed on managing line activities rather than project work which delayed the project and increased budget.

13.1.4.3.1 Recommendations

The Project Leader in SBU1 can convince the top management to examine the project portfolios and take charge of implementing formal project management. An outside consulting firm can be hired for arranging sessions and seminars on project management to all management and supervisors employed in the Division. A formal type of project management can be used so that all departments can be engaged, and can dynamically participate in the planning cycle of the project. This will empower the team members to understand their impact on the working of each department, enable them to prevent overlapping of work, and conform to the schedule, which will finally enhance cooperation, inter-department communication; lessen cost, and improve the attitude of the team member; however implementation of formal project management methodology can face resistance from some departments due to the change in management style. Moreover, better planning and a dynamic and competent project leader will be required, and a need for setting priorities at the divisional level to lessen scheduling variations but being prepared for respond proactively to rapidly changing priorities related to production activities (Kerzner, 2009).

13.1.4.4 Project Leadership and Project team

Project leadership was relatively emotionally intelligent as they showed confidence, trustworthiness, showed organizational commitment, willingness, drove to change and did not make unrealistic self-assessments. Communication between the project team members and project leader was limited to project progress and neither party had time to spend with each other, which showed a lack of social skills on the part of project leadership as well as project teams.

Project direction and project teams were an expert in their respective fields; however, their competency level in project management was not adequate.

For example, the project leadership spent staggeringly less time in evaluating potential project risks, controlling project budget, cost management, managing change control, and had limited proficiency in Project Management tools such as Microsoft Project for planning, scheduling and monitoring project, and was dependent on Project Planners or Finance department for data and reports (Cho & Eppinger, AUGUST 2005).

Project leadership was seen as more of System Designer (Task Master) rather than Systems Integrator (Builder of Learning Organisations) according to the Toyota Leadership Model, because project leader was more involved in problem-solving and instructing the team rather than showing the larger picture of why the task was important, and what impact the results from the task has on overall project outcome. For example, to solve the technical problems, project leader used to spend most of his time in workshop engaged in problem-solving and other task activities that he delegated to his subordinates. Moreover, project leader followed top-down approach for decision-making with less involvement of the team members. However, leader followed bottom-up approach for generating new ideas from the team members through Kaizen events.

Clear-cut job responsibilities were assigned to the project team members, however, due to many unplanned activities, project leader asked team members to perform unplanned activities apart from their regular tasks out of their role. Additionally, each team member had different priorities and goals, which caused conflict and priority clashes among cross-team members leading to frustration among team members finally resulting in a blame culture. This was one of the reasons for high attrition in project planning department.

13.1.4.4.1 Recommendation

It is important that the project leaders and project team members are trained in project management tools and techniques such as scheduling, and access is provided to the financial data for project cost management including, estimating, budgeting, and controlling project cost. For managing project priorities, Project leader should delegate the tasks related to problem-solving to the respective department head or functional head, and involve him only when it is actually required, and concentrate on spending more time with planning department for planning the future activities for reducing unplanned activities, identifying and evaluating future risks, performance monitoring of projects and team members, team building, managing and controlling change, project reviews and stakeholder management. Moreover, to improve the organisation culture, which is more uncooperative, blaming and inflexible, it is required that the SBU head should use bottom-up approach for decision making by involving them, maintain open communication between top executives, middle management and assembly line and machine shop operators for improving morale and increasing productivity, and encourage the cross-functional team members to talk with each other and share information through information sessions, orientation and knowledge sharing and feedback sessions, and through leadership meetings.

13.1.4.5 Project Management Processes

Table 13.1 describes the project management processes.

PM Process	Activities Performed
Project Initiation	Receipt of RFQ.
	Estimation department conducts feasibility study and assessment of current capabilities across people, processes, and systems.
	• Authorize business case. • Send Quotation. • Receive Order.
	Marketing department organizes Project Kick-off meeting (APQP meeting) involving representatives from Methods, Project Planning Department, Machine Shop Department, and Quality Department to understand customer requirements and decide on manufacturing processes.
	Project Leader forms Project cross-functional team.
	• Methods prepare Process Planning. • Methods validate manufacturing process.
	Planning department prepares preliminary project plans.
	Manufacturing teams prepare and approve Mock-ups.
	Project Leaders officially handover project to Project Planning Department.

Project Planning	Project Planning Department creates final project plans.
	Project Planners identifies and documents risks.
	Project Planners perform capacity planning.
	Project Planners create Project schedules are created.
	Project Planners release components and assemblies.
	Project Planners communicate with cross-functional departments is coordinated and maintained.
Project Monitoring and Control	Project Leader monitors project manually however not in an optimized way due to lack of IT tracking systems.
	Project Leader hold weekly divisional level meetings for discussing project progress.
	• Project Leader takes daily morning meetings to discuss daily project progress. • Project Leader conducts a weekly meeting with global customer team for reviewing project progress. • Project Leader creates/send Emails for communicating with global teams. • Project Leader makes customer visits for understanding new customer requirements.
	Project Leader sets KRA for team members.
Project Closing	Prepare documentation. Perform Quality checks Take customer approvals.
	Make delivery.

Table 13.1: Project Management Process followed in SBU 1.

13.1.4.5.1 Project Initiation

Table 13.1 illustrates the project initiation processes followed to implement the project in SBU1. This phase was critical to an improper understanding of the customer requirement could lead to major non-conformances, rework, delays, loss of customer trust, and project failures.

13.1.4.5.2 Project Planning

Project planning department handles this critical phase and plays a major role starting from project initiation phase to project closing phase. Table 13.1 describes the roles handled by project planning department. The Project Planners, apart from the responsibilities of Project delivery, were more involved in operational activities such as capacity management, and other non-value added or unplanned activities that had little relevance to Project management resulting in less time for them for planning project activities.

Demand Management	Fast and accurate retrieval of information.
	Improve decision-making.
Order fulfillment	Improve visibility along with supply chain.
	Improve the quality of information.
Manufacturing flow	Maintain accurate tracking of components.
	Enhance process automation.
Reverse Logistics	Increase productivity.
	Improve quality and reliability.
Supplier Relationship Management	Cut down operating costs.
	Maintain better competitive position.

Table 13.2 Benefits of RFID. Source: Adapted from (Attaran, 2011), (Attaran, 2006), (Hou, 2006), (Reyes, 2007)

Table 13.2 describes the benefit of RFID (Radio Frequency Identification). To avoid wastage of planner's times, Project Leader can employ RFID system to remove internal efficiencies and save firms money in short term. Other benefits of RFID are listed in the Table 13.2. Apart from this, this will improve communication, enable the project planners to track each component while on the production line, and help in carefully scheduled Just in Time (JIT). Moreover, component usage, its availability, location can also be tracked. This will also reduce project planners times in searching "lost" components, decrease inventory carrying capacity and assure faster order-to-cash cycles, however, its implementation has certain issues such as high capital cost, and matters related to integration with the existing ERP system (Attaran, February 2012). This will also allow project planner to concentrate more on project activities rather than non-valued activities.

13.1.4.5.3 Project Monitoring and Control

Project monitoring was also very critical phase of project management in the organization. Daily morning meetings with cross–functional team and weekly review meetings with top management were conducted for reviewing project progress. Measurable Key Performance Indicators (KPI) were set for monitoring the performance of the team members however, performance of the team members was not linked to the project performance, however based on measures such as regular delineation of duties, team member's adherence to quality systems, no's of Kaizens, system conformances, or on the basis of efficiency of the team member in operations such as timely release of material, maintaining updated status of records, etc.

Project Balance Scorecard should be used to evaluate and analyze the performance Scope, Schedule, Quality and Cost against the initially estimated project baseline, and plan should be created to meet those targets either by employing more resources or by controlling cost or by controlling scope creeps and maintain quality. Project Leader should employ 360-degree review procedure for evaluating supervisors, their peers, and their supervisors.

13.1.4.6 Project Risk Management

Project Leaders should identify and document potential risks at the start of the project; sometimes the Project Leader missed to review the risks frequently. The Project Leader should frequently identify the potential project risks, evaluate those risks and add those risks in the risk register. For these risks, Project Leader should prepare proper contingency and mitigation plans.

13.1.4.7 Project Quality

Variability in manufacturing processes along with non-conformances in product quality led to reworks, which further affected project schedule, increased project cost, affected project schedule, caused resource constraints and caused delays in meeting project deadlines.

13.1.4.7.1 Recommendations

Process improvement initiatives should be undertaken such as Lean Six Sigma for reducing variation and reduce non-value added activity; however, this will require top management support along with a mature project leader and team members who are competent in Six Sigma and Lean tools for bringing process improvements. TPM and Kaizen events should organize for continuous improvement and bring new ideas.

13.1.4.8 Project Change Management

Project Leader entertained customer change requests. However, Project Leader did not document these requests either due to top management pressure or due to reluctance on the part of Project Leader to say no to the customer in fear of annoying customer and in the urge to maintain a goody-goody relation with the client, however, ignoring the impact of project cost and schedule. For example, the customer being an institutional organization, the project leader was obliged to entertain their request as a goodwill gesture. However, none of these requests were in the original project scope, and the customer was not charged for these requests.

13.1.4.8.1 Recommendations

The project leader should be tactful to say no to the client requests and tell the customer that any new demands will only be entertained if the customer is willing to pay. The project leader should follow the change request process and get the changes approved by the shift control board and document it.

13.1.4.9 Project Communication

Daily morning meetings and weekly divisional level meetings were conducted for progress review and take decisions. Open-house forums were carried out to communicate the critical issues regarding the project and listen and address related issues of the operators. However, at certain times, meetings headed by project leaders for communicating project priorities neither have a common agenda nor documented, and the actions plans, responsibilities, and timeframes were not identified.

13.1.4.9.1 Recommendations

The project leader should ensure that each meeting must have clear agenda and should document and communicate minutes of the meeting (MOM).

13.1.4.10 Findings

1. There is no single project leadership style adopted by the project leaders in the organization.
2. There is no formal project management methodology.
3. Interconnection of operations management and project management is diverting the attention of project planners.
4. Project Leadership within the organization needs improvement.
5. Project Initiation, Project Planning and Project Monitoring and Control are critical project phases.
6. Project Leader should improve Project Change Management, Project Risk Management, and Project Quality management process.
7. Project Leader should streamline and properly channel Project Communication.

13.1.5 Case Study 2: Projects for Global customers

This case study deals with the projects implemented in the organization for global clients including OEM's located in the USA and the UK. SBU Head 2 manages these projects. We will discuss one of the projects handled by this SBU.

13.1.5.1 Project Definition

13.1.5.1.1 Objectives

The aim is to manufacture successfully and supply aircraft components and assemblies for Aircraft OEM.

13.1.5.2 Project Management Process

The SBU2 follows the common Project Management Process for implementation of global projects as followed by SBU1 for local projects (Refer: Table 13.1). No formal methodology is followed to manage projects.

13.1.5.3 Project Leadership

Project Leadership was more focussed on the operational side rather than concentrating on the strategic aspect of the project and was adopting present-oriented leadership style rather than adopting future-oriented leadership style as he concentrated on meeting short-term monthly targets rather than focusing on future project tasks and customer requirements.

Pace-setting leadership style was also found combined with the participative approach. For example, the project leader used to instruct the project team to perform better and faster rather than achieving competitive advantage and attaining market success (Shenhar, Poli, & Lechler, 2000). The project leader motivated the team member if he/she was skillful but required motivation, however, provided essential instructions to the team member in case team member be motivated but lacked experience. Project Leader recognized and rewarded good performance of the team members. Moreover, leadership was authentic, honest and fair in evaluating and rewarding performance.

13.1.5.3.1 Recommendations

Project Leader should remove non-valued added activities in the project and engage in team building activities. Once that is done, the team will have enough time to participate and increase the value to the project, which will enhance their learning and motivate them. The leader should also encourage their involvement in decision-making and provide training which enhances the knowledge of the team members.

13.1.5.4 Project Team Building

There is a lack of team building activities in the organization. There is more of a blame culture between cross-functional teams, and cross-functional team members are not aligned to achieve one goal. Despite having morning meetings where the team members can communicate, develop relationships and participate in solving each other's problem, project team members engage in blaming each other for project delays. This is because each department has its priorities and departmental goals, and therefore not concerned about the accomplishment of the overall project goal. This can be attributed to the inability of project leadership and Top management to communicate the overall organizational objectives and communicate priorities to each cross-functional team members in spite of the Open house meetings conducted by Top Management to listen and resolve the problems of the staff and team members. Cross-functional team members are unaware of what is essential for the organization and therefore stay within their silos. Communication routed through project leaders and senior management who are high in organization hierarchy have a different impact than that of the project management personnel due to high power distance in Indian culture, however, due to lack of directives from the Top management, there is no focus and pressure of the team members.

Top Management and Project Leader should instruct the cross-functional department heads to give more priority to project goals rather than to departmental objectives. More team-building activities should be encouraged.

13.1.5.5 Project Planning

Macro and Micro plans are prepared and presented to the cross-functional team. Stakeholder management is done by the project planning team. Buy/ Make decisions are also taken by project planning team along with preparation of subcontracting plans for procurement of raw material and outsourcing. Customer communications are also maintained through email and conference calls by the project planning team.

13.1.5.6 Project Monitoring and Control

Project leader monitors the project through daily morning meetings which are attended by SBU, and representatives of Project Planning, Machine Shop, Methods and QC departments, and they report the status of the project, any project related issues. Project Planning informs their presentative of the each department about the day's schedule and the priorities for the day. On the organization level, the evaluation of the project progress is done in the Divisional meeting held once a week. Customer meetings are held weekly through conference calls. Project leader monitors the project progress by settings KRA's for the project team and then measuring those KPIs.

13.1.5.7 Project Risk Management

The project team identifies project risks and documented. Mitigation plans are also prepared. Projects risk are said to be re-evaluated after seven days to identify new project risks. All identified risks are documented with appropriate action to be taken. Near-miss accidents are also reported.

13.1.5.8 Project Quality Management

As per customer requirements, the project follows AS9100 Rev C Standard. Therefore, document requirements are strict, and conformance to the system is imperative. Kaizen events, TPM meetings, and 5S activities are followed by the SBU to improve productivity. Minor product non-conformances are reported during the initial phase of the project due to high precision nature and intricacy of the components, inadequate training of some of the operators, operator mistakes due to lack of proper supervision and guidance, lack of Poka-yoke, however, after certain runs and provision of skills training, non-conformances are minimal. All non-conformances are reported to the customer.

13.1.5.9 Project Communication Management

Regarding maintaining communication with the client, the teleconference is held once a week to discuss project progress, issues and solutions related to project activities. Collaboration is also maintained with the customer through email and phone. However, advanced communication technologies are not used due to issues related to Information Security. Moreover, the organization is certified by ISO 27001 and have NDAs signed with the customers. Communication with local team members is maintained through morning meetings, emails, and phone. Significant project activities, priorities, reminders, project delays, status updates, problem reporting, are done through Email. Senior management is also involved in the fast resolution of project delays. Face to face meetings with the customer are done only once a year through the visit of the Project Leader to the client sites.

13.1.5.10 Training

Skill sets of the personnel working in that SBU are evaluated, and leadership and other management training such as Time Management, Leadership, Presentation Skills are identified by the team members himself/herself or by his/her direct supervisor who is later approved by the Project leader. However, no cultural training is provided to create awareness to the culture of the customer.

13.1.5.11 Project Outcomes

Despite doing so, still the projects miss their scheduled completion date by average 30- 40 days. Cost overruns are appropriately 20% of the planned cost. Most of the delays are reported due to priority clashes, machine breakdown, machining and technical delays.

13.1.5.12 Findings

APQP meeting is a critical phase of this project where requirements are gathered by the Project Leader and team, customer requirements are understood, work breakdown structure is created by dividing the project into small chunks, customer communications are maintained for clarifications and initial project work is completed in collaboration and through participation with cross-functional teams. Adherence to Quality and Aerospace standards is maintained. However, process improvement is required along with a better focus on TPM activities to reduce any product non-conformances.

13.1.6 Findings of Case Study 1 and Case Study 2: Aerospace Organization

- Traditional Project Management approach was followed.
- Project Leadership focused more on the operational side.
- Emotional intelligence was found in Project Leadership.
- There was a limited communication between Project Leadership and Projects Team.
- Team member's KPI was not linked to project process.
- Competency Level in project management was inadequate
- Project Leader was seen as a System Designer(Taskmaster) rather than System Integrator (Builder of Learning Organizations)
- Project leadership gets involved more in solving problems rather than managing projects.
- High attrition was seen in Project Planners due to frustration.
- Identified projects risks, however, did not review frequently.
- High rework was found in the manufacturing process.
- Customer change requests were handled without analyzing the impact on project cost and schedule.

- Open house forums were conducted to resolve problems of the team members
- The daily morning meeting was carried out to review the project process.
- Top management conducted weekly review meetings with project team and their respective SBU (Strategic Business Unit) head.
- Project review meetings with the customers were carried out once in a month.
- Meeting lacked common agenda and was not properly timed.
- Project Leader recorded memorandum/minutes of the meeting for future reference.
- Provided Leadership and Management Training for the team members
- The performance was recognized and rewarded.
- There was variation found in manufacturing processes.

Conclusions of the Case Study 1 are mentioned above

- Project Leadership practiced Pace-setting leadership style along with participative approach.
- Recognized and rewarded accomplishments.
- Project leadership was authentic, honest, and fair in evaluating and rewarding performance.
- Present-Oriented Leadership style was followed by Future-Oriented Leadership style.
- Priority was given to departmental objectives rather than project goals.
- Micro-level and Macro-level plans were prepared by the team.
- Conference calls were used for communicating with global clients.
- Project Leaders identified, documented and reevaluated project risks.
- Some quality issues were also reported.
- Projects reviews were regularly conducted through meetings.
- No cultural training was conducted.
- APQP meetings were conducted for requirement gathering.

Findings from Case Study 2 mentioned above.

13.2 Case Study 3: Project Implementation Framework and Leadership (Toyota)

13.2.1 Roadmap for Project Implementation Process in Toyota

Table 13.3 illustrates the project management framework applied in Toyota for successful implementation of Lean Projects.

Initial Preparation	Preparation Workshop	Lean Organisation	Lean Tools & Technology	Lean Enterprise
Senior Management Support	Identify Key Workstreams	Develop Chief Engineer System	Assess Current Technology Support	Identify Core Supply groups
Appoint of Project Steering Team, and Project Leader	Appoint Workstream Leaders- Team	Define Functional Specialities & Matrix Structure	Define technology needs	Develop Supplier Hierarchy
Identify Outside Sensei	Work Stream - Current - Future (LPDS principles) -Action Plan -Implement (trials and pilots) -Follow-up	Identify Core Engineering Competencies	Customise technology to support Lean processes	Pilot Early Supplier Involvement
Awareness Training	Evaluate & Modify Measurement Systems	Implement Mentoring & Training System	Develop Digital prototype & process design	Expand Supplier Involvement –Resident Engineer -VE VA -Supplier Development

Set up Lean Project Management Obeya	Employ Supportive Lean Tools; A3s, Checklists, etc.	Develop & Implement New Hire Selection Process	Support Lean Support Tool –A3, QualityMatrix standards	Develop Flexible Work Force
		Deploy Policy Deployment System	Institute PD Obeya System	

**Table 13.3: Roadmap for Implementation Process.
Adapted from Morgan & Liker (2006)**

- Initial Preparation: In this phase, Project Leader do some preparatory in consultation with the main executive and manager. Project Leader makes people aware of the project and set up "Obeya" for bringing the change. In this phase, support is required rather than any commitment from Top management. General awareness training shall also be required in this phase. In this phase, Stage needs to build rather than designing any new process.

- Pilot Lean Process: Project Leader initiates parallel communication with the customer. Project Leader identifies key work streams, maps current, and future states, and then proceeds for project implementation. Project Leader defines project metrics for measuring cost, quality, and lead-time of PD projects. Instead of involving everybody in this phase, the leader should concentrate on the pilot project to attain experience and learn the power of lean and develop the cultural change for building momentum. Project teams will experience the same while using and implementing the system.

- Lean organization: After convincing the senior management about the applicability and benefits of lean, the leader puts effort for changing the organization. However, the leader should avoid committing a big mistake of believing that they have mastered lean by only concentrating on Value Stream Mapping or on improvement projects. Project Leader needs to build a broader cultural system that supports lean. Organizations should start with a pilot project and select a leader whose characteristics match with the qualities mentioned in Point 4.

- Lean Tools and Technology: Project Leader concentrates on tools and technologies that require little or no capital investment. Project Leader performs effective reviewing and, regularly engages in digital prototyping for bringing continuous improvements. Project Leader can use the learning to create checklists.
- Lean Enterprise: After attaining stability and mastery in the development process, Project Leaders brings in supplier and customer to create a true lean. Initially, Project Leader should do piloting before creating any enterprise-wide policy. Stable processes will be however required to integrate suppliers and customers for their participation. The flexible pool of resources will also be necessary to be developed.

We can say that Project Leader can accomplish this process through learning, doing and reflecting. Project Leader should employ PDCA at all levels, and complete some preliminary work to bring leaders and resources on the panel. Project Leader should improve and streamline processes by using VSM as a guiding tool and develop people, tools, and technology through the implementation of initial pilot projects. Thereafter, Project Leader can bring broader organizational and technological changes.

The findings or the best practices in the successful implementation of Lean projects in Toyota are listed.

13.2.2 Findings of Case Study 3: Project Leadership in Toyota

Finding from successful implementation of lean projects in Toyota

- Top management should support the project.
- Form Project Steering Committee.
- Select Project Leader (Chief Engineer) matching with project characteristic.
- Identify Organisation's Core Competencies.
- Define team selection process.
- Chief Engineer should encourage team members to learn, act and reflect. Mentor them and develop them.
- Appoint an external person as Sensei or Tutor (Educator or Guide).
- Provide awareness training to the team members and staff.

- Arrange Obeya or Large Rooms for meeting and reviewing project process.
- Employ Value Stream mapping to identify Key work streams to improve and streamline them.
- Regularly communicate with Customers and Stakeholders.
- Prepare detailed project for future actions and project implementation.
- Define Project Matrix of Cost, Quality and Lead Time.
- Create a pilot project and allow the employee to learn through experience.
- Convey message about the benefits of the Lean Project to everyone.
- Concentrate on tools and technologies that require little investment.
- Initiate effective reviewing of project process, progress, and performances.
- Employ PDCA cycle in every phase of the project.
- Encourage participation of team members and Stakeholders.
- Develop flexible project team.
- Create checklists from learning's obtained from the project.

13.3 Case Study 4: Necessity of Project Framework - NASA.

Research by (Bless, 1991) revealed that three areas i.e. over-dependence on the Space Shuttle, poor management, and the propensity of the big project caused the NASA program is to be more costly and less efficient. The Space shuttle accident has resulted in a trend of launch delays, redesigns of spacecraft and infrequent missions. This further led to a culture of risk avoidance, unrealistic budget, political forces, big versus small missions. NASA in its history of project management has created several projects; however, there is no framework to distinguish between different projects (Sauser, Shenhar,& Hoffman, 2005).

Shenhar (2001a) developed a topology based on a rudimentary base in contingency theory for managing project known as Strategic Project Leadership (SPL). SPL framework was developed for Project Leaders for planning and execution phases of the project (Shenhar, 2001b), and to differentiate between different models as he theorized that no two projects are same and that each project should be managed differently (Shenhar, 2001a), (Shenhar, 2000).

As per Shenhar & Dvir (2004), Shenhar (1998) each project has contingencies based on four dimensions of novelty, complexity, technology and space, the NCTP (Novelty, Complexity, Technology and Pace) model. NASA's different projects were differentiated by the dimensions of the NCTP design i.e. Novelty, Complexity, Technology and Pace of the project.

Sauser, Shenhar, & Hoffman (2005) evaluated the four different programs of NASA according to the four dimensions of NTCP Model. The study concluded that NASA must have a unique framework for project and program management; however, exact principles are not defined. However, a single framework can explain the Project Leader about the reasons and various constraints leading to project failure. Moreover, the framework would also advise the Project Leader about what project would not have attained by applying certain practiced or working under certain constraints. However, success is not guaranteed by an efficient framework.

Aerospace projects as executed by NASA require proper management of risks, procedures, and resources, and the projects must evidently evaluate the intricacies and doubts of the task. Through NTCP model, the projects and programs in NASA were properly defined and, therefore, provided a basic framework for analyzing, managing and planning Aerospace projects. Further to this, the Project Leader will get an indication whether the project will be successful within certain constraints. Finally, the NTCP model could be essential for the success of NASA's projects (Sauser, Shenhar, & Hoffman, 2005). Shenhar's (2001) unique framework can be applied for classification and management of different projects.

13.3.1 Findings of Case Study 4: Necessity of Project Framework - NASA.

The findings from the NASA Case Study are listed in Table 13.4.

Findings from NASA Case Study
Organizations must have a unique Project Management Framework.
Differentiate and classify projects based on the dimensions, Novelty, Complexity, Technology, and Pace (NCTP) Model.
Manage risks, procedures, and policies.
Properly define projects and programs.

Plan realistic budgets.
Avoid Risk Avoidance attitude.

Table 13.4. Findings from NASA Case Study.

13.4 Case study 5: LSS Project Implementation in an Aerospace Organisation

13.4.1 History

Formed in 1963 and headquartered in West Michigan, USA, Johnson Technology Inc. (JT) is an aerospace company, which G.E. owned in 1997. JT has 400 hourly and 100 salaried employees. The company is engaged in manufacturing of aircraft engines, heat exchangers, water separators, oxygen equipment, environmental controllers, cooling turbines and fans and aircraft emergency, and power systems. In the early 1990s, Company decided to attain a competitive advantage in the market, and therefore, decided to implement Lean Six Sigma to reduce costs and to increase cash flow. Project Leader formed a new project team to examine practices, benchmark and gather data from existing companies in the global marketplace who have implemented Lean. Project Leader analyzed the gathered data and created the plan to implement Lean. After the company was purchased by G.E., project team received training for Six Sigma (Akbulut-Bailey, Motwani, & Smedley, 2012).

13.4.2 Strategic Initiatives

Top management in JT initiated LSS project in JIT to gain competitive advantage. The project team was, therefore, dedicated and committed to the implementation of LSS. Required resources were provided. The project team for implementation of LSS took a systematic approach, as they believed that LSS would lead to greater advantages (Akbulut-Bailey, Motwani, & Smedley, 2012).

13.4.3 Learning Capacity

Project Leaders created a learning environment by reacting to process change and by sharing the experiences they have learned from other companies.

The approach was to study other companies' culture and the methodology they applied for implementing Lean, and then apply that same method for implementing Lean in their own organization. Vigorous training programs were run for training the employees. Self-training and improvement were also encouraged in building innovative and collaborative teams. Training records were set up for team members, and Project Leaders encouraged team members to review for ensuring if the information was correct and updated. Project Leaders implemented open door suggestion policy and encouraged inputs for improvement from the team members. Suggestions from the customer and customer satisfaction were given top priority (Akbulut-Bailey, Motwani, & Smedley, 2012).

13.4.4 Cultural Readiness

As the senior management was aware of the cultural and structural changes required in LSS improvement project, they incorporated the necessary tools for preparing the organization for change. Several sub-project teams were created for the successful implementation of LSS. The project teams utilized the information they obtained during their preliminary study and created a plan for implementation including input from the project team member as well as the learning programs. A system was planned through which project team members were able to monitor the work and information. Team members were encouraged to participate during the decision-making process. Project Leaders facilitated team members with various tools, which the team members applied and provided inputs to the top management in improving them. As team members realized that their suggestions and ideas were given importance, they further came up with further innovative ideas. This led to increased cooperation and easier change management. After collecting data and associate on board, the company implemented lean, monitored problem and fixed them. Thereafter, Project Leaders provided training to the associates. Later the associates were moved to different lines and departments for knowledge sharing (Akbulut-Bailey, Motwani, & Smedley, 2012).

13.4.5 Network relationships

JT maintained good relationships with suppliers and worked very closely with them. Project Leaders informed suppliers about their needs during the transformation process. Encouragement was given to suppliers interested in

Lean, and necessary help was provided. Project team visited the supplier to assist them in their implementation (Akbulut-Bailey, Motwani, & Smedley, 2012).

13.4.6 Change management practice

Top management periodically met the project team and talked to them. Project team members were encouraged to ask questions and voice their concerns. Through this, Project Leaders built trust between management and associates (Akbulut-Bailey, Motwani, & Smedley, 2012).

13.4.7 Process management practice

Formal techniques and process metrics were designed by the company for process improvement. Tools such as Kanban, One-piece flow, Standard Work, Jidoka were implemented. Six Sigma Project Leaders employed DMAIC methodologies. It is important that the Top management and the project leader provide PM training the team members, and encourage them to use those tools. As the work becomes easier, stress reduces. Team members go home feeling good, and motivation level of team members constantly increases leading to the success of improvement projects. JT through LSS project reduced waste, reduced production cost, decreased manufacturing cycle times, reduced man-hours per part, reduced inventory while increasing customer service levels and higher quality, higher profits, increase efficiency and throughput, increase flexibility in reacting to requirements and customer needs, and more strategic focus (Akbulut-Bailey, Motwani, & Smedley, 2012).

13.4.8 Learning

Learning from the Implementation of Lean Six Sigma in Aerospace Organization
Involve employees in implementation.
Implement LSS. Have patience.
Understand customer requirements and maximize value added activities.
Top Management and Project Leader should pull the entire company together with one vision.
Use Visual controls as a tool for communication and be utilized throughout the company.

Encourage LSS thinking in everything employees do. Invent new ways for eliminating waste, be creative and make a quality priority.
Implement 5s and employees should take care of safety while working.
Train personnel properly on Lean thinking. Provide SS Qualification. Apart from that, send employees to other companies and seminars to improve their knowledge and become LSS experts.
Communicate employees to apply best practices and should be part of their responsibility.
Top Management and Project Leader should adhere to organization principles, and to continuous improvement.

Table 13.4: Learning from LSS Implementation. Source: Adapted from (Akbulut-Bailey, Motwani, & Smedley, 2012)

Table 13.4 describes the learning from LSS implementation. After implementing LSS, sales in JT increased from 30 million dollars per year to 205 million dollars. Sales were 92-95 million dollars. However, the employee count remained 500 since 1999.

13.4.9 Findings of Case Study

The findings from successful implementation of LSS are listed in Table 13.5.

Finding from successful Implementation of Lean Six Sigma project in an Aerospace Organization
Form new project team.
Perform competitor benchmarking to examine practices, and gather data about companies who have implemented Lean Six Sigma in the past.
Create proper project plan.
Concentrate on visual communication.
Build cultural awareness in Project Leadership, team members, and Top management.
Get support from Top management.
Follow a structured well-defined stage-by-stage approach.
Create learning environment.

Provide Project Management training.
Encourage Self-training and improvement for building collaborative and innovative teams.
Encourage suggestions, inputs and feedbacks from employees for improvement.
Encourage new ideas for increasing cooperation.
Incorporate necessary tools for change.
Promote Knowledge sharing.
Create subproject team for each task.
Encourage team members for applying best practices.

**Table 13.5: Findings from Successful Lean Sigma
Project Implementation in Toyota.**

13.5 Case Study 6: Project Leadership Styles in Indian IT Company

As research conducted by Prifling (2010) in a major Indian CMMI-certified IT service provider to comprehend how specific leadership styles of IT Project Leaders can bring success to IT development projects, it was found that leadership styles such as "Collaborative Leadership" and "Directive Leadership" characteristic were found in the Indian IT Project leaders. Project team members, Project Leaders, and Senior Management people were interviewed, and data was analyzed by techniques proposed by grounded theory method (Glaser, 1978), (Glaser, 1998).

13.5.1 Learning

"Collaborative Leadership" and "Directive Leadership" characteristic were found in the Indian IT Project leaders. The research concluded that the style followed by the Project Leader and assistant Project Leaders in leading the subordinates had a substantial impact on project success and timely completion of IT offshore projects.

13.5.1.1 Collaborative Leadership in an Indian IT company

Project Leaders were approachable to the subordinates and always available to solve their problems. Moreover, Project Leaders were also eager to support and contribute to getting them involved in problem-solving. Furthermore, Project Leaders have required expertise in IT field as they started their career from the bottom level i.e. programmer, which enables the Project Leader to develop the team members to become project leaders. Besides this, through collaborative leadership, the Project Leader was able to recognize interdependencies among sub-project and directly engage in project activities at the team level. In addition to this, Project Leader being part of the team was aware of the possible conflicts.

Collaborative leadership increased trust between the team members, which further increased effectiveness since Project Leader could concentrate more on task-related activities rather than interpersonal issues. Trustworthy communication between team members, Project Leaders, and senior management enabled effective collaboration. Project team members in lower hierarchy also appreciated their Project Leader leadership style for the creation of a faithful working environment, trusted, and believed that Project Leader could make the project successful. Through this way, the project leader was able to concentrate on projects related activities, and effectively monitor the project for delivering successful projects rather than wasting time on resolving non-critical and trivial issues (Prifling, 2010).

13.5.1.2 Directive Leadership in an Indian IT company

High power, as well as hierarchical distance, is seen between senior and subordinates in Indian culture. Project Leader gave directions to the subordinates and defined the project milestones, timelines, and deliverables himself/herself that were further communicated to the subordinates without any reflection or having a dialogue with them. The leadership behavior is based on trust and power as an instrument of efficiency for project success.

Respect for hierarchical differences empowers a leader to demand the execution of certain project activities by the project team members since the position of leader just asks for compliance. With the help of this leadership style, Project Leader acts as an arbitrator who further acts as a link to communicate customer issues to project team members. Because of their power and respect, Project Leaders are able to resolve problems through problem-solving initiatives very quickly. Moreover, due to obedience to hierarchy, the Project Leaders are able to get the execution of a task with clear and straightforward objectives. However, the Project Leader practicing this style should be expert in their respective field to earn respect and reputation from the project team members since the expertise of the Project Leader will instill confidence in project team members that their problems can be resolved easily. Setting clear objectives, clear expectation towards project team members, clear directions for setting the roadmap for completion of project tasks, rigorous tracking and control are essential elements of Directive leadership (Prifling, 2010).

13.5.1.3 Summary

Figure 13.1 illustrates the Leadership Model for IT Projects in India

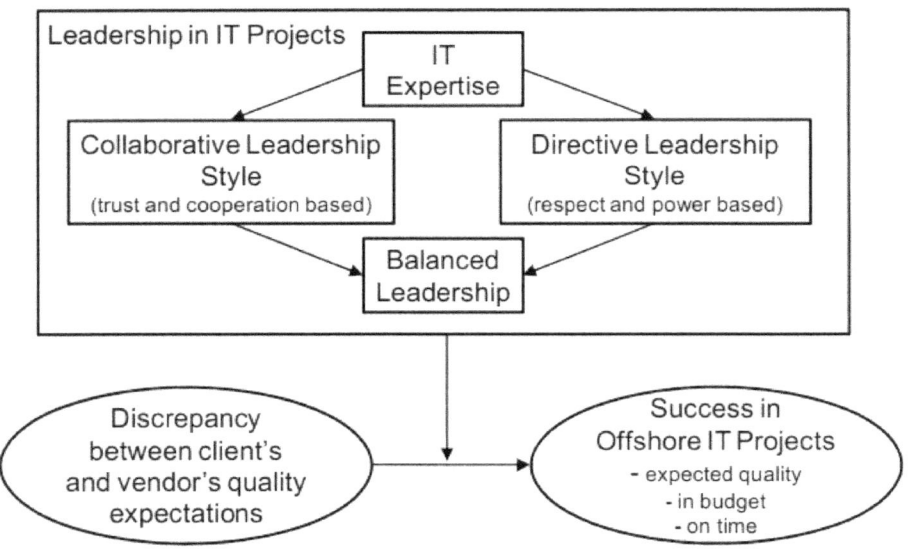

A model of leadership in IT projects

Figure 13.1: Leadership Model for IT Projects in India. Source: Adapted from Prifling (2010)

Collaborative leadership style and Directive Leadership Style are conflicting styles since collaborative leadership propose breaching of hierarchical barriers between Project Leaders and team members and promoting cooperation and trust, whereas directive leadership proposes maintaining the distance between Project Leaders and team members and getting things done through respect and power. Nevertheless, the IT Managers in India have effectively combined the both by changing flexibility in certain situations and by employing right leadership style in proper context. Moreover, it suggests that IT managers should be expert in IT field, adapt continuously and be capable in coalescing trust-based processes with power-based procedures (Prifling, 2010).

13.5.2 Findings of Case Study 6: Project Leadership Style in India.

Case study findings suggest that Indian managers in IT projects should adopt collaborative and directive leadership style for project success. Table 13.5 lists the benefits of cooperative and directive leadership styles. Due to the similarity in culture, project leaders in Aerospace organizations can apply the same leadership practices for successful project management.

Benefits of Collaborative and Directive Leadership Style in India
Better Project Monitoring.
Increased level of trusts between project team members.
Better collaborations between team members.
Fast resolution of problems through problem resolving attitudes.
Settings of clear objectives with clear expectations towards project team members.
Clear directions for completion of project tasks and rigorous tracking and control.

Table 13.5: Benefits of Collaborative and Directive Leadership in India. Source: Adapted from Prifling (2010).

13.6 Case study 7: Successful Implementation of ERP in an Aerospace Organisation

This case describes the successful implementation of SAP R/3 ERP (Enterprise Resource Planning Software) in Pratt & Whitney, Canada (P&WC), a Canadian aerospace organization involved in the manufacturing of aircraft engines, turboprop, and turboshaft. To increase response to the competitive global aerospace marketplace, and to increase productivity and efficiency,

P&WC decided to implement ERP software. Out of BaaN ERP, Oracle ERP, P&WC considered SAP R/3 as it is customer-focused, standardized and *"process-based structure with integrated cross functionality"* (Tchokogue, Bareil, &Duguay, 2005).

Project Information:

Start date: June 1996
End Date: Jan 1999

Project scope listed below:-

- Improve customer response.
- Reduce WIP.
- Increase Inventory Turnover.
- Increase visibility of stocks and operating cost.

13.6.1 Project Implementation Strategy

Project teams were formed which were well structured and consisted of Change Champion, Training teams, and Power Users. Project Leader considered the creation of the Project team, Project Planning, Infrastructure development, training, quality steadiness in quality, and current project management as critical activities (Tchokogue, Bareil, & Duguay, 2005). Phases of Project Implementation listed in Table 13.6

Phases of Project Implementation
Scoping and Planning.
Alignment of Vision with business processes.
Process redesign.
Configuration.
Test and Deliver.

Table 13.6: Phases of Project Implementation

Project Implementation phases are mentioned below-

- Scoping and Planning.
- Alignment of vision with business processes.
- Process Redesign.
- Configuration.
- Test and Deliver.

Scoping and Planning phase was divided into various stages. Major activities performed in the planning stages as researched by Kumar, Maheshwari, & Kumar (2003) are mentioned below-

- Planning: - System Planning, Benefit analysis, Project scoping.
- Configuration: - Architecture, Configuration, Design, Building.
- Testing: - User Training, Product testing.
- Implementation: - Ho Live, Training, and Documentation.

Project Leader followed SAP Methodology (Tchokogue, Bareil, & Duguay, (2005) mentioned below-

- Project Management.
- Technology Architecture.
- Process and Systems Integrity.
- Change Management.
- Knowledge Transfer.

13.6.2 Project Results obtained from SAP Implementation

- The increase in productivity of 11%.
- 30% return on investment.
- Realized 1 million dollars of savings in the year 2000.
- Increased visibility on Inventory cost.
- The increase in business agility.
- Better report generation for managing KPI's.

The project was implemented successfully.

13.6.3 Findings of Case Study 7: Project implementation in Pratt and Whitney

Table 13.7 contains the conclusions of the Case Study involving the successful implementation of SAP R/3 in a Canadian Aerospace and Aeronautics company Pratt and Whitney (Canada).

Findings from Project Implementation of SAP R/3 in Pratt & Whitney
Project Leader applied the complete and proven methodology to project implementation.
Project Leader built a Strong project team.
Project Leader considered Project Planning as a critical process.
Project Leadership showed commitment to ensure employee ownership of the project.
Good change management program.
Project Leadership and Project team had rigor, discipline, and expertise.
Project Leader measured project results.
Project Leader implemented Project with discipline.
Project Leader adopted Risk reduction strategy.
Project Leader applied coordinated deployment of resources.
Project Implementation was consistent with the global vision of the company.
Project Leader appointed Change Agents for bringing change.
Project Leader conducted change sessions and follow-ups sessions for discussion for foreseeable.
Project Leader prepared communication and feedback plans.
Project Leader prepared local actions plans.
Project Leader reviewed business process.
Project Leader created follow-up teams.
Project Leader conducted team feedback forums.
Project Leadership and Top Management encouraged change and identified and disseminated expected employee behaviors and removed obstacles.
Project Leader applied change management techniques.
Project Leader performed extremely rigorous and detailed planning.

| Project Leader developed and deployed change strategy. |
| SAP R/3 implementation optimized performance in large-scale projects. |
| Project Leader focused on knowledge transfer. |

**Table 13:7 Findings from Successful Project involving
Implementation of SAP R/3 in Pratt & Whitney. Source:
Adapted from Tchokogue, Bareil, & Duguay (2005)**

CHAPTER 14

14. Analysis of Survey Results

This chapter will analyze the results of the survey undertaken in an Aerospace organization for understanding and assessing the effectiveness of project leadership in the organization.

14.1 Questionnaire 1 Project Leadership Assessment: Organisation.

14.1.1 Trust and Interdependence

Statements	No of respondents
The success of the organization and success of the project team are interconnected.	14
Trust and interdependence between all the stakeholders regarded as a critical success factor.	12
There is a direct involvement of senior management in the management of the project teams, which is undesirable.	13

Table 14.1: Trust and Interdependence

Table 14.1 illustrates that most of the project leadership and the project team in the organization recognize that project success will bring success for the organization by maintaining trust and mutuality with the stakeholders.

However, project team does not prefer senior managements getting directly involved in the management of the project team.

14.1.2 Decision making and Problem solving

Statements	No of Respondents
Complex and lengthy administrative procedures lead to slow authorization process.	14
Project leaders are driven by the vision of the company for executing daily actions and taking decisions	12
Project leaders take decisions after long and careful consideration.	13
Project leader follows decentralized approach for taking decisions	10
Project leaders are encouraged for developing innovative solutions to business and project problems	10

Table 14.2: Decision Making and Problem Solving

Table 14.2 illustrates that Project leadership and the project team in the organization recognize that administrative procedures should be simple to expedite the project work. Project Leadership keeps the vision of the organization in his mind and thoroughly considers the aspects before taking any decision. Moreover, the organization follows decentralized approach.

Decentralized approach as per Malone (2004) has following benefits-

1. Empowers the team members and project leader to make their decisions without waiting for top management approval.
2. Increases flexibility.
3. Allows team members to collaborate for problem-solving.
4. Improves information flows across the organization.
5. Reduced communication costs.

This approach will also be suitable for the global project in case the communication costs such as email, teleconferencing is very high. In case the communication costs are moderate, an organization can follow centralized approach. Further, in case the communication costs are low, an organization can follow "*connected decentralized*" approach wherein the project leader can use available information, information generated through project meetings, and his/her knowledge to take crucial decisions. This emboldens innovation and creativity and enables Project leader to explore new opportunities (Malone T., 1997). Besides, the organization encourages innovation for problem-solving.

14.1.3 Risk

"Risk" attribute got the minimum score out of all attributes.

Statements	No of Respondents
Problems and risks are an integral part of the projects.	10
Stakeholders are ready to take calculated risk.	10
Senior management encourages calculated risk-taking.	9
Project Leader focuses on risk aversion at all costs.	6

Table 14.3: Risk

Table 14.3 illustrates that project leadership and teams recognize the importance of risk in projects in the organization, encourage team members for calculated risk taking and prepare for the same. These reflect of effective project leadership (Pahal, 1999), however, less than 50% respondent approve of risk aversion which indicates that project direction and team have different attitude towards risk, and the project leadership and project team seem to be more averse about evading loss from project failure than rather than attainment of profit through project success (Hulett, 2006). Project leaders in the organization are seen to more risk averse as they have a constricted view for measuring project success (Krane, Olsson, & Rolstadås, 2012).

It is important that Project Leader maintain a balanced thought towards risk taking and risk aversion.

14.1.4 Communication

"*Communication*" attribute scored less than 3.0 reflects that communication within the organization is not favorable for effective project leadership.

Statements	No of Respondents
The occurrence of project meetings and communication requests surges at the time of project crisis.	13
Project Leaders communicate and explain the team members about the changes in company strategy and project requirements.	10
Project Leader distinctly defines and communicates Project management process.	8
Project Leaders often resolves concerns linked to senior management with open communication.	6

Table 14.4: Communication

Table 14.4 illustrates that the organization follows a strategy of arranging meetings during project crisis through which Project Leader communicates changes in project requirements or overall business strategies. Moreover, definition and communication of project management process in the organization reflect effective project management (Greenberga, et.al, 2011) since project review and crisis meetings enhances attention of the team members towards project crisis (Mahaney & Lederer, 2010). Conversely, lack of open communication hampers trust-building (Jarvenpaa & Keating, 2012) which reveals ineffective leadership (Gillespie & Dietz, 2009).

14.1.5 Teamwork and Interpersonal

"Teamwork and Interpersonal" attribute score maximum score out of all the attributes 3.67.

Statements	No of Respondents
All respondents considered teamwork critical for project success.	14
The relationship between the project team and management is good.	12

Team conflicts have a negative impact on the successful performance of the team.	9
The organization recognizes interpersonal aspects of project leadership.	9
Project team's good performance is recognized and rewarded.	8
Project team celebrates achievements in the projects and shares with other.	7

Table 14.5: Teamwork and Interpersonal

Table 14.5 illustrates that in the organization, project leader and the team considered teamwork critical for success, and the project team maintains a good relationship with management. However, project leadership fails to recognize and reward good performance of the team members, and share their achievement, which reflects ineffective project leadership.

Recognizing team conflict having an adverse impact on team performance is debatable. Team conflict can distract the team members from his/her task, generate tension and therefore affect performance (Wall & Callister, 1995), (Brown, 1983), (Saavedra, Earley, & Van Dyne, 1993). Conversely, low-level conflicts can propel team members to learn, confront and view problems through different perceptions, and thus develop creativity (Levine, Resnick, & Higgins, 1993) and additionally better decision-making (Simons & Peterson, 2000). On the other hand, lack of conflicts tends team members to remain unaware of the inefficiencies (De Dreu & Weingart, 2003,) Therefore; Project Leader needs to understand whether the conflict is task oriented or relationship oriented.

14.1.6 Planning

Statements	No of Respondents
Senior Management shapes the environment and culture, which cultivates the development and growth of the project leaders and the team.	14
Application of formal methodology and tools are vital for successful implementation of the project.	14
Change is essential for bringing organization success.	13

Quality is a vital factor in bringing success to the project.	13
Creativity and innovation are encouraged through the organizational environment.	12
Senior Management concentrates on project results.	12
Project Leader monitors the progress of the project in a systematic and careful manner.	12
Project teams execute the project plan with the help of guidance provided by organizational policies and practices.	12
Project Leader tracks of project deliverables through Project management process.	11
Senior management acts as a project sponsor who encourages and support the project team for delivering high performance	11
Project Leader gives more significance to organizational goals rather than to team or individual goals.	11

Table 14.6: Planning

Table 14.6 illustrates that project leader and project team in the organization consider project tools and methodology critical for project success, along with change and quality. Other factors also reflect that project leadership is effective in those areas.

14.2 Questionnaire 2 Project Leadership Assessment: Individual

The overall average score was 3.61 which reflect that some aspects in the project team members are linked with effective leadership; however, there is room for growth and improvement.

14.2.1 Team Building and Interpersonal skills

Statements	No of Respondents
I can build multifunctional teams.	14
I have the ability to plan and elicit commitments.	14

Project work is conducted by me in an honest and ethical manner	12
I receive the appreciation of all peoples and groups.	12
Project Leader is aware that team motivation increases by rewarding and recognizing team members for good performance.	13
It can be a good thing to have conflict within a project team.	8
Conflicts posts a negative influence on the success of the project	7

Table 14.7 Team Building and Interpersonal skills

Table 14.7 reflects the individual responses of the project leader and team members on team building and interpersonal skills in the organization. 50% respondents deliberate that conflicts have a negative effect on project success, which backs previous similar finding. Project leadership, however, reflect on being strong in areas such team building, authenticity, integrity. In the organization, project leaders motivate the team members through reward and recognizing.

14.2.2 Planning and Risk

"Planning and Risk" attribute got the minimum score out of all the attributes which reflect that certain attributes in project team members are linked with effective leadership. However, there is room for growth and improvement.

Statements	No of Respondents
I can clearly visualize project process.	12
Project leader monitors risk on continuous basis.	10
The project has well-defined work breakdown structure, certain start and end dates, and a financial budget.	10
Selection of the team members based on skills and knowledge is determined by Work Breakdown structure	10

I am able to secure the resources required for completing the project successfully.	9
Project Leader avoids project risks at all cost.	7

Table 14.7: Planning and Risk

Table 14.7 reflects the individual responses of the project leader and team members on planning and risk in the organization. In the organization, project leader manages and monitors risk appropriately. Project leadership shows effectiveness in project planning through a well-defined work breakdown structure, budget and selection criteria.

14.2.3 Communication

Statements	No of Respondents
I develop the vision for the project and enthusiastically communicate to the team.	14
Project Leaders clearly defines expectations from the project.	13
I engage in active listening to analyze all the point of views.	13
I have the ability to look forward, foresee the big picture, and effectively communicate that to stakeholders and team members.	12
Project Leaders maintains daily communication with the project team members.	11
Every project meeting has an agenda; documents minutes and identifies actions, responsibilities, and timeframes.	10
Project Leaders distributes information to all stakeholders with enthusiasm, set expectations, and minimize concerns.	10
Short lines and informal communication are used.	7

Table 14.8 Communication

Table 14.8 reflects the individual responses of the project leader and team members on communication in the organization. Project Leader need to bring improvements in managing meetings and distributing information among team members.

14.2.4 Decision-making and Problem-solving

Statements	No of Respondents
Initiative in problem solving is encouraged by team members.	14
Attaining results is the primary focus of the project.	14
Resolution of individual issues is less important for project success.	6
Success in the project is seen a hindrance by me mainly due to uncertainty and problems.	10
Achievement of project results is possible through the leadership of Project Leader.	13
Project Leader sees problems, issues, and uncertainty as a challenge, which they can overcome.	13
Project Leader assesses the project on the routine basis.	13
The responsibility of meeting the schedule deadlines lies with the Project Leader.	11
Open discussions are held with the senior management regarding project failures, problems, and mistakes.	9
Project Leader evaluates project performance relative to meeting the project goals.	11
I have the ability and skill to filter the information relevant to me required for decision-making.	13
To ensure that project stays on track, Project Leader manages project tasks one at a time.	9
I hold a good professional repute and a record of accomplishment of project success.	14
I can deal effectively with department heads, functional managers, staff, and workers across functional lines, often with little or no formal authority.	13
I contribute in the amalgamation of individuals' demands, their requirements, and their limitations into decisions that benefit the overall project.	13

Table 14.9 Decision Making

Table 14.9 reflects the individual responses of the project leader and team members on decision-making in the organization. There is a need for the organization to maintain open communication with the team members.

14.2.5 Trust and Interdependence

Statements	No of Respondents
Project team members can count on me to assist them to be successful.	14
I maintain a good working relationship with customer and stakeholders.	14
A good relationship is maintained by me with senior management, stakeholders through which mutual trust and respect are developed.	13
Project Leader clearly defines the expectations of the stakeholders at the outset of the project.	10
I can recognize interdependence between the stakeholders.	10
Open communication is used for dealing with problem and uncertainty.	10

Table 14.10: Trust and Interdependence

Table 14.10 reflects the individual responses of the project leader and team members on Trust and Interdependence in the organization.

14.2.6 Cultural and Environment

Statements	No of Respondents
Project Leader should follow procedures and corporate policies.	13
I perceive myself as an enabler for bringing change.	13
Application of project methodology, tools, and techniques is vital for project success.	13
Delivery of the project according to plan is done through the application of organization policies and practices.	13

I am adaptable to diverse circumstances and changing environment.	13
I keep promises and commitments.	12
I have control of the resources necessary for completing the project successfully.	7
Project Leader manages politics and power as a part of the project.	7

Table 14.11: Cultural and Environment

Table 14.11 reflects the personal responses of the Project Leader and team members on Cultural and Environment in the organization.

14.3 Questionnaire 3 Project Leadership Assessment: Team

The overall average score was 3.30 which reflect that some aspects of the project team are linked with effective leadership; however, there is room for growth and improvement.

14.3.1 Planning

Statements	No of Respondents
There is active participation of the project team in project planning.	12
The team leader carefully selects team members.	12
The project team sets clearly defined goals, detailed plans, and attainable milestones.	11
Project Leader does not break the project tasks into work packages, and clearly, communicate the same to the project team members.	8

Table 14.12: Planning

Table 14.12 reflects the group responses on planning in the organization. Project Leader need to give attention in breaking the work packages in small tasks using Work Breakdown structure and communicating the same with the project team members.

14.3.2 Teamwork and Interpersonal Skills

Statements	No of Respondents
During the time of adversity, team members pull together to find solutions for the problem.	12
Project Leader must eliminate Team conflicts, which can be catastrophic.	12
Project team members work as a cohesive group with a full commitment to the project.	12
Team Leader is well concerned about the well-being and the development of the team members.	12
Organization treats project team members with dignity and respect.	11
Senior management provides resources and support to the team.	11
The team is imparted technical as well as interpersonal training.	11
Project Leader practices group activities and open communication to build team spirit and high morale among the team members.	11
Project team members help each other and work towards in best interests of each other.	10
Organization recognizes conflicts within the team as a problem and deals in a timely manner.	10
Project Leader resolves mistakes and errors in the positive and solution oriented way.	10
Accomplishments of the team members are celebrated.	9
The contributions of the team members are recognized and rewarded.	9
Project team does not maintain good repo with the functional department and suppliers.	7

Project teams do not respond changes in requirements and project environment properly.	7

Table 14.13. Teamwork and Interpersonal Skills

Table 14.13 reflects the group responses on teamwork in the organization. Leadership needs to celebrate team success, reward contributions for motivating team members. Project Leader need to increase team-building exercises to improve interactions between the project team and functional departments.

14.3.3 Communication

Statements	No of Respondents
The team leader maintains open and frequent communication with the team members.	13
Project team members understand the strategic importance of the project and their stake in the project's success.	13
Project Leader communicates all the details regarding the status of the project to the project team.	12
The team clearly understands and strictly follows policies applicable to the project.	12
The team members in order to minimize uncertainty and concern distribute information to all stakeholders.	12
Project Leader informs project team members about their responsibilities through kick-off meetings.	11
Project Leader clearly communicates the team members about the project vision and process.	11
Each project team member is clear about his/her assigned roles and responsibilities.	9

Table 14.14. Communication

Table 14.14 reflects the team responses on communication. Project Leader need to further clarify the roles and responsibilities of the team members.

14.4.3 Decision-making and Problem-Solving

Statements	No of Respondents
Project Leader encourages project team members to take the initiative in problem-solving.	12
Project Team members lack authority to make decisions.	12
Project Leader encourages participation of all members for prompt decision-making.	10

Table 14.15. Decision making and Problem-Solving

Table 14.15 reflects the group responses in the organization on decision making which is an ineffective state.

14.2.5 Trust and Interdependence

Statements	No of Respondents
Project Leader maintains a good relationship with the senior management.	14
The team members maintain an atmosphere of mutual respect and trust.	14
There is a cooperative and positive relationship between project team members.	12
Project team members share a strong sense of belonging to each other.	12
Project team members trust team Leader for his/her judgment and have their confidence on him/her.	11
Project team members trust project leader for guidance and support.	10
Senior management and the project team members share a high degree of trust upon each other	10
The team members view criticism courageously in a positive and open manner.	9

There is a lack of enthusiasm in the team members for the project.	9

Table 14.16 Trust and Interdependence

Table 14.16 reflects the group responses in the organization on trust and interdependence. Project leader needs to increase the enthusiasm of the team members through greater participation of the team members in project activities.

14.3.6 Team Performance

Statements	No of Respondents
Project team maintains high quality throughout the project lifecycle.	14
Team members maintain a high level of responsibility towards customer satisfaction.	14
Project Leader encourages project team members to find innovative ways for improving team performance.	12
Project Leader evaluates the team performance based on the project goals.	11
Each project team member takes responsibility for monitoring risk and informing the project leader when they detect risk triggers or events.	11
Application of the project methodology and tools is vital for project success.	11
Project Leader's style is adaptive to the different project phases and the needs of the team.	11
Project Leader delivers the tasks on time and on schedule by the team members with dedication and with quality.	10
Project team members routinely meet project budgets and schedules.	10
The project team members do not take personal responsibility for meeting schedules.	8

Project Leader punishes the team members for their failure in meeting the project objectives.	6

Table 14.17 Team Performance

Table 17.17 reflects the group responses in the organization on team performance. Project Leader needs to set KRA (Key results Areas) to measure team member's performance about the project task and need to be rated about the fulfillment of the project.

14.4 Summary

This chapter analyzed as well as discussed especially the Questionnaire 1 as it reflected the overall effectiveness of the project leadership in the organization.

CHAPTER 15

15. Final Summary

This chapter includes the interview results from the 12 interview respondents. This chapter also consists of Survey findings from an Aerospace Organization to explore the effectiveness of project leadership, and the case studies findings from two projects being executed in the same organization, as well as some other circumstances study's findings related to Project Leadership and Project Management in aerospace as well as other organizations.

15.1 Interview Results

Table 15.1 illustrates the Interview Results.

Critical Processes while Managing Projects	Communication.	Maintaining Interactions with customers.
	Project Initiation and Project Planning	
	Requirements Gathering	
	Risk Management	
	Standardisation of Project Management Processes	
		Two-way stream/ Parallel Communication.

		Frequent Focused Meetings with clear agenda and objective.
Best Practises in Project Management	Communication	Right communication at the right time.
		Latest communication technologies must be used.
		The need of Communication Model and Communication Plan.
	Conduct Stakeholder Analysis	
	Cultural awareness	Understand Cultural background of Team Members.
	Proper Risk Management	Perform Risk Analysis and Risk
		Mitigation Planning
		Need for a Risk Management and Assessment System.
	Develop a Change Request Process	
	Well defined Change Management Process	
		Use Balanced Score
	Regular Project Monitoring	Keep track of Scope, Time, Quality and Cost (STQC)
	Select skilled, experienced and trusted team members	
	Put a Governance Structure	
	Team (People) Management skills	

Qualities of a Project Leader	Perform Appropriate Team (Workplace) Planning	
	Able to take project decisions	
	Effective communicator	
	Cultural Awareness	
	Competency of Project Leader	Hybrid Project Manager
		Competency in Project Management skills
		Leader must have hands-on Skills (Participative)
	Excellent Leadership Skills and Qualities	
	Good Political sense	
	Right Attitude	
	Vision of the Objectives	
	Business Acumen	
	Good negotiator	
	Give constructive and authentic feedback	
	Listen and take feedback	
Team Building Practises	Awards and Appreciation	
	Knowledge Sharing Sessions/Training	
	Allocate Time in Schedule for team-building and knowledge sharing sessions	
	Social Gathering/ Socialising	
Innovative and Collaborative Teams	Promote brainstorming	
	Use collaborative tools	
	Allocate time and resources	

Motivate People	Engage with team member	
	Support team members	
Manage team conflicts	Deal with conflict directly	
	Identify cause	
	Counseling from Project Leader	
Evaluation of Team Performance	Performance measurement through KRA	
	Performance Management Systems	
Cross project learning	Document Lessons Learnt	
Bringing competitive advantage through Project Management	Understanding of the market	
Current Challenges in Project Management	Need for a common Project Management Methodology	
	Improper Project Change Management by Indian Project Managers	
	Incompetency in Project Management skills	
Project Management Methodologies applied in IT and Aerospace Projects	PMI PMBoK(Standardized Project Management Process)	
	Customer Project Management Process	

Table 15.1: Interview Results

15.1. Project Management Methodologies applied in IT and Aerospace Projects

15.1.1 PMI (Standardized Project Management Process):

Project Leaders primarily use PMBoK (PMI) as project management methodology to manage projects in their organization.

> *We are based on PMI. (Respondent 3)*

> *So, I use my methodology. I would say that it is mainly PMBoK. I follow the general steps, the knowledge areas, the process groups and use what we need. In some projects, the standard method was defined, but these are like, we developed our set of processes which were based on PMBOK. There was a hybrid of both processes*

> *The overall guideline for project management is coming from PMI. I am PMP in it. In the US, larger companies and smaller companies have implemented PMI standards.*

15.1.2 Customized Project Management Process

They used customized project management process for managing projects in their organization.

> *We follow internal customized systems. We do not tend to follow PMBOK or Prince2. It is regulated. We have our development process and own customized systems.*

> *It is a mixture. The methodology we have in-house is a structured around PMBOK. However, due to the very nature of the software that we develop and the various markets we deploy that software into, its Business Intelligence systems, and its ERP systems. What we tend to find is that there is a sub-element in the methodology that is perhaps of more technical nature that is aligned itself to the type of products that we deploy. The backbone is PMBoK.*

*For the last few years, I have been working on PMBoK. They try
to follow it closely, but it is tailored to suit its environment.*

*IBM does have its project methodology which is aligned to PMP,
but they have their framework which is used for any customer
IBM caters to.*

Executed in an Aerospace Organisation, the project leadership in the
organization requires improvement for which the project leadership should
adopt collaborative and directive leadership style since the same leadership
styles were applied for project success in an Indian IT organization in India.
Moreover, belonging to the same country, people have common national culture
and a common management style. However, there might be some difference
in the organizational culture for which Project leadership in Aerospace
organization should mix both styles by switching between styles at certain
situations and employ right leadership style in proper context. Furthermore,
apart from literature, project leadership should also try to practise the traits
of transformational leadership along with the role of system integrator with
tractability in their management styles; integration of directing, coaching,
supporting and delegating leadership styles with combination of future and
present-oriented project leadership, visionary and democratic leadership with
high level of self-awareness, motivation, empathy and social skills, depending
upon the project phase and capability of project team member for achieving
maximum team performance.

Regarding the Survey results, project leadership need to improve inter-
departmental communication through open and two-way communications with
the team members to resolve their issues, and to build trust, and communicate
the vision of the organisation and explain the team members' role in the
same through focused meetings with clear agenda to enhance team focus on
project progress. In addition, managers in India are less communicative (Vogel,
2005), and therefore, focused meetings are vital which should be managed in
"Obeya". Moreover, Project leadership should create communication model
and clear communication plans for streamlining communication between
team members, stakeholders, and Top management for increasing their
engagements in project activities. By communicating right project information
at the right time, the project leader should authorize the project members
to take decisions by following "*Connected decentralized*" approach, which

will reduce communication costs and increase employee motivation. For maintaining a good relationship with the project team, project leadership needs to take care not to miss to reward and recognize any team member for their excellent performances as that might demotivate them. Project leader should directly deal with team conflicts rather than avoiding it, through proper conflict resolution strategy, and finding the cause leading to win-win for both parties in order to turn these task-oriented disputes between project teams into cooperative and productive conflicts, however project leadership should step in to reduce relationship conflicts between team members by arranging socialising events, orientation sessions or arranging knowledge sharing sessions for team building, and in order to bring sense of ownership, and develop closeness between team members, however, frequency of these events should depend on upon the length of the project, and therefore time should be allocated in the budget. Development of familiarity and closeness between team members will also increase the performance of the team members as Indian managers team members are culturally collectivist, and tend to perform in teams which means that their performances is low when they work by themselves, or when they work in teams where they don't identify with the team members, and don't feel being part of the team (Earley, 1993). Moreover, the project leader should encourage more teamwork, and support them. Nevertheless, power culture is found in India which hampers the process of building trust between cultures with low power culture since confidence of people in India is built through *"calculative, prediction and capability process"*(Doney, Cannon, & Mullen, 1998). Besides, Indian managers are inclined to sticking to specifications, rather being proactive in generating new ideas. Therefore project leader should facilitate brainstorming sessions involving team members and push them for new ideas for creating a collaborative and innovative teams. It is important that, nonetheless, Project Leader should step aside and listen to team members rather than pass judgments, and allow team members independently come out with new ideas without any hesitancy. In the case of virtual teams, collaborative tools such as Microsoft SharePoint, Skype emails, conference calls should be used. In the same time, Project Leader should allocate time in project schedule for these team-building activities.

Top management should encourage calculated risk taking. Also, more time need to be spent by project leader being more future-oriented rather present-oriented, and involve in planning and identifying potential hazards, regularly updating the risk register, and making mitigation and contingency plans, and executing those plans, which will increase the confidence of the project leadership, and will reduce risk aversion leading to project success and growing organization's profitability through project management. Project leadership should involve the project team and increase their participation.

Combining the results of Case Study 1 and Case Study 2 of the projects being executed in the Aerospace organization, the author as well these research findings suggest that organization must follow a unified joint project management framework that can be applied globally. Amalgamation of Agile project management and Lean Six Sigma project management along with PMBoK and Prince2 cultivates a project management framework through which agility could be brought in the project management with staged reviews. Through this, Project Leader can reduce non-valued added activities, variations in project management processes and reworks. Project Leader focuses on project planning and risk management so that unplanned activities are reduced allowing project leadership and team to spend valuable time in planning activities. Furthermore, project leadership could effectively plan and monitor the project through enhanced communication and by setting project KPIs. There is an urgent need for professional project management training for the team members to enable them to work efficiently and take project decisions. Project Leaders need to manage change requests effectively. However, Indians managers submit to orders, hierarchically adapted, and *"always saying yes"* (Heeks, Krishna, Nicholson, & Sahay, 2001), (Nicholson & Sahay, 2001), but in this case, project leader need to convenience the customer as well as the Project Leader for the impact of these changes on project cost, time and schedule through negotiation.

However, formalizing the project management process could be a challenge as culturally, Indian people being more people oriented than process oriented, therefore, require constant training, motivation, direction or some rewards to motivate and convince them to follow the process for executing project activities. Product Leader should conduct random system audits, and evaluate the performance of the team member by some system non-conformances.

The new improved Project Management Framework is illustrated in next page (A3 Sheet).

Pre-Initiation	Initiation	Project Planning and Control Phase 1	Project Planning and Control Phase 2	Execution	Monitoring and Control	Closing
Identify Organisational vision.	Identify Key Project Stakeholders for getting their input and support.	Define Project Scope and create WBS.	Orient New Team members.	Direct and Manage Project	Monitor and Control Project Work.	Close Project or Phase.
Determine the company culture and existing systems.	Conduct Assessment and technical, operational, financial feasibility studies including assessment of risk from previous projects, identification of new risks, and analysis of other implementation alternatives.	Develop High-Level Schedule (Define activities, estimate durations, and resources and allocate resources) .	Review Project Materials.	Perform Quality Assurance.	Perform Integrated Change Control.	Close Procurements
Collect Processes, procedures and historical information.	Prepare a measurable, comprehensive, transparent, adaptable, business oriented, consistent and accountable Business Case.	Identify Quality Standards.	Conduct Planning Kickoff.	Develop Project Team.	Verify Scope.	Identify WWR, WWW, document and make future enhancements.
Identify business need, issues, problems or oppurtunities, and develop proposed solution to be implemented through projects.	Get consensus on project quality, project controls, get approval of the Business Case, and get commitment to the project from Key stakeholders.	Establish Project Budget	Refine Project Scope	Manage Project Team.	Control Scope.	Project closure report
Present Project Proposals to Project Sponsor.	Decision Gate.	Perform risk identification.	Refine Project Schedule	Communicate and distribute information.	Control Schedule	
Screen Project Proposals.	Prepare a broad statement of the purpose of the project.	Document Risks.	Refine Quality Standards.	Manage Stakeholder expectation	Control Costs.	
Rate Project Proposals.	Delinate clear project objectives.	Document Stakeholder requirements.	Refine Project Budget.	Conduct Procurements.	Perform Quality Control.	
Prioritise project proposals. Perform brainstorming, to select project which delivers maximum value to the businesss and is aligned with business strategy	Identify all the external and internal Stakeholders, and understand their requirements.	Develop Communication Plans.	Identify new Risks and Quantify Risk through Quantatitive and Qualitative Analysis.		Report Performance.	
Decision Gate	Develop a Project charter.	Produce Initial Project Plan.	Develop Risk Management Plan.		Monitor and Control Risks.	
Identify Project Sponsor.	Get formal authorisation from the stakeholders, and document intial requirements which satify stakeholder's needs and expectations.	Review and Refine Project Charter and Business Case.	Define Change Control Process.		Administer Procurements.	
Identify Project Manager.	Decision Gate.	Get approval.	Refine Communications Plan.			
Identify Initial Project Management Team.	Form the team	Decision Gate.	Define Change Management Plan.			
Enable communication between organisation and project team.	Define SIPOC and verify performance		Establish Time/Cost Baseline.			
Prepare project brief outlining what will be achieved by the project.	Convert Charter to contract.		Develop Project Team.			
Define approach for implementing project, and define initial project risks.	Define review process		Develop Implementation Plan.			
Provide justification of the project to Project Sponsors, get approval to proceed.	Decision Gate.		Decision Gate.			
Decision Gate.			Review/Review Business Case.			
Plan for next phase (Initiation Phase).			Prepare for Acceptance and gain Approval Signature.			

Traditional project management framework consists of 5 phases; however, this framework consists of seven steps to have phased reviews for effective monitoring.

Initiation Phase

Project Initiation
Identify internal key stakeholders for securing their support.
Conduct detailed financial and technical assessment studies to gather their detailed requirements.
Assess risk from previous projects for preparing a business case which will be approved by Stakeholder through decision gate.
Prepare purpose statement project along with clear project objectives.
Identify all key stakeholders and gather requirements to prepare the Project Charter.
Take formal authorization from the stakeholder through decision gate for officially initiating the project.
Give concentration in gathering complete project requirement to avoid missing any detail. Until this stage, no initial investments will be required, and there will be minimum spending on overheads.
Form cross-functional team, and define SIPOC "(Supplier, Input, Process, Output, and Customer)."
Convert charter into an official contract.
Define project review process through approval in stage review.
Conduct stakeholder analysis in this phase by determining stakeholders, project leaders (Champion) and Critical to quality (CTQ) outputs.

Table 15.2: Project Initiation Phase

Table 15.2 describes the steps followed by Project Leader for Project Initiation Phase.

Project Planning Phase

Project Planning Phases divided into two phases.

Project Planning - Phase 1
Define project scope and create Work breakdown structure.
Create high-level schedule including the definition of activities, and allocate the resources to them.
Identify quality standards. Identify project risks.
Create budget.
Develop an initial project plan followed by the refining of a project charter and project charter for approval.

Table 15.3: Project Planning. Phase I

Project Planning - Phase II
Give orientation to new team members.
Review project materials, quality and cost to cover estimation errors or price fluctuations.
Conduct planning kick-off meeting followed by a redefinition of project scope, schedule, and quality standards.
Identify new risks in this phase and will be added to the risk register along with the risk identified in the previous phase.
Assess all risks and creates risk management plan.
Create change management process and plan.
Create communication plan.
Provide training to project team.
Develop implementation plan.
Plan and review the business case.

Table 15.4: Project Planning. Phase II

Table 15.4 and 15.5 describes the steps followed in Project Planning Phase I and II.

Project Execution Phase

Execution Phase
Create quality assurance plan.
Use Six Sigma Statistical Tools to measure the processes capabilities.
In the case of any problem, conduct root causes analysis and "5 Whys" Analysis.
Continuously develop and manage project teams through knowledge sharing sessions and training.
Manage stakeholder requirements through communication in "Obeya" and status review meetings, collecting feedback from them, and resolving their issues.
Conduct procurement.
Promote lean practices such as Value Stream Mapping, 5S, Visual Communication. This will reduce non-value added activities and increase flow.
Identify bottleneck resources on the Critical path and remove the bottleneck.

Table 15.5: Execution Phase

Table 15.5 describes the steps followed in Project Execution Phase.

Monitoring and Control Phase

Monitoring and Control
Control changes in the project in this phase along with cost, time and schedule.
Control Quality through Six Sigma Tools.
In the case of any variability, collect data, and measure using statistical tools, charts, and Histograms. Measure process capability.
Verify collected data for any possible cause through Cause and Effects Diagram and Root cause Analysis.
Test solutions. Use SWOT and FMEA tools.

Identify the non-valued added activities through Value Stream Mapping technique.
Run PDCA cycle in each phase of the project to bring continuous improvement.
Monitor risk in this phase.

Table 15.6 Monitoring and Control Phase

Table 15.6 describes the steps followed in Monitoring and Control Phase.

Closing phase

In this phase, Project Leaders records the lessons learned during the project.

To summarize, this framework is front loaded, and project leader concentrates more in the initial phases (Pre-Initiation, Initiation, and Planning Phase 1) of the project to avoid missing any significant detail. Project Leader focuses to gather the support of all the stakeholders since high investments are linked to Aerospace and IT projects.

CHAPTER 16

---

16. Project Management Processes in IT and Aerospace Projects

Today, many organizations adopt PMBoK as a foundation and use its framework structure, and then customize the context according to the business, organizational and project requirements. This means that organizations follow process being followed by PMBoK such as Initiation, Planning, Execution, Monitoring and Control process and then customize them as per the business requirements. Research done by Bauer (2005) demonstrated that competencies of a Project Leader in an Aerospace organization and PMBoK be well integrated for project success. Bauser (2005) recommended using PMBoK as a base foundation, and then customize the process framework according to the business or domain requirement as such approach will be aligned to the operational processes and business strategy leading to higher project success. Therefore, customization of PMBoK as per business requirement is a better approach. Furthermore, PMI certification is very popular and Project Leaders certified or with prior knowledge in PMBoK will be available to Aerospace organization.

It is imperative that Project Leader control the projects within efficacious outputs, aligning with Business strategy, and expending right strategy for managing supply chain, amalgamating Best Practices of Operations Strategy, encompassing Theory of Constraints(TOC) Six Sigma and PM fundamentals with honesty, empathy, sensitivity to Project Comrades ultimately resulting in high "Gross Project Happiness™"

17. REFERENCES

1. A., D. W. (1988). Measurement of project success. *International Journal of Project Management.*

2. Aaltonena, K., Jaakkob, K., & Tuomasa, O. (2008). Stakeholder salience in global projects. *International Journal of Project Management, Volume 26, Issue 5,* 509–516.

3. Aboelmaged, M. (2010). Six Sigma quality: a structured review and implications for future research. *International Journal of Quality & Reliability Management, Vol. 27 Iss: 3,* 268 - 317. [Pdf] Available at: <http://www.pqprc.org/userfiles/groups/Six%20Sigma%20 quality%2-%20astructuredreviewand%20implications%20for%20 future%20research.pdf> [Accessed 26 January 2012].

4. Ackroyd, S., & Hughes, J. (1992). *Data Collection in Context.* New York: Longman.

5. Adair.J. (1988). *Effective Leadership.* London: Pan.

6. Adler, N. (1997). *International dimensions of organizational behavior.* Cincinnati, OH:: South Western.

7. Adler, P., Benner, M., Brunner, D., MacDuffie, J., Osono, E., Staats, B., et al. (2009). Perspectives on the productivity dilemma. *Journal of Operations Management 27,* 99–113.

8. Adnan, H., Shamsuddin, Supardi, A., & Ahmad, N. (2012). Conflict Prevention in Partnering Projects. *Procedia - Social and Behavioral Sciences 35 (2012),* 772 – 781.

9. Adner, R. (2006). Match your innovation strategy to your innovation ecosystem. *Harvard Business Review.,* 1-11.

10. AGI-Goldratt Institute. (2009). Project Management in a Lean World - Translating Lean Six Sigma (LSS) into the Project Environment.

VELOCITY White Paper. [Pdf] Available at: <http://www.emeraldinsight.com/journals.htm?issn=0265-671X&volume=25&issue=8&articleid=1742454&show=pdf> [Accessed 26 January 2012].

11. Ahearn, K., Ferris, G., Hochwarter, W., Douglas, C., & Ammeter, A. (2004). Leader Political Skill and Team Performance. *Journal of Management 30(3),* 309–327.

12. Ahmed, A., Kayis, B., &Amornsawadwatana, S. (2007). A review of techniques for risk management in projects. *Benchmarking: An International Journal, Vol. 14, No. 1, pp.,* 22-36.

13. Ahuja, M., & Galvin, J. (2003). Socialization in virtual groups. *Journal of Management 29 (2),* 161–185.

14. Akbulut-Bailey, A., Motwani, J., & Smedley, E. (2012). When Lean and Six Sigma converge: a case study of a successful implementation of Lean Six Sigma at an aerospace company. *International Journal of Technology Management 2012 - Vol. 57, No.1/2/3,* 18 - 32.

15. Akbulut-Bailey, A., Motwani, J., & Smedley, E. (2012). When Lean and Six Sigma converge: a case study of a successful implementation of Lean Six Sigma at an aerospace company. *International Journal of Technology Management 2012 - Vol. 57, No.1/2/3,* 18 - 32.

16. Akkermans, H., & Oorschot, K. (May 2016). Pilot Error? Managerial Decision Biases as Explanation for Disruptions in Aircraft Development. *Project Management Journal, Volume 47, Issue 2,* 79-102.

17. Alacca, H., & Ceylan, C. (2011). "Value Chain analysis using Value Stream Mapping." *White Good Industry Application Department.*

18. Alexander, S. (2000). Virtual teams are going global. *Infoworld,* 55–56.

19. Ali-Babar, M., Verner, J., & Nguyen. (2007). Establishing and maintaining trust in software outsourcing relationships: an empirical investigation. *Journal of Systems and Software,* 1438–1449.

20. Almeida, B., Correia, I., & Saldanha-da-Gama, F. (2016). Priority-based heuristics for the multi-skill resource constrained project scheduling problem. *Expert Systems With Applications 57,* 91–103.

21. Amalia, M., &Nugroho, Y.(2011) An innovation perspective of knowledge management in a multinational subsidiary. *Journal of Knowledge Management, Vol. 15 Issue: 1,* 71 - 87.

22. Ambler, S. (1998). Process Patterns: Building Large-Scale Systems Using Object Technology (SIGS: Managing Object Technology. Cambridge: Cambridge University Press.

23. AMS. (2003). *Am. Systems Corporation(AMS), Risk Management Process and Implementation.* Chantilly, Va.: Am. Systems Corp.

24. Anantatmula, V. (2010). Project manager leadership role in improving project performance. *Engineering Management Journal, Vol. 22 No. 1,* 13-22.

25. Andersen, E., Grude, K., Haug, T., Katagiri, M., & Turner, R. (2004). *Goal directed project management. 3rd ed.* London: Kogan Page.

26. Anderson, J., Rungtusanatham, M., & Schroeder, R. (1994). A theory of quality management underlying the Deming management method. *Acad. Manag. Rev. 19 (3),* 472-509.

27. Antony, J., Douglas, A., & Antony, F. (2007) Determining the essential characteristics of Six Sigma Black Belts. *The TQM Magazine, Vol. 19,* 274-81.

28. Appelbaum, S. (2004). Critical success factors in the client-consuming relationship. *Journal of American Academy of Business, Cambridge,* 184-91.

29. Ara, A., & Al-Mudimigh, A. (2011) The Role and Impact of Project Management in ERP project implementation life cycle. *Global Journals of Computer Science and Technology.*

30. Argote, L., McEvily, B., & Reagans, R. (2003).] Introduction to the special issue on managing knowledge in organizations: Creating, retaining and transferring knowledge. *Management Science, 49(4),* v-viii.

31. Argyris, C. (1995). *On Organizational Learning.* Oxford, UK: Blackwell.

32. Armstrong, M. (2008). *How to be an even better manager.* London: Kogan Page.

33. Arshad, N., Mohamed, A., & Matnor, Z. (2007). Risk factors in software development projects. *Proceedings of the 6th WSEAS Int. Conf. on Software Engineering Parallel and Distributed Systems,* 51–56.

34. Ashworth, P., Bradbury, J., Feenstra, C., Greenberg, S., Hund, G., Mikunda, T., et al. (2012). Communication, project planning, and

management for carbon capture and storage projects: An international comparison. *Energy Transformed Flagship.*

35. Atkinson, R. (1999). Project management: cost, time and two best guesses and a phenomenon, it's time to accept other success criteria. *International Journal of Project Management Vol. 17, No. 6,* 337±342.

36. Atkinson, R., Crawford, L., & Ward, S. (2006). Fundamental uncertainties in projects and the scope of project management. *International Journal of Project Management, Volume 24, Issue 8,* 687–698.

37. Attaran 2006, 2007, 2011b; Hou and Hung, 2006; Reyes and Frazier, 2007

38. Attaran, M. (2006). The Coming Age of RFID Revolution. Journal of International Technology and Information Management, 15, 4, 77-88.

39. Attaran, M. (2011). "The Supply and Demand for RFID" Industrial Engineer, PP. *The Institute of Industrial Engineers (IIE), 43, 12,* 26-31.

40. Attaran, M. (February 2012). Critical Success Factors and Challenges of Implementing RFID in Supply Chain Management. *Journal of Supply Chain and Operations Management, Volume 10, Number 1.*

41. Atwater, D., & Bass, B. (1994). 'Transformational leadership in teams. In. In B. Avolio, & B. Bass, *Improving Organizational Effectiveness through Transformational Leadership* (pp. 48–83.). Thousand Oaks, CA: Sage.

42. Awamleh, R., & Gardner, W. (1999). Perceptions of leader charisma and effectiveness: The effects of vision content, delivery, and organizational performance. *The Leadership Quarterly.*

43. Babbie, E. (2007). The Practise of Social Research (11th Edition). Belmont, CA: Wadsworth.

44. Baccarini, D., Salm, G., & Love, P. (2004). Management of risks in information technology projects. *Industrial Management & Data Systems,* 286-295.

45. BADIRU, A., BADIRU, A., & BADIRU, A. (2007). *Industrial Project Management - Concepts, Tools, and Techniques.* Boca Raton: CRC Press.

46. Bailey, K. (1987). *Methods of Social Research (3rd Edition).* New York: Free Press.

47. Baker, B., Murphy, D., & Fisher, D. (1983). Factors affecting project success. In D. Cleland, & W. King, *Project Management Handbook*. New York: Van Nostrand Reinhold.

48. Baker, B., Murphy, D., & Fisher, D. (1988). Factors Affecting Project Success. *Project Management Handbook*.

49. Baker, F. T. (1972). Chief programmer team management of production programming. *IBM Systems Journal, 11(1)*, 56–73.

50. Ballard, G. (1999). *Work Structuring White Paper #4*. Las Vegas, Nevada: Lean Construction Institute.

51. Ballard, H. (2000). THE LAST PLANNER SYSTEM OF PRODUCTION CONTROL. *Ph.D. Thesis. Faculty of Engineering. School of Civil Engineering. Birmingham, AL: The University of Birmingham*. [Pdf] Available at: <http://wvvw.leanconstruction.org/pdf/ballard2000-dissertation.pdf> [Accessed 26 January 2012].

52. Baptista, A., Santos, F., & Páscoa, J. (March 2016). Project Management Methodologies as Main Tool for Current Challenges in Global Economy Driving Historical Changes. *Journal of Advanced Management Science Vol. 4, No. 2*.

53. Barczak, G., McDonough, E., &Athanassiou, N. (2006). So you want to be Global Project Leader? *Research Technology Management*.

54. Barge, J. (2004). Reflexivity as managerial practice. *Communication Monographs, 71*, 70-96.

55. BARKEMA, H., BAUM, J., & MANNIX, E. (Oct 01, 2002). Management challenges in a new time. *Academy of Management Journal, Vol. 45, No. 5*, 916-930.

56. Barnett, J. (2009). Room with a view. INTEGRATED DEFENSE SYSTEMS / BOEING FRONTIERS.

57. Bartram, P. (2012). *Perfect Project Manager*. Random House eBooks.

58. Bass, B. (1985). Leadership and performance beyond expectations. New York: Free Press.

59. Bauer, B. (2005). A SUCCESS PARADIGM FOR PROJECT MANAGERS IN THE AEROSPACE INDUSTRY. *PhD. Thesis*.

60. Bedi, H. (1992). *Understanding the Asian Manager*. New Delhi: Allen & Unwin.

61. Belassi, W., & Tukel, O. (1996). A new framework for determining critical success/failure factors in projects. *International Journal of Project Management, Vol. 14 No. 3*, 141-51.

62. Belassi, W., & Tukul, O. (1996). A new framework for determining critical success and failure factors in project management. *International Journal of Project Management, 14(3)*, 141-51.

63. Belbin, R. (1981). *Management Teams: Why they Succeed or Fail.* London: Butterworth Heinemann.

64. Belout, A., & Gauvreau, C. (January 2004). Factors Influencing Project Success: the Impact of Human Resource Management. *International Journal of Project Management, Vol. 22, No 1*, 1-11.

65. Ben-David, I., & Raz, T. (2001). An integrated approach for risk response development in project planning. *Journal of the Operational Research Society 52*, 14-25.

66. Benner, M., & Tushman, M. (Apr. 2003). Exploitation, Exploration, and Process Management. *The Academy of Management Review, Vol. 28, No. 2*, 238-256.

67. Bennis, W. (1989). *On Becoming the Leader.* New York: Addison-Wesley.

68. Bentley, C. (2010). *Prince2 - A Practical Handbook - Third Edition.* Burlington: Butterworth-Heinemann

69. Bharat, V. (2012). Managing Cultural Differences. Strategic Outsourcing - Management for Professionals.

70. Biedenbach, T., & Muller, R. (2012). Absorptive, innovative and adaptive capabilities and their impact on project and project portfolio performance. *International Journal of Project Management, 30(5)*, 621-635.

71. Binder, J. (2008). Global Project Management: Communication, Collaboration, and Management Across Borders. Burlington: Gower Publishing Limited.

72. Bird, A. (2008). *Assessing global leadership competencies. In M. Mendenhall, J. S. Osland, A. Bird, G. R. Oddou, & M. L. Maznevski (Eds.), Global leadership: Research, practice, and development (pp. 64–80).* New York: Routledge.

73. Blackstone, J., Cox, J., & Schleier, J. (2009). A tutorial on project management from a theory of constraints perspective.

International Journal of Production Research. DF]. Available at <http://0-www.tandfonline.com.pugwash.lib.warwick.ac.uk/doi/pdf/10.1080/00207540802392551> accessed on [15 May 2012]

74.   Blaney, J. (1989). Managing software development projects. *Project Management Seminar/Symposium, Atlanta, GA.*

75.   Blaxter, L., Hughes, C., & Tight, M. (2010). *How to research. Fourth Edition.* Berkshire: Open University Press.

76.   Block, R. (1983). *The Politics of Projects.* Yourdon Press: Prentice-Hall.

77.   Blomkvist, P., &Uppvall, L. (2012). A Chain is only as Strong as its Weakest Link: Managing Change in the Curriculum of Industrial Management Education. *International Journal of Industrial Engineering and Management (IJIEM), Vol. 3 No 2,* 53-65.

78.   Boadle, W. (2004). Project Failure and Success Factor

79.   Boehm, B., & Turner, R. (2003). Using Risk to Balance Agile and Plan-Driven Methods. *IEEE.*

80.   Boh, W., Ren, Y., Kiesler, S., & Bussjaeger, R. (2007). Expertise and collaboration in the geographically dispersed organization. *Organization Science, 18(4),* 59

81.   Bouti, A., & Kadi, A. (1994). A State-of-the-Art Review of FMEA/FMECA. *Int'l J. Reliability, Quality and Safety Eng., vol. 1,* 515-543.

82.   Bozeman, B. (2007). Public values and the public interest: Counterbalancing economic individualism. Washington, D.C: Georgetown University Press

83.   Brady, T., & Davies, A. (2014). Managing structural and dynamic complexity: a tale of two projects. *Project Management Journal Volume 45, Issue 4,* 21-38.

84.   Brady, T., Davies, A., & Nightingale, P. (2012). Dealing with uncertainty in complex projects: Revisiting Klein and Meckling, special issue: Classics of project management. *International Journal of Managing Projects in Business Volume 5, Issue 4,* 661-679.

85.   Bresnen, M. (2006). Conflicting and conflated discourses? Project management, organizational change, and learning. In D. Hodgson, & S. Cicmil, *Making Projects Critical.* (pp. 68-89). Basingstoke: Palgrave Macmillan.

86.   Bresnena, M., Edelmanb, L., Newellb, S., & Scarbrougha, H. (2003). Social practices and the management of knowledge in

project environments. *International Journal of Project Management 21,* 157–166.

87. BREUKELEN, W., LEEDEN, R., WESSELIUS, W., & HOES, M. (2012). Differential treatment within sports teams, leader–member (coach–player) exchange quality, team atmosphere, and team performance. *Journal of Organizational Behaviour, J. Organiz. Behav. 33,* 43–63.

88. Breyfogle III, F. (2003). Implementing Six Sigma: Smarter Solutions Using Statistical Methods. New York: John Wiley & Sons

89. Brill, J., Bishop, M., & Walker, A. (2006). The competencies and characteristics required of an effective project manager: A web-based Delphi study. *Educational Technology Research and Development. V. 54. No. 2.,* 1042-1629.

90. Briner, W., Hastings, C., & Geddes, M. (2004). *Project Leadership - Second Edition.* Hampshire: Gower.

91. Briner, W., Hastings, C., & Geddes, M. (2011). *Project Leadership.* Burlington: Gower Publishing Limited

92. Brinkkemper, S., & Jansen, S. (2012). *Collaboration in Outsourcing: A Journey to Quality.* Basingstoke, Hampshire: Palgrave McMillan.

93. Brinkkemper, S., & Jansen, S. (2012). *Collaboration in Outsourcing: A Journey to Quality.* Basingstoke: Palgrave McMillan.

94. Brooks, F. (1975). *The mythical man-month.* Addison-Wesley Publishing Company.

95. Brown, J., & Duguid, P. (1991). Organizational learning and communities-of-practice: *Organization Science, Vol. 2, No. 1,* 40–57.

96. Brown, K., Huettner, B., &Jame, C. (2006). Managing Virtual Teams: Getting the Most from Wikis, Blogs, and Other Collaborative Tools. Sudbury: Jones and Bartlett.

97. Brown, L. (1983). *Managing conflict at organizational interfaces.* Reading, MA: Addison-Wesley.

98. Brown, L., & Grundy, T. (2011). *Project Management for the Pharmaceutical Industry.* Farnham: Gower.

99. Buchan, D. (1994.). Risk analysis—some practical suggestions. *Cost Eng. 36,* 29–34.

100. Bunderson, J. (2003). Recognizing and Utilizing Expertise in Work Groups: A Status Characteristics Perspective. *Administrative Science Quarterly, 48*, 557–591.

101. Burke, R., & Barron, S. (2007). Project Management Leadership - Building Creative Teams. Burke Publishing.

102. Burnes, B. (2004). Managing change: a strategic approach to organisational4th edition. Prentice Hall.

103. Burns, J. (1978). *Leadership.* New York: Harper & Row.

104. Burns, R. (1997). *Introduction to Research Methods - 2nd Edition.* Melbourne: Longman Cheshire.

105. Bush, A., Tiwana, A., & Tsuji, H. (2008). An empirical investigation of the drivers of software outsourcing decisions in Japanese organizations. *Softw. Technol. 50*, 499–510.

106. Byrne, G. (2003). Ensuring optimal success with Six Sigma implementations. *Journal of Organizational Excellence, Vol. 22*, 43.

107. Cain, S. (2012). The creative power of one. Retrieved 08 16, 2012, from The creative power of one: http://heresthenews.blogspot.co.uk/2012/01/creative-power-of-one.html

108. Calvert, S. (1995). Managing stakeholders. In J. Turner, *The commercial project manager.* Maidenhead: McGraw-Hill.

109. Carmel, E. (1999.). Global Software Teams: Collaboration Across Borders and Time. Saddle River, NJ: Prentice Hall.

110. Carmel, E., & Abbott, P. (2006). Configurations of global software development: Offshore versus nearshore. *Proceedings of the 2006 International Workshop on Global Software Development for the Practitioner*, 3-7.

111. Caroll, J. (2012). Effective Project Management in Easy Steps - Second Edition. Lemington Spa: Easy Steps Limited.

112. Cascio, W. (2014). *Looking back, looking forward: Technology in the workplace. In M. D. Coovert & L. F. Thompson (Eds.), The psychology of workplace technology.* New York: Routledge.

113. Casey, V., & Richardson, I. (2005). Virtual Software Teams: Overcoming the Obstacles. *3rd World Congress for Software Quality, Munich, Germany.*

114. Casey, V. (2009). *Software Testing and Global Industry: Future Paradigms.* Newcastle, UK: Cambridge Scholars Publishing.

115. Casey, V., & Richardson, I. (2006). Uncovering the reality within virtual software teams, ICSE 2006. Shanghai: ACM Press.

116. Casey, V., & Richardson, I. (2008). A Structured Approach to Global Software Development. *European Systems and Software Process Improvement and Innovation.*

117. Casey, V., & Richardson, I. (2008). The impact of fear on the operation of virtual teams. *IEEE International Conference on Global Software Engineering.*

118. CERF - Civil Engineering Research Foundation. (2004). Independent Research Assessment of Project Management Factors Affecting Department of Energy Project Success - Final Report. Office of Engineering and Construction Management U.S. Department of Energy.

119. Cerpa, N., & Verner, J. (December 2009). Why did your project fail? *Communications of the ACM Finding the Fun in Computer Science Education Volume 52 Issue 12*, 130-134.

120. Cerpa, N., Bardeen, M., Kitchenham, B., & Verner, J. (September 2010). Evaluating logistic regression models to estimate software project outcomes. *Information and Software Technology, Volume 52, Issue 9*, Pages 934–944.

121. Cervone, H. (2011). Understanding agile project management methods using Scrum. *OCLC Systems & Services: International digital library perspectives Vol. 27 No. 1*, 18-22.[Pdf] Available at: <http://impact.asu.edu/cse598fall/PapersPresented/Understanding_agile.pdf> [Accessed 26 January 2012].

122. Chakravorty, S. (2010). Where Process-Improvement Projects Go Wrong. *Wall Street Journal - Eastern Edition*. [Pdf] Available at: <http://0-proquest.umi.com.pugwash.lib.warwick.ac.uk/pqdweb?index=0&did=1946677101&SrchMode=1&sid=2&Fmt=3&VInst=PROD&VType=PQD&RQT=309&VName=PQD&TS=1337199022&clientId=9678> [Accessed 26 January 2012].

123. Chan, A., & Chan, A. (2004). Key Performance Indicators for measuring construction success. *Benchmarking: An International Journal. Vol 11 No 2*, 203-221.

124. Chandler, A. (1962). Strategy and Structure: Chapters in the History of the Industrial Enterprise. Cambridge, MA: MIT Press.

125. Charvat, J. (2002). How to identify a failing project.

126. Chelcea, S. (2010). Sociological research methodology. methods quantitative and qualitative. Bucharest: Economic.

127. Chen, G., & An, R. (2006). *A Chinese model of intercultural leader competence. In D. K. Deardorff (Ed.), The Sage handbook of intercultural competence.* Thousand Oaks, CA: Sage.

128. Chen, G., & An, R. (2009). *Chen, G., & An, R. (2009). A Chinese model of intercultural leader competence. In D. K. Deardorff. The Sage handbook of intercultural competence.* Thousand Oaks, CA: Sage.

129. Chen, G., Liu, C., &Tjosvold, D. (March 2005). Conflict Management for Effective Top Management Teams and Innovation in China. *Journal of Management Studies 42:2.*

130. Cheng, C.-Y., & Chang, P.-Y. (2012). Implementation of the Lean Six Sigma framework in non-profit organizations: A case study. *Total Quality Management & Business Excellence,* 431-447.

131. Chin, G. (2004). *Agile Project Management.* NY: AMACOM.

132. Christiansen, J., & Varnes, C. (2008). From models to practice: decision-making at portfolio meetings. *International Journal of Quality & Reliability Management,* 87-101. [PDF]. Available at <http://0-www.emeraldinsight.com.pugwash.lib.warwick.ac.uk/ journals.htm?issn=0265-671X&volume=25&issue=1&articleid=164 1965&show=pdf> accessed on [15 May 2012]

133. Christianson, J., & Varnes, C. (2006). The ignorance of information at gate meetings. *13ᵗʰ International Product Development Management Conference,* 1519-1536. [PDF]. Available at <http://www.mendeley. com/research/ignorance-information-gate-meetings/> accessed on [15 May 2012]

134. CII. (1995). Qualitative Effects of Project Changes. Construction Industry Institute, the University of Texas at Austin, Austin, TX.

135. Cioffi, D. (2001). Adopt Hacker Rules To Increase Project Success. *First Caribbean & Latin American Conference On Project Management.*

136. Clark, K., & Fujimoto, T. (1991). *Product development performance: Strategy, organization and management in the world auto industry.* Boston: Harvard Business School Press.

137. Clark, T. (2012). The Employee Engagement Mindset: The Six Drivers for Tapping into the Hidden Potential of Everyone in Your Company. London: McGraw-Hill.

138. Clarke, N. (2010). Emotional intelligence and its relationship to transformational leadership and key project manager competencies. *Project Management Journal, Vol. 41 No. 2*, 5-20.

139. Cleland, D. I. (1986). Project Stakeholder Management. *Project Management Journal, 17(4), 36.*

140. Cleland, D., & King, W. (1968). *Systems analysis and project management.* New York: McGraw-Hill.

141. Cleland, D., & King, W. (1983). *System Analysis and Project Management.* New York: McGraw-Hill.

142. Cohen, B., &Thias, M. (2009). The Failure of the Off-shore Experiment: A Case for Collocated Agile Teams. *Agile Conference (Chicago, USA, 2009),* 251-256.

143. Cohen, S., & Bailey, D. (1997). What makes teams work: Group effectiveness research from the shop floor to the executive suite. *Journal of Management, 23(3),* 239–264.

144. Collis, J., & Hussey, R. (2009.). Business research : a practical guide for undergraduate & postgraduate students. 3rd ed. London: Palgrave Macmillan.

145. Connaughton, S., & Shuffler, M. (2007). Multinational and Multicultural Distributed Teams: A Review and Future Agenda. *Small Group Research, 38 (3),* 387–412.

146. Contract management

147. Cooke-Davies, T. (2002). The real project success factors. *International Journal of Project, Vol. 20 No. 3, pp.,* 185-190. [PDF], Available at <https://www.surfgroepen.nl/sites/Ontwerpprojecten/DC/Onderzoek/Refw%2075.%20map%2013.%20The%20real%20success%20factors%20on%20projects.pdf> Accessed on [14 June 2011]

148. Cooper, R. (2001). Winning at new products: Accelerating the process from Idea to Launch. Reading: Perseus Books.

149. Cooper, R. (2008). Perspective: The Stage-Gate® Idea-to-Launch Process—Update, What's New, and NexGen Systems. *Journal of Product Innovation Management.* [PDF]. Available at <http://www.

proakatemia.fi/wordpress/wp-content/uploads/2009/11/Stage-Gate-what-is-new.pdf> accessed on [15 May 2012]

150. Cooper, R., Edgett, S., & Kleinschmidt, E. (1997a). Portfolio management in new product development: Lessons from the Leaders I. *Research Technology Management*. [PDF]. Available at <http://0-proquest.umi.com.pugwash.lib.warwick.ac.uk/pqdweb?index=1& did=13917194&SrchMode=1&sid=1&Fmt=6&VInst=PROD&V Type=PQD&RQT=309&VName=PQD&TS=1337197990&clien tId=9678> accessed on [15 May 2012]

151. Cooper, R., Edgett, S., & Kleinschmidt, E. (2000). New Problems, New Solutions: Making Portfolio Management More Effective. *R&D Management*. [PDF]. Available at<http://www.stage-gate.com/downloads/Making_Portfolio_Management_More_Effective.pdf> accessed on [15 May 2012]

152. Cooper, R., Edgett, S., & Kleinschmidt, E. (2001). Portfolio management for new product development: results of an industry practices study. *R&D Management*. [PDF]. Available at <http://www.prod-dev.com/downloads/working_papers/wp_13.pdf> accessed on [15 May 2012]

153. Cooper, R., Edgett, S., & Kleinshmidt, E. (1997b). Portfolio management in new product development: Lessons from the Leaders II. *Research Technology Management*, 43. [PDF]. Available at <http://0-proquest.umi.com.pugwash.lib.warwick.ac.uk/pqdweb ?index=0&did=22999496&SrchMode=1&sid=1&Fmt=6&VInst=P ROD&VType=PQD&RQT=309&VName=PQD&TS=13371979 90&clientId=9678> accessed on [15 May 2012]

154. COSO. (2004). *Enterprise Risk Management: Integrated Framework*. COSO (Committee of Sponsoring Organisations of the TreadwayCommission),.

155. Crabtree, B., & Miller, W. (1999). Using codes and code manuals: A template organizing style of interpretation. In B. Crabtree, & W. Miller, *Doing qualitative research, 2nd Edition* (pp. 163-178). Newbury Park, CA: Sage.

156. Crawford, J. (2011). The Strategic Project Office - Second Edition. Boca Raton: CRC Press.

157. Crawford, L. (2005). Senior management perceptions of project management competence. *International Journal of Project Management,* 7-16.

158. Crawford, M., & Di Benedetto. (2006). *New products management, Eighth edition.* Ridge, IL: McGraw-Hill/Irwin.

159. Crosby, B., & Bryson, J. (2010). Integrative leadership and the creation and maintenance of cross-sector collaborations. *The Leadership Quarterly,* 211-230.

160. Cross, R., Ehrlich, K., Dawson, R., & Helferich, J. (2008). Managing Collaboration at the Point of Execution: Improving Team Effectiveness with a Network Perspective. *California Management Review, 50(4).*

161. CUMMINGS, J., & HAAS, M. (2012). So many teams, so little time: Time allocation matters in geographically dispersed teams. *Journal of Organizational Behavior, J. Organiz. Behav. 33,* 316–341.

162. Dahlin, K., Weingart, L., & Hinds, P. (2005). Team Diversity and Information Use. *The Academy of Management Journal, Vol. 48, No. 6 (Dec., 2005),* 1107-1123.

163. Daim, T., Ha, A., Reutiman, S., Hughes, B., Pathak, U., Bynum, W., et al. (2012). Exploring the communication breakdown in global virtual teams. *International Journal of Project Management, Volume 30, Issue 2,* 199–212.

164. Damian, D., Izquierdo, L., Singer, J., & Kwan, I. (2007). Awareness in the Wild: Why Communication Breakdowns Occur. *International Conference on Global Software Engineering (ICGSE 2007), Munich,* 81-90.

165. Davari, M., & Demeulemeester, E. (2016). *The proactive and reactive resource-constrained project scheduling problem.* Retrieved 5 5, 2016, from Available at SSRN: http://ssrn.com/abstract=2771609

166. Davies, A., & Brady, T. (2015). Explicating the dynamics of project capabilities. *International Journal of Project Management* `.

167. Davies, A., & Mackenzie, I. (2014). Project complexity and systems integration:constructing the London 2012 Olympics and Paralympics Games. *International Journal of Project Management Volume 32, Issue 5, July 2014.* 773–790.

168. Davies, A., Gann, D., & Douglas, T. (2009). Innovation in Megaprojects: Systems Integration at London Heathrow Terminal 5. *California Management Review, Vol. 51 No. 2*, 101-125.

169. De Vries, R., Bakker-Pieper, A., & Oostenveld, W. (2010). Leadership = Communication? The Relations of Leaders' Communication Styles with Leadership Styles, Knowledge Sharing and Leadership Outcomes. *Journal of Business Psychology, 25*, 367-380.

170. De Wit, A. (1988). Measurement of project success. *International Journal of Project Management*.

171. Delamont, S. (1992). Delamont, S (1992) Fieldwork in Educational Settings: Methods, Pitfalls and Perspectives. London, Falmer.

172. DeLone, W., & McLean, E. (2003). The DeLone and McLean model of information systems. *Journal of Management Information Systems Vol. 19 No. 4*, 9-30.

173. Demeulemeester, E., & Herroelen, W. (2011). Robust project scheduling. Foundations and Trends in Technology. *Information and Operations Management, 3*, 201-376.

174. Demir, K. (2009). A Survey on Challenges of Software Project Management. *Proceedings of the 2009 International Conference on Software Engineering Research Practice*, 13–16.

175. Den Hartog, R., & Verburg, R. (1997). Charisma and Rhetoric: Communication Techniques of International Business Leaders. *The Leadership Quarterly 8(4)*.

176. Desai, D. (2008). Improving productivity and profitability through Six Sigma: experience of a small-scale jobbing industry. *nternational Journal of Productivity and Quality Management, Vol. 3 No. 3*, 290-310. [Pdf] Available at: <http://www.inderscience.com/search/index.php?action=record&rec_id=17500> [Accessed 26 January 2012].

177. Desai, D., Antony, J., & Patel, M. (2012). An Assessment of the Critical Success Factors for Six Sigma Implementation in Indian Industries. *International Journal of Productivity and Performance Management, Vol. 61 Iss: 4*, 426 - 444. [Pdf] Available at: <http://www.emeraldinsight.com/journals.htm?issn=1741-0401&volume=61&issue=4&articleid=17031067&show=pdf> [Accessed 26 January 2012].

178. Detert, J., & Burris, E. (2007). Leadership behavior and employee voice: is the door really open? *Academy of Management Journal, 50,* 869–84.

179. Dewan, T., & Myatt, D. (2008). The Qualities of Leadership: Direction, Communication, and Obfuscation. *American Political Science Review Vol. 102, No. 3,* 351.

180. Dietrich, P., &Lehtonen, P. (2005). Successful management of strategic intentions through multiple projects—reflections from empirical study. *International Journal of Project Management 23 (5),* 386–391.

181. Dillon, R., & Tinsley, C. (2008). How near-misses influence decision making under risk: A missed opportunity for learning. *Management Science, Vol. 54, No. 8,* pp. 1425-1440.

182. Dinsmore, P., & Rocha, L. (2012). Enterprise Project Governance: A Guide to the Successful Management of Projects across the Organization. New York: AMACOM.

183. Dinur, A. (2012). Common and uncommon sense in managerial decision making under task uncertainty. *Management Decision Vol. 49 Iss: 5 pp.,* 694 - 709.

184. Doney, P., Cannon, J., & Mullen, M. (1998). Understanding the influence of national culture on the development of trust. *Academy of Management Review (2),* 610-620.

185. Dowson, P. (1994). *Organizational change: a processual approach.* London: Sage Publications

186. Druskat, V., & Wheeler, J. (2003). Managing from the boundary: The Effective leadership of self-managing work teams. *Academy of Management Journal, 46(4),* 435-457.

187. DTI (Department of Trade and Industry, UK). (2003). Inspired Leadership [PDF], Available at <http://webarchive.nationalarchives. gov.uk/+/http://www.berr.gov.uk/files/file10989.pdf> Accessed on [4 August 2012]

188. DTI. (n.d.). Inspirational Leadership. [Online], Available at <http:// berr.gov.uk/files/file10989.pdf> accessed on [02 Feb 2011] Fitzgerald, B. (1997). The use of systems development methodologies in practice: a field study. *Information Systems Journal Volume 7, Issue 3,* 201±212.

189. DuBrin, A. J. (2011). Leadership: Research Findings, Practise and Skills - 3ʳᵈ Edition. Boston, MA; Houghton-Mifflin

190. Dulewicz, V., & Higgs, M. (2005). Assessing leadership dimensions, styles and organizational. *Journal of Managerial Psychology, Vol. 20 No. 2*, 105-23.

191. Duncan, W. (1987). Get out from under. *Computerworld*, 89-93.

192. Earley, P. (1993). East meets West meet Mideast: Further explorations of collectivistic and individualistic work groups. *Academy of Management Journal, 36(2)*, 319-348.

193. Eckhause, J., Hughes, D., & Gabriel, S. (2009). Evaluating real options for mitigating technical risk in public sector R&D acquisitions. *International Journal of Project Management, Vol. 27, No. 4*, 365-377.

194. Edmondson, A., &Nembhard, I. (2009). Product Development and Learning in Project Teams:*Journal of Product Innovation Management 26*, 123–138.

195. Egorova, E., Torchiano, M., & Morisio, M. (October 2010). Actual vs. perceived effect of software engineering practices in the Italian industry. *Journal of Systems and Software, Volume 83, Issue 10*, 1907–1916.

196. Ehsani, M., Koozechian, H., & Mora, H. (June 2012). Athlete' Satisfaction with Coach in Iran's Professional Handball. *Asian Social Science Vol. 8, No. 7*

197. Elenkov, D., Judge, W., & Wright, P. (2005). Strategic leadership and executive innovation an international multi-cluster comparative study. *Strategic Management Journal, 26*, 665–82.

198. Elias, A., &Cavana, R. (2006). Elias AA, Cavana RY, Jackson LS. Stakeholder analysis for R&D project management. 32(4). *R&D Manage*, 301–10.

199. Emam, E., & Koru, A.G. (2008). A replicated survey of IT software project failures. *IEEE Software Volume 25, Issue 5*, 84-90.

200. Engwall, M. (2003). No project is an island: linking projects to history and context. *Res. Policy 32*, 798–808.

201. Evgenia, E., Torchiano, M., & Morisio, M. (October 2010). Actual vs. perceived effect of software engineering practices in the Italian

industry. *Journal of Systems and Software Volume 83, Issue 10,* 1907–1916.

202. Fact Finders, Inc. (1996). Southwestern Bell Telephone Product Development. *Fact Finders, Inc.*

203. Finkelstein, S. (1992). Power in top management teams: dimensions, measurement, and validation. *Academy of Management Journal, 35,* 505–38.

204. Finkelstein, S., & Hambrick, D. (1990). Top-management-team tenure and organizational outcomes: *Administrative Science Quarterly, 35,* 484–503.

205. Fisher, E. (2011). What practitioners consider to be the skills and behaviours of an effective people project manager. *International Journal of Project Management 29,* 994–1002.

206. Flyvbjerg, B. (2014). Whats you should know about megaprojects and why. An overview. *Project Management Journal, 45(2),* 8-19.

207. Flyvbjerg, B., Bruzelius, N., & Rothengatter, W. (2003). *Megaprojects and Risk: An Anatomy of Ambition.* Cambridge University Press.

208. Follet, M. (1927). Leader and expert. In H. Metcalf, *The psychological foundations of management* (pp. 220–243). Chicago: Shaw.

209. Fontaine, M. (2016). *Enterprise Risk Management-A Common Framework for the Entire Organization.* New York: Butterworth-Heinemann.

210. Forbes, L., & Ahmed, S. (2011). Modern Construction - Lean Project Delivery and Integrated Practises. Baco Raton: CRC Press.

211. Fortune, J., & White, D. (2006). "Framing of Project Critical Success Factors by a Systems Model." *International Journal of Project Management, Vol. 24, No.,* 53–65.

212. Frese, M., Beimel, S., & Schoenborn, S. (2003). Action training for charismatic leadership: Two evaluations of studies of a commercial training module on inspirational communication of a vision. *Personnel Psychology.*

213. Frese, R., & Sauter, V. (2003). Project Success and Failure: What is success, what is failure, and how can you improve your odds for success?

214. Fui-Hoon Nah, F., Lee-Shang Lau, J., &Kuang, J. (2001). Critical factors for successful implementation of enterprise systems. *Business Process Management Journal Volume 7, No 3,* 285-296.

215. Fuqua, H., Paynex, K., & Cangemi, J. (1998). Leadership and the Effective Use of Power. *National FORUMS Journals, 15 E(4)*.

216. Gabelica, C., Bossche, P., Segers, M., & Gijselaers, W. (2011). Feedback, a powerful lever in teams: A review. *Educational Research Review*. [Pdf] Available at: <http://www.sciencedirect.com/science/article/pii/S1747938X11000492> [Accessed 26 January 2012].

217. Garcla, R., & Calantone, R. (2002). A critical look at technological innovation typology and innovativeness terminology: A literature review. *Journal of Product Innovation Management 19(2)*, 110-132.

218. Gardner, W., Cogliser, C., Davis, K., & Dickens, M. (2011). Authentic leadership: A review of the literature and research agenda. *The Leadership Quarterly 22,* 1120–1145.

219. Garel, G. (2013). A history of project management models: From pre-models to the standard models. *Elsevier-International Journal of Project Management, vol. 31*, 663-669.

220. Gaspersz, V. (2007). *"Lean Six Sigma for Manufacturing and Service Industries."* Jakarta: Gramedia Pustaka Utama.

221. Gauthier-Villars., D., & Michaels, D. (2007, July 9). *EADS considers a simpler management structure.* Retrieved September 25, 2008, from Wall Street Journal: http://online.wsj.com/article/SB118393055196560256.html

222. Geert-hofstede.com. (2012, June 21). *National cultural dimensions.* Geert-hofstede.com: [Online], Available at <http://geert-hofstede.com/national-culture.html> Accessed on [14 June 2011]

223. Geoghegan, L., & Dulewicz, V. (2008). Do project managers' leadership competencies. *Project Management Journal, Vol. 39 No. 4*, 58-67.

224. George, M. (2003). *Lean Six Sigma for Services.* New York: McGraw-Hill.

225. Gibb, C. (1954). Leadership. In G. Lindzey, *Handbook of social psychology, Vol. 2* (pp. 877-917). Reading, Massachusetts: Addison-Wesley.

226. Gibson., C., & Cohen, S. (2003). *Virtual teams that work: Creating conditions for virtual team effectiveness.* San Francisco, CA: Jossey-Bass.

227. Giezen, M. (2012). Keeping it simple? A case study into the advantages and disadvantages of reducing complexity in megaproject planning. *International Journal of Project Management.*

228. Gitlow, H., & Levine, D. (2005). Six Sigma For Green Belts And Champions: Foundations, Dmaic, Tools, Cases, And Certification. Upper Saddle River, NJ: Prentice-Hall.

229. Globerson, S., & Zwikael, O. (2002). The impact of the project manager on project management. *Project Management Journal, Vol. 33 No. 3*, 58-64.

230. Goldratt, E. (1997). *Critical Chain*. Great Barrington, MA: North River Press.

231. Goleman, D. (1998). What makes a leader? *Harvard Business Review, Vol. 76 No. 6*, 93-103.

232. Goleman, D., Boyatzis, R., & McKee, A. (2001). Primal Leadership The Hidden Driver of Great Performance. *Harvard Business Review.*

233. Gordon, B. (1997). Japan's Aerospace Industry. [PDF], Available at <http://wgordon.web.wesleyan.edu/papers/aerosp.pdf> Accessed on [15 May 2012]

234. Graham, R. (1999). Managing the project management process in Aerospace and Construction: a comparative approach. *International Journal of Project Management Vol. 17, No. 1*, 39±45.

235. Greenberga, S., Gauvreaub, L., Hnottavange-Telleen, K., Finley, R., & Marsteller, S. (2011). Meeting CCS communication challenges head-on: Integrating communications, planning, risk assessment, and project management. *Energy Procedia 4 (2011)*, 6188–6193.

236. Grinnell, R. (1993). *Social Work Research and Evaluation (4th Edn).* Itasca (IL): F.E. Peacock.

237. Group EFO. (1995). *Innovation Survey: Report on New Products.* Weston, CT : EFO Limited.

238. Group., S. (1995). *Chaos.* Retrieved from http://standishgroup.com/visitor/chaos.htm

239. Grover, V., Jeong, S., Kettinger, W., &Teng, J. (1995). The Implementation of Business Process Reengineering. *Journal of Management Information Systems, 12, 1*, 109-144.

240. Grundy, T. (2000). Strategic Project Management and Strategic Behaviour. *International Journal of Project Management, Vol 18, No.2*, 93-104.

241. Gundling, E., Hogan., T., & Cvitkovich, K. (2011). *What is global leadership?: 10 behaviors that define great global leaders.* Boston: Nicholas Brealey.

242. Gurung, A., & Prater, E. (2006). A research framework for the impact of cultural differences on IT outsourcing. *Journal of Global Information Technology Management, 9 (1),* 24–43.

243. H., K. (2000.). *Applied project management. Best practices on implementation.* New York : John Wiley.

244. Hackman, J. (1987). The design of work teams. In J. Lorsch, *Handbook of organizational behavior* (pp. 315–342). Englewood Cliffs, NJ: : Prentice-Hall.

245. Hahn, G., Hill, W., Hoerl, R., &Zinkgraf, S. (Aug., 1999). The Impact of Six Sigma Improvement-A Glimpse into the Future of Statistics. *The American Statistician, Vol. 53, No. 3,* 208-215. [Pdf] Available at: <http://www.jstor.org/stable/pdfplus/2686099.pdf> [Accessed 26 January 2012].

246. Hamel, G., & Prahalad, C. (1994). *Competing for the Future.* Boston. : Harvard Business School Press.

247. Hammer, M., & Champy, J. (1993). *Reengineering the Corporation: A Manifesto for Business Revolution.* London: Nicholas Brearley Publishing.

248. Haverila, M., & Fehr, K. (2016). The impact of product superiority on customer satisfaction in project management. *International Journal of Project Management 34,* 570–583.

249. Heeks, R., Krishna, S., Nicholson, B., & Sahay, S. (2001). Synching or sinking: Global software outsourcing relatioships. *IEEE software,* 54-60.

250. Heeks, R., Krishna, S., Nicholson, B., &Sahay, S. (2001). Synching or sinking: Global software outsourcing relationships. *IEEE software,* 54-60.

251. Henderson, K., & Evans, J. (2000). Successful implementation of Six Sigma: benchmarking General Electric Company. *Benchmarking: An International Journal,* 260-282. Pdf] Available at: <http://0-www.emeraldinsight.com.pugwash.lib.warwick.ac.uk/journals. htm?issn=1463-5771&volume=7&issue=4&articleid=843007&sho

w=pdf&PHPSESSID=c1vjs1mldlnl3jmm20uce1j9j0> [Accessed 26 January 2012].

252. Herroelen, W. (2005). Project scheduling: Theory and practice. *Production and Operations Management 14(4)*, 413-432.

253. Hersey, P., Blanchard, K., & Johnson, D. (1988). *Management of Organizational Behaviour, 9th Editon*. New Jersey: Prentice Hall.

254. Hersy, P., & Blanchard, K. (2001). *Management of Organisational Behaviour*. London: Prentice- Hall.

255. Hidding, G., & Nicholas, J. (2014). Reducing I.T. Project Management Failures: Early Empirical Results. *47th Hawaii International Conference on System Science*.

256. Hillson, D. (2011). Extending the Risk Process to Manage Opportunities. *Proc. Fourth European Project Management Conf.*

257. Hinds, P., & Mortensen, M. (2005). Understanding conflict in geographically distributed teams: The moderating effects of shared identity, shared context, and spontaneous communication. *Organization Science, 16 (3)*, 290–307.

258. Hoerl, R., & Gardner, M. (2010). Lean Six Sigma, creativity, and innovation. *International Journal of Lean Six Sigma, Volume: 1 Issue: 1.*

259. Hofstede, g. (1980). *Cultural consequences: International differences in work-related values*. Beverly Hills, CA:: Sage.

260. Hofstede, G. (1980). Culture's consequences: International differences in work-related values. Beverly Hills, CA: Sage.

261. Hou, J.-L. a.-H. (2006). Quantitative Performance Evaluation of RFID Applications in the Supply Chain of the Printing Industry. *Industrial Management and Data Systems, 106(1)*, 96-120.

262. Howell, J., & Avolio, B. (1993). 'Transformational leadership, transactional leadership, locus of control, and support for innovation: key predictors of consolidated-business-unit performance. *Journal of Applied Psychology, 78*, 891–902.

263. Huang, Z., Poli, M., & Mithiborwala, H. (August 2-6 2009). Project Strategy: Success Themes for Strategic Projects. *PICMET 2009 Proceedings*. Portland, Oregon USA.

264. Hulett, D. (2006). Decision Tree Analysis for the Risk Averse Organization. *Presented at the PMI EMEA Congress in Madrid.*

265. Hur, Y., Berg, P., & Wilderom, C. (2011). Transformational leadership as a mediator between emotional intelligence and team outcomes. *The Leadership Quarterly 22*, 591–603.

266. Hussey, J., & Hussey, R. (1997). *Business Research: A practical guide for graduates and post-graduate students.* Basingstoke: Palgrave. Şimandan, M. (2010). Methodology and Method in Scientific Research. *Journal Plus Education Vol VI (2010), No. 2*, 73-80.

267. Hwang, B.-G., & Low, L. (2012). Construction project change management in Singapore: Status, importance and impact. *International Journal of Project Management 30*, 817–826.

268. Ilies, R., Morgeson, F., & Nahrgang, J. (2005). Authentic leadership and eudaemonic well-being: Understanding leader–follower outcomes. *The Leadership Quarterly, Volume 16, Issue 3*, 373–394.

269. Indrawati, S., & Ridwansyah, M. (2015). Manufacturing Continuous Improvement Using Lean Six Sigma: An Iron Ores Industry Case Application, Industrial Engineering and Service Science. *Procedia Manufacturing 4*, 528 – 534.

270. Introna, L., & Whitley, E. (1997). Against method-ism: exploring the limits of. *Information Technology & People, Vol 10, No 1*, 31-45.

271. Isaac, S., &Navon, R. (2008). Feasibility study of an automated tool for identifying the implications of changes in construction projects. *Journal of Construction Engineering and Management 134 (2)*, 139–145.

272. Ishikawa, K. (1985). *What is Total Quality Control? the Japanese Way.* Englewood Cliffs, NJ: Prentice-Hall.

273. Ivory, C. (2005). Can Project Management learn anything from studies of failure in Complex Systems? *Project Management Journal*

274. Jablin, F., Cude, R., House, A., J., L., & Roth, N. (1994). Communication competence in organizations: Conceptualizations and comparison across multiple levels of analysis. In L. Thayer, & G. Barnett, *Emerging Perspectives in Organizational Communication Vol. 4, pp.* (pp. 114-140). Norwood, NJ: Ablex.

275. Jamison, S., Cardarelli, M., & Hanley, S. (2007). *Essential sharepoint® 2007: delivering high-impact collaboration.* Addison-Wesley Professional.

276. Jani, A. (2011). Escalation of commitment in troubled IT projects: Influence of project risk factors and self-efficacy on the perception of risk and the commitment to a failing project. *International Journal of Project Management, Vol. 29, No. 7*, 93.

277. Jankowicz, A. (2005). *Business Research Projects - Fourth Edition.* London: Thomas Learning.

278. Janssen, M., van der Voort, H., & van Veenstra, A. (2014). Failure of large transformation projects from the viewpoint of complex adaptive systems- Management principles for dealing with project dynamics. *Information System frontiers.*

279. Jarvenpaa, S., & Leidner, D. (1999). Communication and trust in global virtual teams. *Organization Science, 10 (6)*, 791–815.

280. Jarvenpaa, S., Knoll, K., & Leidner, D. (1998). Is anybody out there? Antecedents of trust in global virtual teams. *Journal of Management Information Systems, 14*, 29-64.

281. Javidan, M., Dorfman, P., Sully de Luque, M., & House, R. (2006). In the eye of the beholder:Cross-cultural lessons in leadership from project. *Academy of Management Perspectives, 20*, 67–90.

282. Jing-wu, C., & Xian, Z. (2010). PRINCE2 Based Project Management Maturity Model. *IEEE.*

283. Johansson, C., D Miller, V., &Hamrin, S. (2011). Communicative Theories, Concepts, and Central Communication Behaviour. *Research Project, Department of Media and Communication, Mid Sweden, University.*

284. Johnson, W., & Luo, C. (2008). NPD project timeliness: the project-level impact of early engineering effort and customer involvement. *International Journal of Product Development - Volume 6, Number 2/2008*, 160-176.

285. Jones, C. (April 2008). Software Tracking: The Last Defense Against Failure. *CROSSTALK The Journal of Defense Software Engineering.*

286. Jones, C., & Lichtenstein, B. (2008). Temporary inter-organizational projects: How temporal and social embeddedness enhance coordination and manage uncertainty. *The Oxford Handbook of Inter-Organizational Relations*, 231-255.

287. JR, T. (1993). *The handbook of project-based management.* England: McGraw-Hill.

288. Judge, T., Bono, J., Ilies, R., & Gerhardt, M. (2002). Personality and Leadership: A Qualitative and Quantitative Review. *Journal of Applied Psychology, 87*, 765–780.

289. Jugdev, K. (2003). *Jugdev, K. (2003). Developing and sustaining project management as a strategic asset: A multiple case study using the resource-based view (Ph.D. dissertation).* Alberta, Canada: University of Calgary.

290. Jugdev, K., & Muller, R. (2005). A retrospective look at our evolving understanding of project success. *Project Management Journal, Vol. 36 No. 4*, pp. 19-31. [PDF], Available at <http://www.iei.liu.se/fek/svp/723g18/articles_and_papers/1.107461/JugdevandMuller 2005PMJ.pdf> Accessed on [14 June 2011]

291. Jurison, J. (1999). SOFTWARE PROJECT MANAGEMENT. *Communications of AIS Volume 2, Article 17.*

292. K. Molokken-Ostvold, & M. Jorgensen. (Sept. 2005). A comparison of software project overruns - flexible versus sequential development models. *IEEE Transactions on Software Engineering (Volume:31, Issue: 9)*, 754 - 766.

293. Kandemir, D., Calantone, R., & Garcia, R. (2006). An exploration of organizational factors in new product development success. *Kandemir, D. journal of business and industrial marketing. V. 21. No. 5*, 300.

294. Kanter, R. (1984). *The Change Masters. London: Unwin Hyman.* London: Unwin Hyman.

295. Kanter, J., & Walsh, J. (2004). Toward more successful project management. *Information System Management*, 16-21.

296. Kaplan, R., & Norton, D. (1996). *The balanced scorecard. Translating strategy into action.* Cambridge, Mass: Harvard Business School.

297. Kappelmana, L., McKeemanb, R., & Zhan, L. (2006). Early Warning Signs of it Project Failure: The Dominant Dozen. *Information Systems Management Volume 23, Issue 4*, 31-36.

298. Karlsen, J. (2002). Project stakeholder management. 14(4). *Eng Manage J*, 19–24.

299. Kärnä, S. (2014). Analysing customer satisfaction and quality in construction—the case of public and private customers. *Nordic Journal Of Surveying and Real Estate Research 2*, 67-80.

300. Kaur, R., & Sengupta, D. (February 2012). Software Process Models and Analysis on Failure of Software Development Projects. *IJSER, Volume 2, Issue 2.*

301. Keegan, A., & Den Hartog, D. (2004). Transformational leadership in a project-based environment: a comparative study of the leadership styles of project managers and line managers. *International Journal of Project Management, Vol. 22 No. 8,* 609-17.

302. Keil, M., Cule, P., Lyytinen, K., & Schmidt, R. (Nov. 1998). A framework for identifying software project risks. *Communications of the ACM Volume 41 Issue 11,* 76-83.

303. Keizer, J., &Halman, J. (2009). Risks in major innovation projects, a multiple case study within a world's leading company in the fast-moving consumer goods. *International Journal of Technology Management, Vol. 48, No. 4,* 499-517.

304. Keller, R. (1992). Transformational leadership and the performance of research and development. *Journal of Management, Vol. 18 No. 3,* 489-501.

305. Kendrick, T. (2012). Results Without Authority: Controlling a Project When the Team Doesn't Report to You -- A Project Manager's Guide. New York: AMACOM.

306. Kerr, S., & Jermier, J. (1978). Substitutes for leadership: Their meaning and measurement. *Organisational Behaviour and Human Performance,* 375-403.

307. Kertzner, H. (2000). Applied Project Management: Best Practices on Implementation. New York: Wiley.

308. Kerzner, H. (1987). In search of excellence in project management. *Journal of Systems Management, Vol. 38 No. 2,* 30-9.

309. Kerzner, H. (2009). Project Management - A systematic Approach to Planning, Scheduling, and Controlling. Hoboken, New Jersey: John Wiley & Sons.

310. Kerzner, H. (2010). Project Management Best Practises - Achieving Global Excellence. Second Edition. New Jersey: John Wiley & Sons.

311. Kerzner, H., &Belack, C. (2010). *Managing Complex Projects.* Hoboken, New Jersey: John Wiley &Sons.Kerzner, H. (2009). *Project Management - Case Studies. Third Edition.* New York: John Wiley and Sons.

312. Keyes, J. (2010). Implementing the Project Management Balanced Scorecard. Boca Raton, FL: CRC Press, Inc.

313. Khan, S., & Niazi, M. (2012). Critical challenges in offshore software development outsourcing: an empirical study. *International IASTED Conference on Software Engineering SE 2012, Greece.*

314. Killen, C., Hunt, R., & Kleinschmidt, E. (2008). Project portfolio management for product innovation. *International Journal of Quality & Reliability Management, 25(1)*, 24-38.

315. King, N. (1998). Template Analysis. In C. Cassell, & G. Symon, *Qualitative methods and analysis in organizational research* (pp. 118-134). London: Sage.

316. King, N. (2004). Using templates in the thematic analysis of text. In C. Cassell, & G. Symon., *Essential guide to qualitative methods in organizational research* (pp. 256-270). London: Sage.

317. King, N. (2012). Being creative around health : participative methodologies in critical community psychology. In C. Horrocks, & S. Johnson, *Advances in Health Psychology: Critical Approaches.* London: Palgrave Macmillan.

318. King, N., Carroll, C., Newton, P., & Dornan, T. (2002). "You can't Cure it so you have to Endure it": The Experience of Adaptation to Diabetic Renal Disease. *Qualitative Health Research.*

319. King, R. (2005). Research strategy. Thirteen courses on Research Strategy. Iaşi: Editura Polirom.

320. Kirkpatrick, S., & Locke, E. (1996). Direct and indirect effects of three core charismatic leadership components on performance and attitudes. *Journal of Applied Psychology. V. 81., No. 1.*, 36.

321. Kleindorfer, P., &Saad, G. (2005). Managing disruption risks in supply chains. *Production and Operations Management, Vol. 14, No. 1*, 53- 68.

322. Kloppenborg, T., Shriberg, A., & Ventatraman, J. (2003). *Project Leadership*. Vienna: Management Concepts.

323. Kochan, T., & Rubinstein, S. (2000). Toward a stakeholder theory of the firm. *The Saturn partnership. Organization Science 11(4)*, 367–386.

324. Koene, B., Vogelaar, A., & Soeters, J. (2002). Leadership effects on organizational climate and financial performance: Local leadership effect in chain organizations. *The Leadership Quarterly, 13,* 193–215.

325. Kolltveit, B., Karlsen, J., & Gronhaug, K. (1997). Perspective on Project Management, *International Journal of Project Management, Vol. 25,* 3-9.

326. Koo, C., Hong, T., Hyun, C., & Koo, K. (2010). A CBR-based hybrid model for predicting a construction duration and cost based on project characteristics in multi-family housing projects. *Canadian Journal of Civil Engineering, 37(5),* 739-752.

327. Koonce, L., Anderson, U., &Marchant, G. (1995). Justification of decisions in Auditing. *Journal of Accounting Research, 33,* 369-384.

328. Koskela L, & Howell, G. (2002). The underlying theory of project management is obsolete. *Project Management Institute.*

329. Kostelac, D., Vukomanović, M., & Ikonić, M. (2012). INTEGRATING ENTERPRISE PROJECT PORTFOLIO MANAGEMENT WITH THE BALANCED SCORECARD: A CASE FROM THE PHARMACEUTICAL INDUSTRY. *Technical Gazette 19, 2,* 303-316.

330. Kotler, J. (1990). A Force of Change: How leadership Differs from Management. New York: Free Press.

331. Kotler, P. (1990). What leaders really do. 68(3),. *Harvard Business Review,* 103–111.

332. Kozlowski, S., & Ilgen, D. (2006). Enhancing the Effectiveness of Work Groups and Teams. *Psychological Science in the Public Interest, 7(3),* 77–124.

333. Krane, H., Olsson, N., & Rolstadås, A. (2012). How Project Manager– Project Owner Interaction Can Work Within and Influence Project Risk Management. *Project Management Journal. Volume 43, Issue 2.*

334. Kravchenko, M. (2012). The Employee Engagement Mindset: The Six Drivers for Tapping into the Hidden Potential of Everyone in Your Company. *Master Thesis, Department of Development and Planning, Alborg University.*

335. Krippendorff., K. (2003.). Content Analysis: An Introduction to Its Methodology., 2nd edition. London, UK: Sage Publications.

336. Kuen, C., & Zailani, S. (June 2012). Critical Factors in Successful New Product Development: An Empirical Study of Malaysian Manufacturing Companies. *International Journal of Management Vol. 29 No. 2 Part 1,* 429 -449. [PDF], Available at <http:// encore.lib.warwick.ac.uk:50080/ebsco-web/bsi/pdfviewer/ pdfviewer?sid=a518e97a-4c10-4bba-a581-12d4378e2d04%40sessio nmgr112&vid=2&hid=108> Accessed on [14 June 2011]

337. Kumar, M., Antony, J., Madu, C., Montgomery, D., & Park, S. (2008). Common myths of Six Sigma demystified. *International Journal of Quality & Reliability Management Vol. 25 Iss: 8,* 878 - 895. [Pdf] Available at: <http://www.emeraldinsight.com/journals. htm?issn=0265-671X&volume=25&issue=8&articleid=1742454&s how=pdf> [Accessed 26 January 2012].

338. Kumar, R. (2011). Research methodology : a step-by-step guide for beginners. 3rd ed. London: SAGE.

339. Kumar, V., Maheshwari, B., & Kumar, U. (2003.). An investigation of critical management issues in ERP implementation: Empirical evidence from Canadian organizations. Technovation 23, 793–807.

340. Kume, H., & Loftus, J. (1985). *Statistical Methods for Quality Improvement.* Tokyo: AOTS, The Association for Overseas Technical.

341. Kwak, Y., & Stoddard, J. (2004). Project risk management: lessons learned from software. *Technovation 24,* 915–920.

342. Kwak, Y. (2003). *The Story of Managing Projects,* Carayannis: Quorum Books.

343. Kwan, T., & Leung, H. (2007). Improving Risk Management Practices for IT Projects. *ACST'07 Proceedings of the third conference on IASTED International Conference: Advances in Computer Science and Technology,* 443-448.

344. Kwan, T., & Leung, H. (2011). A Risk Management Methodology for Project Risk Dependencies. *IEEE TRANSACTIONS ON SOFTWARE ENGINEERING, VOL. 37, NO. 5,* 635-648.

345. Lacey, H. (2012). Powerful Win Win Solutions: A Practical Toolkit for Resolving Conflict in the Workplace. Bloomington, IN: AuthorHouse.

346. Lamas, P., & Demeulemeester, E. (2015). A purely proactive scheduling procedure for the resource constrained project scheduling problem with stochastic activity durations. *Journal of Scheduling.*

347. Larson., E., & Gobeli, D. (May 1989). Significance of project management structure on development success. *IEEE Transactions onEngineering Management, Volume 36, Issue 2.*

348. Latham, G. (2000). *Cultural awareness and cross cultural communication: Combat multipliers for leaders in the next millennium.* Leavenworth, KS: Army Command and General Staff College Fort School of Advanced Military Studies.

349. Lawler, E., Mohrman, S., & Ledford, G. (1995). *Creating high-performance organizations: Practices and results of employee involvement and total quality management in Fortune 1000 companies.* San Francisco, CA: Jossey-Bass.

350. LCI. (2008). Lean Construction Opportunities Ideas Practices. SPEECH PRESENTED TO THE CASCADIA LCI "INTRODUCTION TO LEAN DESIGN" WORKSHOP

351. Lechler, T., Ronen, B., &Stohr, E. (2005). Critical Chain: A New Project Management Paradigm or Old Wine in New Bottles? *Engineering Management Journal.* [Pdf] Available at: <http://boazronen.org/PDF/Critical%20Chain%20-%20A%20New%20Project%20Management%20Paradigm%20or%20Old%20Wine%20in%20New%20Bottles.pdf> [Accessed 26 January 2012].

352. Lee-Kelley, L., &Sankey, T. (2007). Global virtual teams for value creation and project success: A case study. *International Journal of Project Management 26 (2008),* 51–62.

353. Legris, P., &Collerette, P. (2006). Roadmap for it project implementation - Integrating stakeholders and change. *Project Management Journal.*

354. Lehtinen, T., Mäntylä, M., & Vanhan, J. (2014). Perceived causes of software project failures – An analysis of their relationships. *Information and Software Technology 56,* 623–643.

355. Leinonen, P. (2005). Conceptualizing the Awareness of Collaboration: A Qualitative Study of a Global Virtual Team. *Computer Supported Cooperative Work 14:* 301–322.

356. Lenfle, S. (2008). Exploration and project management. *International Journal of Project Management, 28(5)*, 469-478.

357. Lenfle, S., & Loch, C. (2010). Lost roots: How project management came to emphasize control over flexibility and novelty. *California Management Review, 53(1)*, 32-55.

358. Lenfle, S., & Loch, C. (2010). Lost Roots: How Project Management Came to Emphasize Control Over Flexibility and Novelty. *California Management Review, Vol. 53 No. 1*, 32-55.

359. Leus, R. (2003). *The generation of stable project plans. Ph.D. thesis.* KU Leuven.

360. Li, H., & Womer, K. (2009). Scheduling projects with multi-skilled personnel by a hybrid MILP/CP benders decomposition algorithm. *Journal of Scheduling, 12*, 281–298.

361. Lia, T., Nga, S., & Skitmo, M. (January 2013). Evaluating stakeholder satisfaction during public participation in major infrastructure and construction projects: A fuzzy approach. *Automation in Construction, Volume 29*, 123–135.

362. Lianying, Z., Jing, H., &Xinxing, Z. (2012). The Project Management Maturity Model and Application Based on PRINCE2. *Procedia Engineering*, 3691 – 3697. PDF], Available at < http://www.sciencedirect.com/science/article/pii/S1877705812005644> Accessed on [15 May, 2012]

363. Liker, J. (2004). The Toyota Way: 14 Management Principles from the World's Greatest Manufacturer. New York: Mc-Graw Hill.

364. Liker, J., & Morgan, J. (2006). The Toyota Way in Services: The Case of Lean Product Development. *Academy of Management Perspectives.*

365. Lindermana, K., Schroeder, R., Zaheer, S., Liedtkeb, C., &Choo, A. (2004). Integrating quality management practices with knowledge creation processes. *Journal of Operations Management 22 (2004) 589–607*, 589–607[Pdf] Available at: <http://140.118.1.131/teaching/2009%20KM/paper%202009%5CIntegrating%20quality%20management%20practices%20with%20knowledge%20creation%20processes.pdf> [Accessed 26 January 2012].

366. Ling, F., Low, S., Wang, S., & Lim, H. (2009). Key project management practices affecting Singaporean firms' project performance in China. *International Journal of Project Management 27*, 59-71.

367. Liu, J., Derzsi, Z., Raus, M., &Kipp, A. (2008). eGovernment Project Evaluation: An Integrated Framework. *Electronic Government.*

368. Liu, J.-C., Chen, V., Chan, C.-L., & Lie, T. (2008). The impact of software process standardization on software flexibility and project management performance:control theory perspective. *Information and Software Technology 50 (9–10)*, 889–896.

369. Lo, C.-H. (2011). Better Project Management Practice in East Asia Using Revised Transformational Leadership Theories. *PhD. Thesis, University of Maryland University College.*

370. Lock, D. (2007). *The Essentials of Project Management, 3rd Edition.* London: Gower Publishing.

371. Locke, A., Alavi, M., & Wagner, J. (1997). Participation in decision making: an information exchange. In G. Gerris, *Research in Personnel and Human Resource Management.* Greenwich, CT.: JAI Press.

372. Loewe, P., &Dominiquini, J. (2006). Overcoming the barriers to effective. *STRATEGY & LEADERSHIP VOL. 34 NO. 1,* 24-31.

373. Lomas, C., Burke, M., & Page, C. (2008). Collaboration Tools. *Educause Learning Initiative*

374. Loo, R. (2002). Working towards best practices in project management- a Canadian study. *International Journal of Project Management,* 93-98.

375. Lundberg, G. (1942). Social Research: A Study of Methods of Gathering Data (2nd Edition). Monterey, CA: Brooks/Cole.

376. Lussier, R., & Achua, C. (2001). *Leadership: Theory, Application, Skill Building.* Cincinnati, OH: South-Western.

377. Luu, V., Kim, S.-Y., & Huynh, T.-A. (2008). Improving project management performance of large contractors. *International Journal of Project Management 26,* 758–769.

378. Lyons, N., &Wilker, M. (2012). Interactive Project Management: Pixels, People, and Process. New Riders.

379. Madsen, S. (2012). *Project Management Coaching Workbook.* Tysons Corner, VA: Management Concepts.

380. Mahanti, R., & Antony, J. (2009). Six Sigma in the Indian software industry: some observations and results from a pilot survey. *The TQM Journal,* 549 - 564. [Pdf] Available at: <http://www.emeraldinsight.

com/journals.htm?issn=1754-2731&volume=21&issue=6&articleid= 1817318&show=pdf> [Accessed 26 January 2012].

381. Malone, T. (1997). Is Empowerment Just a Fad? *Sloan Management Review*.

382. Malone, T. (2004). Bringing the Market Inside. *Harvard Business Review*.

383. MarketWatch (2012). Reliance Industries may invest $1B in aerospace. [Web], Available at <http://www.marketwatch.com/ story/reliance-industries-may-invest-1b-in-aerospace-2012-07-29> Accessed on [19 August 2012]

384. Marshall, C., & Rossman, G. (2006). *Designing Qualitative Research, 4th Edition*. Thousand Oaks: Sage.

385. Martin, A., & Bal, V. (2006). *The state of teams*. Greensboro, NC: Center for Creative Leadership.

386. Martin, C. (1976). *Project Management*. New York: Amaco.

387. Mascia, S. (2012). Project Psychology - Using Psychological Models and Techniques to Create a Successful Project. Farnham: Gower Publishing Limited.

388. MAST, J. (2006). Six Sigma and Competitive Advantage. *Total Quality Management, Vol. 17, No. 4*, 455–464. [Pdf] Available at: <http://mail.ibisuva.nl/assets/files/demast2006b.pdf> [Accessed 26 January 2012].

389. Masticola, S. (2007). A Simple Estimate of the Cost of Software Project Failures and the Breakeven Effectiveness of a Project Risk Management. *First International Workshop on the Economics of Software and Computation (ESC'07)*.

390. Mathur, P. (2009). Managing projects utilizing self-managed teams. *MSc Dissertation - University of Massachusetts*.

391. Matlack, C. (2006, October 5). *Airbus: First blame the software*. Retrieved September 25, 2008, from Businessweek Online: http://www.businessweek. com/globalbiz/content/oct2006/ gb20061005_846432.htm?campaign_id=rss_daily

392. May, L. (1988). Major causes of software project failures. *Crosstalk. Volume 11, Issue 6*, 9-12.

393. McCartney, W., & Campbell, C. (2006). Leadership, management, and derailment: A model of individual success and failure. *Leadership & Organization Development Journal, Vol. 27 Iss: 3*, 190 - 202.
394. McElroy, B., & Mills C., B. (2003). Managing stakeholders. In R. Turner, *People in Project Management.; 2003.* (pp. 99–118). Aldershot: Gower.
395. McFarlan, F. W. (1981). Portfolio approach to information systems. *Harvard Business Review, 59(5)*, 142–150.
396. McGrath, J. (1984). *Groups: Interaction and performance.* Englewood Cliffs, NJ: Prentice-Hall.
397. Mckinsey& Company, (2009). Building India- Accelerating Infrastructure Projects. *Infrastructure Practise.* [Online], Available at <http://www.mckinsey.com/locations/india/mckinseyonindia/pdf/Building_India_Executive_Summary_Media_120809.pdf> Accessed on [02 Feb 2011]
398. McLaughlin, L. (May-June 2003). An eye on India: outsourcing debate continues. *IEEE Software, vol. 20, no. 3*, 114-117.
399. McLeod, L., & MacDonell, S. (October 2011). Factors that affect software systems development project outcomes: A survey of research. *ACM Computing Surveys (CSUR) Volume 43 Issue 4 Article No. 24.*
400. Means, J., & Adams, T. (2005). *Facilitating the Project Lifecycle.* San Francisco: Josey-Bass.
401. Mendenhall, M., Osland, J., Bird, A., Oddou, G., & Maznevski, M. (2008). *leadership: Research, practice and development.* New York: Routledge.
402. Mengesha, W. (2004:45). Performances for Public Construction Projects in Developing Countries: Federal Road & Educational Building Projects in Ethiopia. *Norwegian University of Science and Technology: Doctoral Thesis.*
403. Meredith, J., & Mantel, S. (2012). *Project Management - A Managerial Approach. Eighth Edition.* Hoboken, NJ: John Wiley & Sons.
404. Meyer, A., Loch, C., & Pich, M. (2002). Managing project uncertainty: from variation to chaos. *MIT SLOAN MANAGEMENT REVIEW WINTER.*

405. Midler, C., & Navarre, C. (2004). Project management in automotive industry. In P. Morris, & J. Pinto, *The Wiley Guide to management projects* (pp. 1368-1388). Hoboken, NJ: Wiley.

406. Midler, C., Killen, C., & Kock, A. (2016). Project and Innovation Management: Bridging Contemporary Trends in Theory and Practice. *Project Management Journal Volume 47, Issue 2*, 3-7.

407. Mignerat, M., &Rivard, S. (2012). The institutionalization of information system project. *Information and Organization 22*, 125-153.

408. Milgrom, P., & Roberts, J. (1992). *Economics, organization, and management.* Englewood Cliffs, NJ: Prentice-Hall.

409. Miller, K., &Monge, P. (1986). Participation, satisfaction, and productivity:A meta-analytic review. *Academy of Management Journal, 29*, 727-753.

410. Miller, R. (2015). The migration of methodologies for Project Management research. *Project Management Journal 46(2)*, 3-5.

411. Miller, R., & Lessard, D. (2001). Understanding and managing risks in large engineering projects. *International Journal of Project Management Volume 19, Issue 8*, 437–443.

412. Milosevic, D., &Patanakul, P. (2004). Standardized project management may increase development project success. *International Journal of Project Management. Vol. 23*, 181-192.

413. Milosevic, D., &Patanakul, P. (2010). Standardized project management may increase management and its success - a conceptual framework. *International Journal of Project Management 28 (8)*, 807–817.

414. MindTools.com. (2012). Team Management Skills. Retrieved August 14, 2012, from MindTools.com: http://www.mindtools.com/pages/article/newTMM_92.htm

415. Minevich, M., & Richter, F. (2005). *Global outsourcing report.*

416. Mintzberg, H. (1983.). *Power in and around organizations.* Englewood Cliffs, NJ: Prentice-Hall.

417. Mintzberg, H. (1985). The organization as political arena. *Journal of Management Studies, 22:* 133–154.

418. Mitchell, R., Agle, B., & Wood, D. (1997). Toward a theory of stakeholder identification and salience: Defining the principle of who and what really counts. *Academy of Management Review, 22(4)*, 853–888.

419. Miyamoto, M. (2015). Leadership in ITC project management in Japan. *Procedia Computer Science Volume 64*, 32-39.

420. Molhanec, M. (2010). Agile Project Management Framework. *33rd Int. Spring Seminar on Electronics Technology.*

421. Moløkken-Østvold, K., & Jørgensen, M. (2005). A comparison of software project overruns – flexible versus sequential development models. *IEEE Trans. Softw. Eng. 31*, 754-766.

422. Moran, R., & Youngdahl, W. (2008). Leading Global Projects : For Professional and Accidental Project Leaders. London: Elsevier

423. Moran, R., Harris, P., & Moran, S. (2010). *Managing cultural differences: Global leadership ship strategies for cross-cultural business success (8th ed.).* Oxford, England: Butterworth-Heinemann.

424. Moran, R., Harris, P., & Moran, S. (2011). Managing Cultural Differences - Leadership Skills and Strategies for Working in a Global world - Eight Edition. Oxford: Elsevier.

425. Morgan, J., & Liker, J. (2006). The Toyota Product Development System : Integrating People, Process, and Technology. NY: Integrating People, Process, and Technology.

426. Morris, P. (1986). Project Management: a view from Oxford. *International Journal or Construction Management and Technology,* 36-52.

427. Morris, P. (ed). *The Project Management, paperback ed.* London: Thomas Telford.

428. Morris, P. W. (2004). The Validity of Knowledge in Project Management and the Challenge of Learning and Competency Development. In P. W. Morris, & J. K. Pinto, *The Wiley Guide to Managing Projects* (pp. 1137 - 1149). Hoboken, New Jersey.: John Wiley & Sons, Inc.

429. Morris, P., & Hough, G. (1987). *The Anatomy of Major Projects: A Study of the Reality of Project Management.* Chichester: John Wiley & Sons.

430. Morris, P., & Pinto, J. (2007). *Project Organisation & Project Management Competencies.* New Jersey: John Wiley & Sons.

431. Moscovici, S., & Buschini, F. (2007). *The methodology of socio-human sciences.* Iași: Editura Polirom.

432. Moser, R., von der Gracht, H., & Gnatzy, T. (2010). The Indian Aerospace Industry 2019: An Analysis of the Political, Technological and Economic Conditions. Wiesbaden: BrainNet Supply Management Group AG.

433. Motawa, I., Anumba, C., Lee, S., & Peña-Mora, F. (2007.). An integrated system for change management in construction. *Automation in Construction 16 (3)*, 368–377.

434. Mu¨ller, R., & Turner, R. (2010). Leadership competency profiles of successful project managers. *International Journal of Project Management 28,* 437–448.

435. Muller, R. (2001). BUFFERS & RISK: Critical Chain Project Management. International Conference On Software Management & Applications of Software Measurement.

436. Muller, R., & Turner, J. (2010). Project-Oriented Leadership - Advances in Project Management. Surrey: Gower Publishing.

437. Mumford, E. (1981). Participative systems design: Structure and method. *Systems, Obkective, Solutions V. 1, No -1,* 5-19.

438. Munns, A., & Bjeirmi, B. (February 1996). "The Role of Project Management in Achieving Project Success." *International Journal of Project Management, Vol. 14, No. 2,* pp. 81-M.

439. Murphy, D., Baker, B., & Fisher, D. (1974). Determinants of project success. *Project Management Journal*, 1215-8. [PDF], Available at <http://www.mendeley.com/research/determinants-construction-project-success/> Accessed on [15 May 2012]

440. Murphy, T. (2002). *Achieving Business Value from Technology: A Practical Guide for Today's Executive.* John Wiley & Sons.

441. Nadeem, M., Qureshia, M., Asim, M., Nadeem, M., &Mehmood, A. (2012). A New Teaching Model For The Subject Of Software Project Management. *Department of Computer Science, COMSATS Institute of Information Technology, Lahore.*

442. Naidoo, L., & Lord, R. (2008). Speech imagery and perceptions of charisma: The mediating role of positive affect. *The Leadership Quarterly Volume 19, Issue 3,* 283–296.

443. Nasina, J., & Nallam, S. (2016). Analysis of cost escalations in pharmaceutical projects. *International Journal of Managing Project in Business, Volume 9(2).*

444. Nasir, M., & Sahibuddin, S. (May 2011). Critical success factors for software projects: A comparative study. *Scientific Research and Essays Volume 6, Issue 10*, 2174-2186.

445. Newbold, R. (1998). *Project Management in the Fast Lane*. Miami: The St. Lucie Press.

446. Niazi, M., Mahmood, S., Alshayeb, M., Qureshi, A., Faisal, K., & Cerpa, N. (2016). Toward successful project management in global software development. *International Journal of Project Management 34*, 1553–1567.

447. Nicholas, J., &Steyn, H. (2008). Project Management for Business, Engineering and Technology - 3rd Edition. London: Butterworth-Heinemann.

448. Nicholson, B., & Sahay, S. (2001). Some political and cultural Issues in globalization of software development: Case experience from Britain and India. *Information and Organisation 11*, 25 - 43.

449. Nicholson, B., &Sahay, S. (2001). Some political and cultural Issues in globalization of software development: Case experience from Britain and India. *Information and Organisation 11*, 25 - 43.

450. Nidhraa, S., Yanamadalaa, M., Afzalb, W., & Torkara, R. (2013). Knowledge transfer challenges and mitigation strategies in global software development—a systematic literature review and industrial validation. *Int. J. Inf. Management -33*, 333-355.

451. Nidiffer, K., & Dolan, D. (2005). Evolving Distributed Project Management. *IEEE Software 22 (5)*, 63–72.

452. Nidumolu, S. (1996). Standardization, requirements uncertainty and software project performance. *Information Management 31 (3)*, 135–150.

453. Nixon, P. (2012). Leadership performance is significant to project success or failure: a critical analysis. *International Journal of Productivity and Performance Management. v. 61. no. 2., ISBN: 1741-0401*, 204 -.

454. Nixon, P., Harrington, M., & Parker, D. (2012). Leadership performance is significant to project success or failure: a critical analysis. *International Journal of Productivity and Performance Management, Vol. 61 Iss: 2*, 204 - 216. [PDF], Available at <http://0-www.emeraldinsight.com.pugwash.lib.warwick.ac.uk/journals.

htm?issn=1741-0401&volume=61&issue=2&articleid=17010521&show=pdf&PHPSESSID=7ghehpra1ie67upkn3c8sqltt7> Accessed on [14 June 2011]

455. Nokes, S., & Kelly, S. (2007). The Definitive Guide to Project Management - The Fast Track to Gettings the Job Done on Time and On Budget. Harlow, UK: Pearson Education.

456. Norton, D., & Kaplan, R. (1992). The balanced scorecard: measures that. *Harvard Business Review, 70, 1,* 71-79.

457. Note, M. (2016). *Project Management for Information Professionals.* Elsevier Ltd.

458. Nurkertamanda, D., & Wulandari, F. (2009). Failure Modes and Effects Analysis (FMEA) in Chitose Folding Chairs Product Yamato HAA. *Journal of Industrial Engineering, University of Diponegoro Vol. IV.*

459. O'Connor, M., & Reinborough, L. (May 1992). "Quality Projects in the 1990's: A Review of Past Projects and Future Trends". *Trends", International Journal of Project Management, Vol. 10, No.2,* 107-114.

460. O'LEARY, M., MORTENSEN, M., & WOOLLEY, A. (2011). Multiple team membership: A theoretical model of its effects on productivity and learning for individuals and teams. *Academy of Management Review, 36(3).*

461. O'Leary, T., & Williams, T. (2008). Making a difference? Evaluating an innovative approach to the project management Centre of Excellence in a UK government department. *International Journal of Project Management 26,* 556–565.

462. Office of Government Commerce. (2009). *Managing Successful Projects with PRINCE2,* The Stationary Office, Norwich, UK.

463. OGC. (2002). *Prince2.* London: Crown Copyright.

464. Olander, S. (2007). Stakeholder impact analysis in construction project management. *Construction Management and Economics 25,* 277–287.

465. Olanders, S., &Landin, A. (2005). Evaluation of stakeholder influence in the implementation of construction projects. *International Journal of Project Management.*

466. Oshri, I., Kotlarsky, J., & P. Willcocks, L. (2007). Global software development: Exploring socialization and face-to-face meetings in

distributed strategic projects. *Journal of Strategic Information Systems 16*, 25–49.

467. Oshri, I., Kotlarsky, J., & Willcocks, L. (2007). Global software development: Exploring socialization and face-to-face meetings in distributed strategic projects. *Journal of Strategic Information Systems, Vol.16 (No.1)*, 25-49.

468. P., D. (1999). *Winning in business through enterprise project management.* New York: American Management Association.

469. Pahal, D. (1999). Effective Leadership--An IT Perspective. *Online Journal of distance learning administration.*

470. Pamfilie, R., Petcu, A., & Draghici, M. (2012). The importance of leadership in driving a strategic Lean Six Sigma management. *International Strategic Management Conference, Procedia Social and Behavioral Sciences, 58*, 187-196.

471. Papke-Shields, K., Beise, C., & Quan, J. (2010). Do Project Managers Practice What They Preach, and Does it Matter to Project Success?". *International Journal of Project Management, Vol. 28*, 650–662.

472. Parka, J., Lee, J., Lee, H., & Truexb, D. (2012). Exploring the impact of communication effectiveness on service quality, trust and relationship commitment in IT services.g. *Int. J. Inf. Management.*

473. Parry, K. (2004). The Seven Sins and Seven Virtues of Leadership: Which Path Do We Follow. *CLME Leading Matters Symposium, 17 August 2005, Griffith University Ecocentre, Nathan, Australia.* Available at<http://griffith.edu.au/.../report-parry-leadershop.pdf> [Accessed on 18th June 2012]

474. Passenheim, O. (2009). *Project Management.*Ventus Publishing.

475. Pass, S., and B. Ronen, "Management by the Market Constraint in the Hi-Tech Industry," International Journal of Production Research, 41:4 (2003), pp. 713–724

476. Patanakul, P., & Shenhar, A. (February 2012). What Project Strategy Really Is: The Fundamental Building Block in Strategic Project Management. *Project Management Journal*

477. Patanakul, P., & Shenhar, A. (February 2012). What is really project strategy? The fundamental building block in strategic project management. *Project Management Journal.*

478. Paul, S., Samarah, I., Seetharaman, P., & Mykytyn, P. (2005). An empirical investigation of collaborative comflict management style in group support system-based global virtual teams. *Journal of Management Information Systems, 21 (3)*, 185–222.

479. Payne, J., &Turner, J. (1999). 1999. Company-wide project management: the planning and control of programmes of projects of different type. *International Journal of Project Management 17 (1)*, 55–59.

480. Penley, J., & Hawkins, B. (1985). Studying Interpersonal Communication in Organisation: A Leadership application. *Academy of Management Journal*, 309-380.

481. Pepper, M., & Spedding, T. (2010). The evolution of lean Six Sigma. *International Journal of Quality & Reliability Management*, 138-155.

482. Pereira, Z., & Requeijo, J. (2008). *Qualidade: Planeamento e Controlo Estatístico de Processos*. Lisboa: Prefácio.

483. Peters, T., & Waterman, R. (1984). *In Search of Excellence*. New York: Warner Books.

484. Phillips, E., & Pugh, D. (2006). *How to Get a Ph.D.: A Handbook for Students and Their Supervisors*. Berkshire: Open University Press

485. Phillips, J., Bothell, T., & Snead, G. (2002). *The Project Management Scorecard: Measuring the Success of Project Management Solutions*. Butterworth-Heinemann.

486. Pillai, A., Joshi, A., &Rao, K. (2002). Performance measurement of R&D projects in a multi-project, concurrent engineering environment. *International Journal of Project Management*, 165–177.

487. Pinto, J., & Slevin, D. (1988b). Critical success factors in effective project implementation. In D. Cleland, & W. King, *Project Management Handbook, 2nd ed.* (pp. 479-512.). New York, NY: Van Nostrand Reinhold. [PDF], Available at <http://gspa.grade.nida.ac.th/pdf/PA%20780%20(Pakorn)/8.Critical%20Success%20Factors%20in%20Effective%20Project%20Implementati.pdf > Accessed on [14 June, 2011]

488. Pinto, J. (1996). *Power and politics in project management*. USA: Project Management Institute.

489. Pinto, J. (2007). Project Management - Achieving Competitive Advantage - Second Edition. New Jersey: Pearson Education.

490. Pinto, J. (2010). Project Management - Achieving Competitive Advantage : Second Edition. Upper Saddle River: Pearson.

491. Pinto, J., & Kharbanda, O. (1995). Lessons for an Accidental Profession. *Bus Horizons*, 41–51.

492. PINTO, J., & PRESCOTT, J. (May 1990). PLANNING AND TACTICAL FACTORS IN THE PROJECT IMPLEMENTATION PROCESS. *Joumat of Management Studies 27:3*.

493. Pinto, J., & Slevin, D. (1987). Balancing Strategy and Tactics in Project Implementation. *Sloan Management Review*, 33-41.

494. Pinto, J., & Slevin, D. (1987). Critical factors in successful project implementation. *IEEE Transactions on Engineering Management*, 22-7.

495. Pinto, J., & Slevin, D. (1988). Critical Success Factors across the Project Life Cycle. *Project Management Journal, Vol. 19, No. 3*, 67-75.

496. Pinto, J., & Slevin, D. (1988a). Project success: definition and measurement techniques. *Project Management Journal, Vol. 19 No. 1*, 67-71. [PDF], Available at <http://gspa.grade.nida.ac.th/pdf/PA%20 780%20(Pakorn)/8.Critical%20Success%20Factors%20in%20 Effective%20Project%20Implementati.pdf > Accessed on [14 June, 2011]

497. PMI (2012). Sectors to watch. Aerospace and Defence. Outlook – Very Promising. [Web], Available at <http://www.pmi.org/ Professional-Development/~/media/PDF/Professional-Development/ PMN0112%20Sectors.ashx> Accessed on [19 August 2012]

498. PMI. (2008). A Guide to Project Management Body of Knowledge (PMBOK Guide) - Fourth Edition. PA: Project Management Institute.

499. PMI. (2010). *Project Management Practices in India*. Retrieved from http://www.indiaprwire.com/pressrelease/education/20100624 54558.htm. [Online], Available at <http://www.indiaprwire.com/ pressrelease/education/2010062454558.htm> accessed on [02 Feb 2011]

500. PMI. (2011). Taking Project Management Learning to Higher Level. *PMI Case Study*.

501. Podsakoff, P., Bommer, W., & Podsakoff, N. (2006). Relationships between leader reward and punishment behavior and subordinate

attitudes, perceptions, and behaviors: a meta-analytic review of existing and new research. *Organizational Behavior & Human Decision Processes, 99*, 113–42.

502. Poli, M., Mithiborwala, H., Shabbir, H., & Lalic, B. (August 2-6). Project Strategy: Selecting the Best Project Structure. *PICMET 2009 Proceedings*, 2009.

503. Post, J., Preston, L., & Sachs, S. (2005). *Redefining the Corporation Stakeholder Management and Organizational Wealth.* Stanford, CA.: Stanford University Press.

504. Powell, A., Piccoli, G., & Ives, B. (2004). Virtual teams: A review of current literature and direction for future research. *ACM SIGMIS Database, 35 (1)*, 6–36.

505. Prifling, M. (2010). EXPLORING LEADERSHIP STYLES IN SOFTWARE DEVELOPMENT PROJECTS. *E-Finance Lab, House of Finance, Goethe University Frankfurt, Germany.* Available at <http://www.pacis-net.org/file/2010/S03-04.pdf> Accessed on [4 August 2012]

506. Procaccino, J., Verner, J., Overmyer, S., & Darter, M. (15 January 2002). Case study: factors for early prediction of software development success. *Information and Software Technology, Volume 44, Issue 1*, 53–62.

507. Project Manager Institute-PMI. (2013). *A Guide to the Project Management Body of Knowledge, 5ᵗʰ ed.* Newtown Square, PA: Project Manager Institute, Inc.

508. Punch, K. (1998). Introduction to Social Research: Quantitative and Qualitative Approaches. London: Sage.

509. Punch, K. (2005). Introduction to Social Research: Quantitative and Qualitative approaches. 2ⁿᵈ Edition. London: Sage.

510. Purvanova, R., & Bono, J. (2009). Transformational leadership in context: Face-to-face and virtual teams. *The Leadership Quarterly 20*, 343–357.

511. Pusch, M. (2009). *The interculturally competent global leader. In D. K. Deardorff (Ed.), The Sage handbook of intercultural competence.* Thousand Oaks, CA: Sage.

512. PWC (PricewaterhouseCoopers) (2012). Changing Dynamics – Indian Aerospace Industry. [Web], Available at <http://www.pwc.

com/gx/en/aerospace-defence/pdf/india-aerospace.pdf> Accessed on [19 August 2012]

513. Qu, L., Ma, M., & Zhang, G. (2011). Waste Analysis of Lean Service. *International Conference on Management and Service Science (MASS)*, 1-4.

514. R, G. (1990). *Handbook of management by projects.* Vienna: Manz.

515. Rajanayakam, J. (2010). LEADERSHIP SHARING AMONG MULTI-VENDOR IT PROJECT LEADERS IN A MULTISOURCING ORGANIZATIONAL ENVIRONMENT. *Ph.D. Dissertation Organizational Leadership - Indiana Wesleyan University.*

516. Raz, T., Barnes, R., &Dvir, D. (2003). A critical look at critical chain project management. *Project Management Journal.* [Pdf] Available at: <http://www.pmir.com/html/pmdatabase/file/pmjournals/dec03.pdf#page=26> [Accessed 26 January 2012].

517. Rand, G.K., "Critical Chain," Journal of the Operational Research Society, 49:2 (1998), p. 181

518. Rand, G.K., "Critical Chain: The Theory of Constraints Applied to Project Management," International Journal of Project Management, 18:3 (2000), pp. 173–177

519. Redmill, F. (1987). Software Projects: Evolutionary vs. Big-bang Delivery, Wiley Series in Software Engineering Practice, Chichester: Wiley.

520. Remington, K. (2012). *Leading Complex Projects.* Surrey: Gower.

521. Research Councils UK. (2011). Integrity, Clarity and Good Management. *RCUK Policy and Code of Conduct on the Governance of Good Research Conduct.* [PDF], Available at <http://www.rcuk.ac.uk/documents/reviews/grc/goodresearchconductcode.pdf> Accessed on [4 August 2012]

522. Reyes, P. a. (2007). Radio frequency identification: Past, present, and future business applications. *International Journal of Integrated Supply Management, 3, 2*, 125-134.

523. Richardson, I., Casey, V., McCaffery, F., Burton, J., & Beecham, S. (2012). A Process Framework for Global Software Engineering Teams. *Information and Software Technology.*

524. Riggio, R., Riggio, H., Salinas, C., & Cole, E. (2003). The Role of Social and Emotional Communication Skills in Leader Emergence and Effectiveness. *Group Dynamics: Theory, Research, and Practice., Vol. 7, No. 2,* 83–103.

525. Robinson, H., & Richards, R. (2010). Critical Chain Project Management: Motivation & Overview. *IEEE.* [Pdf] Available at: <http://www.siriusconseils.com/_pdf/chainproject.pdf> [Accessed 26 January 2012].

526. Rodrigues, A. (May 2007). The Impact of Project Management on Business Performance in the Portuguese Market. *PM World Today - May 2007 (Vol. IX, Issue V).* [Pdf] Available at: <http://www.pmforum.org/library/RegionalReports/2007/PDFs/Rodrigues-5-07.pdf> [Accessed 26 January 2012].

527. Rothwell, W., Graber, J., & McCormick, N. (2012). *Lean but Agile: Rethink Workforce Planning and Gain a True Competitive Edge.* New York: AMA - American Management Association.

528. Rubin, R., Munz, D., & Bommer, W. (2005). Leading from within: the effects of emotion recognition and personality on transformational leadership behavior. *Academy of Management Journal 48*, 845-58.

529. Rule, D., & Galaskiewicz, J. (2000). Distribution of Knowledge, Group Network Structure, and Group Performance. *Management ScienceVol. 46, No. 5 (May 2000), pp. 612-625*, 612-625.

530. Ryan, R. (2008). Leadership Development - A Guide for HR and Training Professionals. Oxford: Butterworth-Heinemann.

531. S. I., T., Smith-Jentsch, K., &Behson, S. (1998). (1998). Training team leaders to facilitate team learning. In C.-B. Janis A. (Ed), & E. Salas, *Making decisions under stress: Implications for individual and team training (pp. 17-38)., xxiii, 447* (pp. 247–270). Washington, DC, US: American Psychological Association.

532. Salazar, M., & Salas, E. (2013). Reflections of cross-cultural collaboration science. *Journal of Organizational Behavior, 34 (6)*, 910–917.

533. Sandersa, D., & Hilda, C. (2000). SIX SIGMAON BUSINESS PROCESSES: COIVIMON ORGANIZATIONAL ISSUES. *Quality Engineering 12 (4)*, 603-610. Pdf] Available at: <

http://0-www.tandfonline.com.pugwash.lib.warwick.ac.uk/doi/abs/10.1080/08982110008962625> [Accessed 26 January 2012].

534. Sapolsky, H. (1972). *The Polaris System Development: Bureaucratic and Programmatic Success in Government.* Cambridge, Mass: Harvard University Press.

535. Sauser, B., Shenhar, A., & Hoffman, E. (2005). Identifying Differences in Space Programs. In T. Anderson, T. Daim, D. Kocaoglu, D. Milosevic, & C. Weber, *Technology Management: A Unifying Discipline for Melting the Boundaries,* (pp. 392–402.). Piscataway, NJ: IEEE Press.

536. Sayles, L., & Chandler, M. (1971). *Chandler, M.K., 1971. Managing Large Systems.* New York: The Free Press.

537. Sayles, L., & Chandler, M. (1971). *Managing Large Systems: Organisation for the Future.* New York: Harper & Row.

538. Schindlera, M., &Epplerb, M. ((2003)). Harvesting project knowledge: a review of project learning methods and success factors. *International Journal of Project Management 21,* 219–228.

539. Schriesheim, C., Castro, S., &Cogliser, C. (1999). Leader-member exchange (LMX) research: A comprehensive review of theory, measurement, and data-analytic practices. *Leadership Quarterly, 10,* 63–113.

540. Schroedera, R., Lindermana, K., Liedtkeb, C., &Chooc, A. (2008). Six Sigma: Definition and underlying theory.*Journal of Operations Management.* [Pdf] Available at: <http://www.iem.unifei.edu.br/turrioni/PosGraduacao/PQM07/Six_sigma_aula_10_e_11/six%20sigma%202.pdf> [Accessed 26 January 2012].

541. Schultz, R., Slevin, D., & Pinto, J. (1987). Strategy and Tactics in a Process Model of Project Implementation. *Interfaces 16:3,* 34-46.

542. Schwab, A., & Miner, A. (2008). Learning in hybrid-project systems: the effects of project performance on repeated collaboration. *Academy of Management Journal 51 (6),* 1117–1149.

543. Schwalbe, K. (2004). *Information Technology Project Management, 3rd ed.,.* Boston, MA.: Course Technology.

544. SEI. (Aug. 2006). *CMMI for Development, Version 1.2.* Carnegie Mellon Software Engineering Institute(SEI).

545. Sense, A. (2003). A model of the politics of project leader learning. *International Journal of Project Management, 2003.*

546. Shachaf, P. (2008). Cultural diversity and information and communication technology impacts on global virtual teams: An exploratory study. *Information & Management, 45 (2)*, 131–142.

547. Shamir, B., Arthur, M., & House, R. (1994). The rhetoric of charismatic leadership: A theoretical extension, a case study, and implications for research. *The Leadership Quarterly. Volume 5, Issue 1.*, 25–42.

548. Shehu Z, (2008). The framework for effective adoption and implementation of programme management in the UK construction industry. In: Built and natural environment. Ph.D. thesis. Glasgow Caledonian University: Glasgow; 2008

549. Shehu, Z., & Akintoye, A. (2010). Major challenges to the successful implementation and practice of programme management in the construction environment: A critical analysis. *International Journal of Project Management 28,* 26–39.

550. Shenhar, A. (1998). From Theory to Practice: Toward a Typology of Project Management Styles, *IEEE Transactions of Engineering Management vol. 45(1)*, 33-47.

551. Shenhar, A. (2000). Strategic Project Leadership: How to Lead Projects as Strategic,.*Competitive Weapons, Stevens Institute of Technology.*

552. Shenhar, A. (2001a). One Size Does Not Fit All Projects: Exploring Classical Contingency Domains,.*Management Science, vol. 47(3)*, 394-414

553. Shenhar, A. (2001b). Contingent management in temporary, dynamic organizations: The comparative analysis of projects, *Journal of High Technology Management Research, vol. 12*, 239-271.

554. Shenhar, A. (2004). Strategic Project Leadership: Toward A Strategic Approach to Project Management. *R&D Management.*

555. Shenhar, A., & Dvir, D. (2004). How Projects Differ, and What to Do About It. In P. Morris, & J. Pinto, *The Wiley Guide to Managing Projects,* (pp. 1265-1286, 2004). Hoboken, NJ: Wiley & Sons.

556. Shenhar, A., & Dvir, D. (2004). Project management evolution: Past history and future research directions. *PMI research conference preceedings, PMP, Vol 2*, London: England.

557. Shenhar, A., & Dvir, D. (2007). *Reinventing Project Management.* Boston, MA: Harvard Business School Press.

558. Shenhar, A., & R. Max Wideman. (1996). *Improving PM: Linking Success Criteria to Project Type. A paper presented to the Southern Alberta Chapter, Project Management Institute, Symposium "Creating Canadian Advantage through Project Management."* Calgary.

559. Shenhar, A., Dvir, D., Guth, W., Lechler, T., Milosevic, D., Patanakul, P., et al. (2007). *Project strategy—The missing link. In A. Shenhar D. Milosevic, & H. J. Thamhain (Eds.), Linking project management to business.* Newtown Square, PA: Project Management Institute.

560. Shenhar, A., Dvir, D., Levy, O., & Maltz, A. (2001). Project success: a multidimensional strategic concept". *Long Range Planning, Vol. 34 No. 6*, 699-725.

561. Shenhar, A., Holzmann, V., Melamed, B., & Zhao, Y. (2006). The Challenge of Innovation in Highly Complex Projects: What can we learn from Boeing's Dreamlines Experience? *Project Management Journal, Volume 47(2),*.

562. Shenhar, A., Poli, M., & Lechler, T. (2001). *A New Framework for Strategic Project Management Pergamon, Management of Technology: The Key to Prosperity in the Third Millennium, PICMET - Ninth International Conference on Management Technology,* Thousand Oaks, CA.

563. Shenhar, A., Tishler, A., Dvir, D., Lipovetsky, S., & Lechler, T. (2002). Refining the search for project success factors: a multivariate typological approach. *R&D Management Vol. 32 No. 2*, 111-26.

564. Shimizu, T., Park, W., & Hong, P. (2012). Project Managers for Risk Management: Case for Japan. *Benchmarking: An International Journal, 19(3)*.

565. Shimizu, T., Park, Y., & Hong, P. (2012). Project Manager and Risk Management: A Comparative Study between Japanese and Korean Firms. *The 5th International Symposium and Workshop in Global Supply Chains, University of Tokyo, Japan.*

566. Shore, B. (2008). Systematic Biases and Culture in Project Failures. *Project Management Journal Vol 39 No 4*, 5-16.

567. Sicotte, H., Drouin, N., & Delerue, H. (2014). innovation portfolio management as a subset of dynamic capabilities: Measurement and impact on innovative performance. *Project Management Journal, 45(6)*, 58-72.

568. Siddique, L., & Hussein, B. (June 2014). Practical insight about choice of methodology in large complex software projects in Norway. *Technology Management Conference (ITMC), 2014 IEEE International*, 1-4.

569. Silva, A., & Rocha, J. (2012). Towards a Two-Way Participatory Process. Computational Science and Its Applications – ICCSA. Lecture Notes in Computer Science, 571-582.

570. Şimandan, M. (2010). Methodology and Method in Scientific Research. *Journal Plus Education Vol VI (2010), No. 2*, 73-80.

571. Simpson, J., Kollmannsberger, C., Schmalen, H., & Berkowitz, D. (2002). New product development in German and US technology firms. *European Journal of Innovation Management, Vol. 5 Iss: 4*, 194 - 207.

572. Simpson, W., & Lynch, W. (1999). Critical Success Factors in Critical Chain Project Management. *Proceedings of the 30th Annual Project Management Institute 1999 Seminars & Symposium.* [Pdf] Available at: <http://www.stottlerhenke.com/papers/IEEE_Aerospace_2010_critical_chain.pdf> [Accessed 26 January 2012].

573. Singer, S., & Edmondson., A. (2008). When learning and performance are at odds: Confronting the tension. In P. Kumar, & P. Ramsey, *Performance and learning matters:* (pp. 33–60). Singapore: World Scientific.

574. Singgih, M., & Tjiong, W. (2011). Singgih M, L., Tjiong, W., "Repair Production Systems Division of Plastic Injection and Blow." *Proceedings of the National Seminar on Technology Management XIII, 2011.*

575. Singh, G. (February 2012). LEADERSHIP IN THE ERA OF GLOBAL PRESSURES Volume 2, Issue 2. *International Journal of Research in IT & Management, Volume 2, Issue 2.*

576. Smite, D., & Borzovs, J. (2010). New forms of work in light of globalization in software development. In M. Pankowska, *Infonomics for Distributed Business and Decision Making Environment: Creating Information Systems Ecology in* (pp. 1-390). Hershey PA: IGI Global.

577. Smite, D., Wohlin, C., & Feldt, R. (2010). *Empirical evidence in global software engineering: a systematic review.* 91-118: Empirical Software Engineering, Volume 15, Issue 1,

578. Snee, R. (2010). Lean Six Sigma – getting better all the time. *International Journal of Lean Six Sigma, Vol. 1 Iss: 1, 9 – 29.*

579. Snee, R., &Hoerl, R. (2003). Leading Six Sigma: A Step-by-Step Guide Based on Experience with GE and other Six Sigma companies. Upper Saddle: Prentice-Hall.

580. Soderholm, A. (2008). Project management of unexpected events. *International Journal of Project Management,* 80-86.

581. Söderlund, J. (2004). Building theories of project management: past research, questions for the future. *International Journal of Project Management 22,* 183–191.

582. Soliman, F. (2011). Appraisal of Innovation Leaders. *UTS Business School, University of Technology, Sydney*

583. Spangler, W., & House, R. (1991). Presidential Effectiveness and the Leadership Motive Profile. *Journal of Personality and Social Psychology. Vol. 60, No. 3.,* 439-455.

584. Spector, R. (2006). How constraints management enhances lean and six sigma. *Chain Management Review, Vol.10 No.1,* 42-7.

585. Srivastava, A., Bartol, K., & Locke, E. (2006). Empowering leadership in management teams: Effects on knowledge sharing, efficacy, and performance. *Academy of Management Journal; Dec2006, Vol. 49 Issue 6,* 1239-1251.

586. Stacey, R. (2007). Strategic management and organisational dynamics: the challenge of complexity : Fifth Edition. Essex: FT Prentice Hall.

587. Steffey, R., &Anantatmula, V. (2011). International Projects Proposal Analysis: Risk Assessment Using Radial Maps. *Project Management Journal, Vol. 42, No. 3,* 62-74.

588. Stein, S., Lauer, Y., & Kharbili, M. (2012). Using Template Analysis as Background Reading Technique for Requirements Elicitation. *IDS Scheer AG*.

589. Steiner, I. (1972). *Group process and productivity.* New York: Academic Press.

590. Stokker, J., &Hallam, G. (2009). The right person, in the right job, with the right skills, at the right time. A workforce-planning model that goes beyond metrics. *Library Management, 30(8/9).*, 561-571.

591. Stork, F. (2001). *Stochastic resource-constrained project scheduling. Ph.D. thesis, TU Berlin.*

592. Stork, F. (2001). *Stochastic resource-constrained project scheduling. Ph.D. thesis.* TU Berlin.

593. Sturdivant, J. (2004). The CNSI Requirements Analysis Proces.

594. Summer, M. (99). Critical Success Factors in Enterprise Wide Information Information Management Systems Projects. *SIGCPR.*

595. Tang, C. (2006). Perspectives in supply chain risk management. *International Journal of Production Economics, Vol. 103, No. 2,* 451-488.

596. Tas, E., & Yaman, H. (2005). A building cost estimation model based on cost significant work packages. *Engineering, Construction and Architectural Management, 12(3),* 251-263.

597. Tate, B. (2008). A longitudinal study of the relationships among self-monitoring, authentic leadership, and perceptions of leadership. *Journal of Leadership and Organizational Studies, 15,* 16-29.

598. Taylor, S., & Bogdan, R. (1998). Introduction to qualitative research methods : a guidebook and resource - Third Edition. New York: Wiley.

599. Taylora, A., Cocklin, C., Browna, R., & Wilson-Evered, E. (2011). An investigation of champion-driven leadership processes. *The Leadership Quarterly 22,* 412-433

600. Tchokogue, A., Bareil, C., &Duguay, C. (2005). Key lessons from the implementation of an ERP at Pratt & Whitney Canada. Int. J. Production Economics 95, 151–163.

601. Teller, J., & Kock, A. (2013). An empirical investigation on how portfolio risk management influences project portfolio success.

International Journal of Project Management Volume 31, Issue 6, August 2013, 817–829.

602. Tenera, A., & Pinto, L. (19 March 2014). A Lean Six Sigma (LSS) project management improvement model. *Procedia - Social and Behavioral Sciences Volume 119*, 912–920.

603. Thamhain, H. (2004). Team leadership effectiveness in technology-based project environments. *Project Management Journal*.

604. Thiétart, R.-A. (2001). Doing management research : a comprehensive guide. London: SAGE,.

605. Thompsen, J. (2000). Effective Leadership of Virtual Project Teams. *IEEE*.

606. Tiwana, A., & Keil, M. (Nov. 2004). "The One-Minute Risk Assessment Tool." *Communications of the ACM, Vol. 47, No. 11*, 73-77.

607. Tjosvold, D. (1998). The cooperative and competitive goal approach to conflict: accomplishments and challenges. *Applied Psychology: An International Review, 47*, 285–313.

608. Todd, P., & McGrath. (1995). Product Development Leadership for Technology-based Companies: Measurement and Management–A Prelude to Action. MA: Weston.

609. Tommelein, I., Ballard, G., & Kaminsky, P. (2009). Supply Chain Management for Lean Project Delivery. In W. O'Brien, C. Formoso, V. Ruben, & K. London, *Construction Supply Chain Management Handbook*. Boca Raton: CRC Press. [Pdf] Available at: <http://ieor.berkeley.edu/~kaminsky/Reprints/*PROOF_IT_GB_PK_08.pdf*> [Accessed 26 January 2012].

610. Torbica, Z., & Stroh, R. (2001). Customer satisfaction in home building. *J. Constr. Eng. Manag. 127*, 82–86.

611. TOWLER, A. (2003). Effects of charismatic influence training on attitudes, behavior, and performance. *Personnel Psychology - 56*, 363-381.

612. Truexa, D., Baskervilleb, R., & Trav, J. (2000). Amethodical systems development: the deferred systems development methods. *Accounting, Management and Information Technologies Volume 10, Issue 1*, 53-79.

613. Tsai, H., Moskowitz, H., & Lee, L. (European Journal of Operational Research 151). Human resource selection for software development projects using Taguchi's parameter design. *2003*, 167-180.

614. Tsai, W.–H., Hwang, E., Chan, J.–C., Lai, C.–W., & Lin, S.–J. (2012). Turning around troubled projects in an ERP implementation project from consultancy project leaders' perspectives. *International Journal of Business and Systems Research*.

615. Tu, C.-H., Sujo-Montes, L., Yen, C.-J., Chan, J.-Y., &Blocher, M. (2012). The Integration of Personal Learning Environments & Open Network Learning Environments. *TechTrends, Volume 56, Number 3*, 13-19.

616. Tuckman.B. (1965). Development Sequence in small groups. *Psychological Bulletin*, 384-399.

617. Tukel, O., & Rom, W. (1995). Analysis of the Characteristics of Projects in Diverse Industries, *Working Paper, Cleveland State University, Cleveland, OHIO*.

618. Turner, J., & Cochrane, R. (1993). Goals and methods matrix: Coping will projects with ill-defined goals and/or methods of achieving them. *International Journal of Project Management, 11(2)*, 93-102.

619. Turner, J., Kristoffer., V., &Thurloway. (2002). *The project manager as change agent*. London: McGraw-Hill.

620. Turner, R. (1999). The Handbook of Project-based Management: Improving the Processes for Achieving Strategic Objectives. London.: McGraw-Hill.

621. Turner, R., & Muller, R. (2005). The project manager's leadership style as a success factor on projects: a literature review. *Project Management Journal, Vol. 36 No. 1*, 49-61. [PDF], Available at <https://www.surfgroepen.nl/sites/Ontwerpprojecten/DC/Onderzoek/refw%20135.%20Leadership%20style%20as%20a%20succes%20factor%20(overlap%20met%20boek).Pdf > Accessed on [14 June, 2011]

622. Uhl-Bien, M., Marion, R., & McKelvey, B. (2007). Complexity leadership theory: Shifting leadership from the industrial age to the knowledge era. *The Leadership Quarterly, 18*, 289-318.

623. Umble, M., and E. Umble, "Manage Your Projects for Success: An Application of the Theory of Constraints," Production and Inventory Management Journal, 41:2 (2000), pp. 27–32

624. Unger, B., Rank, J., & Gemunden, H. (2014). Corporate innovation culture and dimensions of project portfolio: The moderating role of national culture. *Project Management Journal, 45(6)*, 38-57.

625. University of Warwick. (2012). Research Governance & Ethics. *Research Code of Practice.* [PDF], Available at <http://www2.warwick.ac.uk/services/rss/researchgovernance_ethics/research_code_of_practice/120228_research_code_of_practice.pdf> Accessed on [4 August 2012]

626. Vaccaro, I., Jansen, J., Van Den Bosch, F., & Volberda, H. (January 2012). Management Innovation and Leadership: The Moderating Role of Organizational Size. *Journal of Management Studies 49:1,* 29-58.

627. Valenzuela, D., &Shrivastava, P. (n.d.). Interview as a Method for Qualitative Research. [Online], Available at <http://www.public.asu.edu/~kroel/www500/Interview%20Fri.pdf> Accessed on [02 Feb 2011]

628. Van Scoy, R. (1992). Software Development Risk: Opportunity, Not Problem. *Software Eng. Inst., Carnegie Mellon University.*

629. Verner, J. (2008). What factors lead to software project failure? *Second International Conference on Research Challenges in Information Science,* 71 - 80.

630. Verner, J., &Cerpa, N. (2005). Australian Software Development: What Software Project Management Practices Lead to Success? *Australian Software Engineering Conference (ASWEC'05).*

631. Verner, J., Sampson, J., & Cerpa, N. (2008). What factors lead to software project failure. *Proceedings of Research Challenges in Information Science 2008,* 71-80.

632. Verzuh, E. (2005). *The Fast Forward MBA in Project Management, Second Edition.* Hoboken, New Jersey: John Wiley & Sons, Inc.

633. Visitacion, M. (2003). Project Management Best Practices: Key Processes and Common Sense. *Giga Information Group.* [Pdf] Available at: <http://www.slideshare.net/walkerswu/project-management-best-practices/download> [Accessed 26 January 2012].

634. Vlăsceanu, L. (1998). Sociological research methodology. In C. Zamfir şi, *Dictionary of Sociology*. Bucharest: Editura Babel.

635. Vogel, M. (2005). Einmel Indien und zuruck. *CIO*.

636. Vose, D. (2008). Risk Analysis: A Quantitative Guide - Third Edition. West Sussex: John Wiley & Sons

637. WALKER, D., & SHEN, Y. (2002). Project understanding, planning, management action and construction time performance: two Australian case studies. *Construction Management and Economics 20*, 31–44.

638. Walter, F., Humphrey, R., & Cole, M. (2012). Unleashing leadership potential: Toward an evidence-based management of emotional intelligence. *Organizational Dynamics 41*, 212—219.

639. Welman, Kruger, & Mitchell. (2005). *Research Methodology - Third Edition*. Oxford: Oxford University Press.

640. Wen-Der, Y. (2006). Wen-Der, Y. (2006). PIREM: a new model for conceptual cost estimation. *Construction Management and Economics, 24(3)*, 259-270.

641. West, D. (2010). Project Sponsorship- An Essential Guide for Those Sponsoring Projects Within their Organisations. Franham: Gower Publishing Company.

642. Westerveld, E. (2003). The Project Excellence Model: linking success criteria. *International Journal of Project Management 21*, 411–418.

643. Wheelright, S., & Clark, K. (1992). *Creating project plans to focus product development*. Cambridge, MA: Harvard Business School Publishing.

644. White, D., & Fortune, J. (2002). Current practice in project management – an empirical study. *International Journal of Project Management 20*.

645. Wildman, J., & Griffith, R. (2015). *Leading Global teams - Translating Multidisciplinary Science to Practice*. New York : Springer.

646. Williams, R., Walker, J., & Dorofee, A. (1997). Putting Risk Management into Practice. *IEEE Software, Vol. 14, No. 3*, 75-82.

647. Williams, T. (2005). Assessing and Moving on From the Dominant Project Management Discourse in the Light of Project Overruns. *IEEE TRANSACTIONS ON ENGINEERING MANAGEMENT, VOL. 52, NO. 4*.

648. WILSON, C. (2006). Brainstorming Pitfalls and Best Practices. Interactions - Gadgets, part 2: T he science of gadgetry Volume 13 Issue 5, 50 - 63.

649. Winters-Miner, L., Bolding, P., Hilbe, J., Goldstein, M., Hill, T., Nisbet, R., et al. (2015). Root Cause Analysis, Six Sigma, and Overall Quality Control and Lean Concepts. *Practical Predictive Analytics and Decisioning Systems for Medicine*, 143-164.

650. WONG, C., LASCHINGER, H., & CUMMINGS, G. (2010). Authentic leadership and nurses' voice behavior and perceptions of care quality. *Journal of Nursing Management, 18*, 889-900.

651. Wysocki, R., &Rafeq, A. (2007). Effective Project Management—Traditional, Adaptive, Extreme. *Information Systems Control Journal, Volume 5*.

652. Xenidis, Y., & Stavrakas, E. (2013). Risk Based Budgeting of Infrastructure Projects. *Procedia - Social and Behavioral Sciences 74*, 478 – 487.

653. Yammarino, F., Dubinsky, A., Comer, L., & Jolson, M. (1997). Women and transformational and contingent reward leadership: a multiple-levels-of-analysis perspective. *Academy of Management Journal, 40*, 205–22.

654. Yammarino, F., Spangler, W., & Dubinsky, A. (1998). Transformational and contingent leadership: individual, dyad, and group levels of analysis. *Leadership Quarterly, 9*, 27–54.

655. Yang, J., & Peng, S. (2008). Development of a customer satisfaction evaluation model for construction project management. *Building Environment, 43*, 458-468.

656. Yang, L.-R. (2012). Key practices, manufacturing capability and attainment of manufacturing goals: The perspective of project/engineer-to-order manufacturing. *International Journal of Project Management*.

657. Yang, Q., Kherbachi, S., Hong, Y., & Shan, C. (2015). Identifying and managing coordination complexity in global product development project. *International Journal of Project Management Volume 33, Issue 7*, 1464–1475.

658. Yanga, L.-R., Huang, C.-F., & Wu, K.-S. (2011). The association among project manager's leadership style, teamwork and project success. *International Journal of Project Management 29*, 258–267.

659. Yedidia, M., Gillespie, C., Kachur, E., Schwartz, M., Ockene, J., & Chepaitis, A. (2003). Effect of Communications Training on Medical Student Performance. *IAMA: Journal of the American Medical Association 290(9)*, 1157-1165.

660. Yeh, J.-Y., Wei, C.-C., & Wei, C.-S. (2012). The impact of team personality balance on project performance. *African Journal of Business Management Vol. 6(4)*, 1674-1684.

661. Yin., R. (2009). Case study research : design and methods. 4th ed.. London: Sage Publications.

662. Yoo, J., Choi, M., Hyang, N., Woo, S., Kim, S.-S., Kim, S., et al. (2011). Implementation of best practice for chemotherapy-induced nausea and vomiting in an acute care setting. *International Journal of Evidence-Based Healthcare.*, 32–38.

663. Youker, R. (2002). The difference between different types of projects. *PMI, 30th Annual Seminar Symposium.* Philadelphia, PA, USA.

664. Yourdon, E. (2004.). *Death March, Second Editio.* Upper Saddle River, NJ: Prentice Hall.

665. Yu1, J.-H., & Kwon, H.-R. (2011). Critical success factors for urban regeneration projects in Korea. *International Journal of Project Management 29*, 889 – 899.

666. Zaccaro, S., Rittman, A., & Marks, M. (2001). Team leadership. *The Leadership Quarterly 12*, 451–483.

667. Zaleznik, A. (1977). Managers and leaders: Are they different? *Harvard Business Review, 55(3)*, 67–78.

668. Zhang, Q., Irfan, M., Khattak, M., Zhu, X., & Hassan, M. (2012). Lean Six Sigma: A Literature Review. *INTERDISCIPLINARY JOURNAL OF CONTEMPORARY RESEARCH IN BUSINESS.* [Pdf] Available at: <http://journal-archieves15.webs.com/599-605.pdf> [Accessed 26 January 2012].

669. Zhang, Y. (2016). Selecting risk response strategies considering project risk interdependence. *International Journal of Project Management 34*, 819–830.

670. Zhou, J., & George, J. (2003). Awakening employee creativity: the role of leader emotional intelligence'. *Leadership Quarterly, 14,* 545–68.

671. Zika-Viktorsson, A., Sundström, P., & Engwall, M. (2006). Project overload: An exploratory study of work and management in multi-project settings. *International Journal of Project Management,* 385–394.

672. Zou, P., Zhang, G., & Wang, J. (2007). Understanding the key risks in construction. *International Journal of Project Management, Volume 25, Issue 6,* 601–614.

673. Zou, Y., & Lee, S. (2008). The impacts of change management practices on project change cost performance. *Construction Management and Economics 26 (4),* 387–393.

www.ingramcontent.com/pod-product-compliance
Lightning Source LLC
Chambersburg PA
CBHW071359170526
45165CB00001B/110